Islamic Societies in Practice, Second Edition

Florida A&M University, Tallahassee
Florida Atlantic University, Boca Raton
Florida Gulf Coast University, Ft. Myers
Florida International University, Miami
Florida State University, Tallahassee
University of Central Florida, Orlando
University of Florida, Gainesville
University of North Florida, Jacksonville
University of South Florida, Tampa
University of West Florida, Pensacola

Islamic Societies in Practice

SECOND EDITION

CAROLYN FLUEHR-LOBBAN

University Press of Florida

Gainesville · Tallahassee · Tampa · Boca Raton
Pensacola · Orlando · Miami · Jacksonville · Ft. Myers

09 08 07 06 05 04   6 5 4 3 2 1

Library of Congress Cataloging-in-Publication Data
Fluehr-Lobban, Carolyn.
Islamic societies in practice / Carolyn Fluehr-Lobban.—2nd ed.
p. cm.
Previously published as: Islamic society in practice.
Includes bibliographical references and index.
ISBN 0-8130-2721-7 (pbk.: alk. paper)
1. Islam—Africa, North. 2. Islam—Sudan. 3. Islam—Egypt. 4. Islam—Tunisia.
5. Africa, North—Religious life and customs. 6. Sudan—Religious life and
customs. 7. Egypt—Religious life and customs. 8. Tunisia—Religious life and
customs. I. Fluehr-Lobban, Carolyn. Islamic society in practice. II. Title.
BP64.A4F58 2004
297'.0962—dc22   2004042563

The University Press of Florida is the scholarly publishing agency for the State
University System of Florida, comprising Florida A&M University, Florida Atlantic
University, Florida Gulf Coast University, Florida International University, Florida
State University, University of Central Florida, University of Florida, University of
North Florida, University of South Florida, and University of West Florida.

University Press of Florida
15 Northwest 15th Street
Gainesville, FL 32611-2079
http://www.upf.com

Contents

Figures and Maps

Figures

Maps

Acknowledgments

This second edition, like the first, is dedicated to my mother, Anne Wolsonovich Fluehr, still going strong at age eighty-five. She remains an inspiration in my life for her independence and self-sufficiency now, as she was in her personal travels and love of adventure in the previous decades of her life. She wonders if she read to me from *The Thousand and One Nights* to make me interested in the Middle East, Africa, and the Islamic world. But the fact is that I followed her example—dreaming, following an inner compass.

As I reflect upon my mother's influence, I think about my daughters and the effects that living in the Arab and Muslim world has had upon them, and so I have them in my mind and heart as I prepare this revised edition. Their stories as children in the field are related in the first chapter, and now as young women they have selected career paths and goals that echo those experiences. Josina—who lived in Sudan, Egypt, and Tunisia—has chosen a career in experiential and outdoor education and tells her parents that a significant part of her childhood learning was gained from experiencing the cultural life of northern Africa. Nicki spent her junior semester abroad at the American University in Cairo in 2001 during the tragic fall when the attacks of September 11 changed our worlds, Arab, Muslim, and Western. She plans a career in international and peace studies. Their father, Richard Lobban, fellow anthropologist, researcher, and companion through all of these adventures, is likewise lovingly acknowledged.

My students have been a continuing source of inspiration. Their engagement with the challenging subject matter confronting American ignorance and the blinders of prejudice that exist about the Arab and Muslim world reflects an honest effort to change this unfortunate reality.

I acknowledge with deep respect and gratitude the unconditional hospitality that my family and I have received over the decades in Muslim, Arab, and African homes, as well as in offices and institutions too numerous to mention individually. The easy access and generosity characteristic of these visits may not be the experience of the Americans who will visit the region in the post 9/11 world.

I thank my student at Rhode Island College Saʿada Hussein from Lamu for providing some of the details of Habib Swela's life. I thank Ogüz Bozkurt for introducing me to the lineal descendant of Maulana Jalálu-ʿd-Din Muhammad i Rúmi in Istanbul; I thank Ahmed Shahi for the Shayqiya proverb "When you are losing your patience, try a little more patience"; and I thank Mahmoud Khojasteh for the information on the Persian Nouruz festival.

Finally, I wish to thank colleagues at Colgate University, where I was NEH humanities professor in the spring of 2003 as the second edition was being completed. Michael Peletz of the Sociology and Anthropology Department was especially helpful in adding material on Malaysia, and Omid Safi introduced me to a number of new progressive Muslims who are developing innovative interpretations of Islam and Shariʿa. I also wish to thank the Colgate University Research Council for its support of the production of two new maps for this second edition.

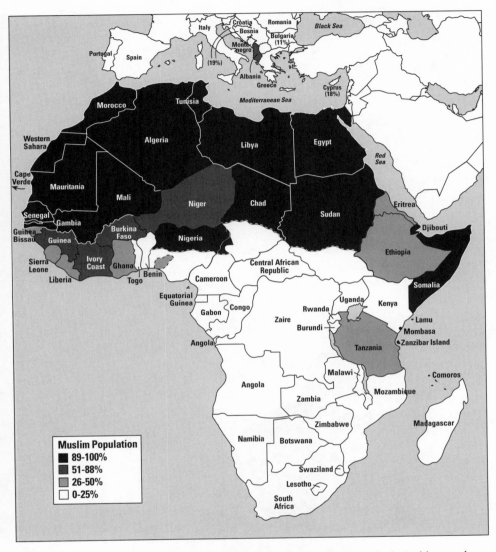

Map 1. Islam in Africa and Europe. Map developed by Carolyn Fluehr-Lobban and Ellen Walker.

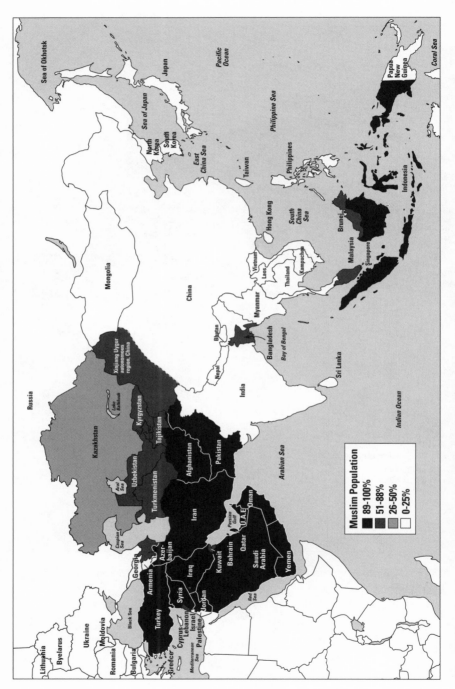

Map 2. Islam in Asia. Map developed by Carolyn Fluehr-Lobban and Ellen Walker.

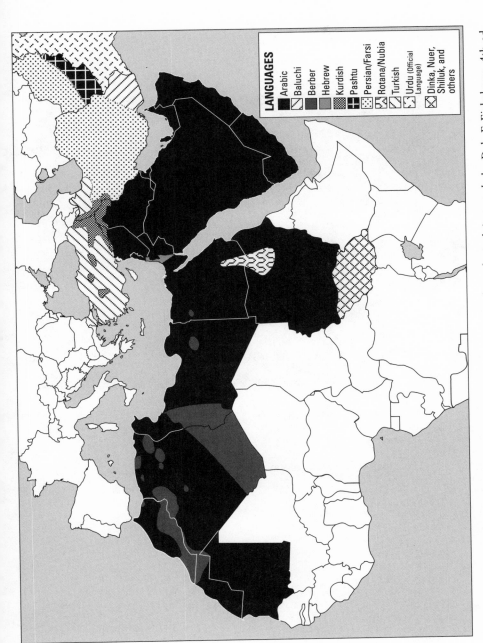

LANGUAGES

- ■ Arabic
- ◩ Baluchi
- ▨ Berber
- ▨ Hebrew
- ▦ Kurdish
- ✚ Pashtu
- ▨ Persian/Farsi
- ▧ Rotana/Nubia
- ▨ Turkish
- ▨ Urdu (Official Language)
- ⊗ Dinka, Nuer, Shilluk, and others

Map 3. Middle Eastern Languages. From *The Middle East: An Anthropological Approach*, by Dale F. Eickelman. 4th ed. Upper Saddle River, N.J.: Prentice Hall, 2002. Reprinted by permission of the publisher.

For my mother, Anne Wolsonovich Fluehr,
whose keen eye and love of geography, history,
and travel have always been an inspiration.

Introduction

The interconnected relationship between the West and the Arab-Islamic world changed after the September 11, 2001, attacks on the World Trade Center towers and the Pentagon, and relations among Arab and Muslim nations became vastly more complex. The crises deepened as the United States launched its "war on terrorism" in the fall of 2001, then invaded Afghanistan later that year and Iraq in 2003, while Americans struggled to understand why Middle Easterners and Muslims are so angry with the United States. The media and the American general public grew more concerned with understanding Islam and Muslims after President George W. Bush announced that the United States was fighting a war against terrorists, not Muslims. At the same time Reuters, a major European and international news agency, announced that it would no longer use the words *terrorism* or *terrorist* in reference to actions or actors, as these are highly subjective terms that depend upon the perspective of those using them. Calling to mind the adage that one man's terrorist is another's freedom fighter, their position was one that sought to maintain the greatest objectivity.

The second edition of this book seeks to accomplish the same ends as the first edition, that is, to humanize the peoples of the Middle East and the diverse societies in which Muslims live. The first edition was begun in the wake of the 1991 Gulf War when the U.S. "star wars" offensive directed against a demonized individual, Saddam Hussein, failed to take any account of the "collateral damage" done to the Iraqi people. It did not seem to matter how many Iraqis died, and in the decade after the war the United States turned a blind eye to the suffering of Iraqis, especially women and children, who were harmed by the total embargo imposed upon Iraq. The second edition is written as another war on Iraq has been waged. In the face of strong international and domestic opposition, the fate of the Iraqi people became more of a factor in the political equation.

This perceived attitude toward Iraqis and the conditions that Palestinians chronically suffer are recognized as issues that have inflamed anger at the United States. It is clear that we must study the region and understand its history and worldviews. This second edition is dedicated to the hope for peace that might flow from a more enlightened understanding of Middle Eastern perspectives.

The current complicated relations and associated tension between the Western world and Christianity and the Arab world and Islam are deeply rooted in history and have been marked by political and cultural struggles often waged in the name of religion. The last decades of the twentieth century reawakened this tension and struggle between the East and the West with many dramatic events, most notably the Arab defeat in the June 1967 war; the 1979 popular Islamic revolution in Iran and the taking of American hostages; the assassination of the West's most charismatic Arab ally, Anwar al-Sadat, in 1981; the attacks on American barracks in Lebanon and Saudi Arabia in the 1980s; the Gulf War of 1991; the two major intifadas, or uprisings, of Palestinians in Israel—1987–93 and resuming in 2000 after the failure of the Oslo Peace talks; the bombings of the American embassies in East Africa in 1998, allegedly by followers of Osama bin Laden; and the spread of extremist groups, such as the Taliban in Afghanistan or the National Islamic Front in Sudan, who directly threatened the United States. The attacks on the World Trade Center, with limited damage in 1993 and with devastating effect in 2001, were indisputable turning points, the effects of which are still unfolding as this second edition goes to press. As the first decade of the twenty-first century unfolds, we in the West will have to decide whether we will demonize the Muslim and Arab worlds or humanize them.

The Islamist upsurge has as much to do with political realities internal to Arab and Muslim states and their failed undemocratic regimes as it has to do with anti-Western and anti-American attitudes. The term *Islamism* has evolved from the term *Islamic fundamentalism*, meaning the use of Islamic ideas in the political realm. Many in the West do not distinguish between Islamism, or political Islam, in the Muslim world and Arab nationalism (one nation of the Arabic-speaking peoples) in the Middle East, and they tend to make facile generalizations and stereotypes that associate Islam with terrorism and Arab politics with an automatic anti-Western bias. As Edward Said pointed out in *Covering Islam*, for the general public in Europe and America, Islam is news of a particularly unpleasant sort (1981, 136). Islam is perceived as a threat to Western civilization. The "clash of civilizations" view appeared to assume the upper hand in the wake of the attacks on the

World Trade Center, while the divide between the civilized "us" and the uncivilized "them" has become more pronounced as the whole of the Arab-Islamic world is judged by the actions of the violent extremists. Americans have not judged Christianity by the violent actions of a few extremist anti-abortionist groups or the racist attacks by members of the World Church of the Creator. And it was homegrown terrorism that was responsible for the bombing of the Murra Federal Building in Oklahoma City in 1995.

Tied to this perception is a fear of Islam in the West, a fear rooted in the complex history of contact and conflict between the Islamic world and Europe. Before European hegemony on the eve of 1492, the global economic system was dominated by empires to the east, a significant portion of which were Islamic (Abu-Lughod 1989). From the eleventh through the thirteen centuries, the Crusades pitted the Christian West against the Muslim East in an effort to regain the Holy Land and Jerusalem. The Muslim occupation of the Iberian peninsula for eight centuries is viewed as an aberration from which Christianity was liberated after the 1492 expulsion of Muslims and Jews and the ensuing Inquisition. Orientalist scholar Bernard Lewis has asked "What Went Wrong?" (2002) in the fall of the once grand Islamic civilization that it has devolved to despotic regimes and terrorist cells. European colonial occupation of most of the Middle East and much of the Islamic world during the nineteenth and twentieth centuries set the tone of European-Christian superiority and Muslim-Arab inferiority that has yet to be fundamentally altered. Today, fear of Islam has added the negative stereotypes of fanaticism, terrorism, and barbarism to the Arab and Muslim.

Although militant political Islamic movements, now widely referred to as Islamist, have captured the attention of the West, the overwhelming majority of the world's 1.2 billion Muslims have nothing to do with these events. Most Muslims are not Arabs, and they live outside the Middle East, mainly in countries that were colonized by one of the European powers and possess knowledge and experience with the West, yet are among the world's poorest countries. The mantle of European imperialism has been largely inherited by the United States.

Islam is now the second most practiced faith in the United States, after Christianity. While all are part of the world community of Muslims, the *Umma*, each region has distinctive ties to the spread of Islam, and cultural and linguistic diversity is the norm rather than the exception. The faith of Islam is a basic unifier, as is the Arabic language, valued by all Muslims because it was the language in which the Holy Book, the Qur'an, was revealed to Muhammad nearly six centuries after the introduction of Christianity. Islam has been a powerful unifier because its theology has been, perhaps, less subject to the doctrinal disputes that Christianity has witnessed, and because its teachings blend religious, moral, and social practice into an indivisible whole for the believer-practitioner.

Islam, as lived and practiced by Muslims in everyday life and society, is the focus of this book. My principal goal is to bring out the human dimension of regions and cultural traditions that have been stereotyped and maligned in the West, on the one hand, or simplified and romanticized, on the other. This book is an effort to get behind the headlines that have focused on war, conflict, terrorism, and religious fanaticism and to make accessible to a Western audience the everyday lives of the people of the Arab and Muslim worlds.

I

Islam and Muslim Societies in Practice

The Middle East, Arab, and Islamic Worlds

There is a tendency in the West to homogenize the East and lump together Arabs, Muslims, and Middle Easterners. Islam is a global faith with most of its 1.2 billion practitioners living in Asia. Christians make up significant minorities in Egypt, Sudan, and Syria, and they form nearly half of Lebanon's population. In Europe, historical populations of Muslims are found in the former Yugoslavia and Bulgaria, and they are a 70 percent majority in Albania. In contemporary Europe and North America, immigration from Asia and Africa has infused Euro-American society with a new Muslim face, as in the United States, where it is the second most practiced faith. The largest Muslim country is Indonesia, which was headed by a woman, Megawati Sukarnoputri, in 2003. Turks and Iranians are not Arabs, and the most troubled country in the region is the Jewish state of Israel. The most populous of Africa's nations, Nigeria at 100 million, is more than half Muslim.

The "Middle East" is a geographical referent that was coined in the West as a mercantile and colonial strategy whereby traders from London and Boston viewed the region as closer to itself, the Near or Middle East in contrast to the "Far East" of India and China. In contemporary usage the Middle East stretches from Rabat in Morocco to Tehran in Iran, a distance of about 3,400 miles, equal to that between New York and Fairbanks, Alaska. The Middle East includes territories on three continents: Asia, Africa, and Europe (the European part of Turkey) (Eickelman 1998, 1–2). Central Asia was shaped by the great caravan routes of the Middle Ages silk trade, which brought luxury goods from China to Europe. Central Asia comprised the eastern borders of the former Soviet Union, which officially banned the practice of Islam and made museums and archaeological parks of its great mosques of Bukhara and Samarkand. I visited these Muslim monuments in 1975 and was surprised to see that Central Asian Muslims still observed Friday prayers.

A Eurocentric designation, "Middle East" is a geographical idea with decided colonial roots that do not reflect regional perspectives. Regional geographical references point to a different center, that of Mecca and Medina, the birthplace and heartland of Islam in the Hijaz, the Arabian peninsula. As one prays facing Mecca in the Hijaz, to the right (*al-Yamin*) of the Muslim praying is what has come to be known as Yemen. The lands to the west in the direction of the setting sun are the Maghrib, also the reference for the evening sunset prayer and the Arabic reference for Morocco. As one faces Mecca, the north is on the left, hence the term *shemaal* refers to both north and left-hand side. Al-Sahara means desert, and the Levant (meaning "to rise up," as in the sunrise) reflects the French colonial past of Lebanon and Syria, referring to the place of the rising sun.

The Middle East and Muslim Asia are arid or semiarid, with desert cultures and ancient riverain cultures providing the major motifs. Agriculture originated in this region with the domestication of wheat and barley and of goats, sheep, cattle, and dogs all occurring in prehistory from about 10,000 B.C.E. (Before the Common Era) in the Fertile Crescent areas of Mesopotamia—between the Tigris and Euphrates Rivers—and the Nile Valley including the White and Blue Niles of Sudan, as well as the Egyptian Nile. Pastoralism, as well as agriculture, originated in these regions, and in certain remote areas it still prevails as a major livelihood. However, the major stereotype of Arabs living in desert tents with their camels and veiled wives is a myth that persists in Western fantasies. Today most people in these regions live in cities, although ties to agrarian society are still strong. Many are relatively recent migrants who maintain ties to land and family in the rural areas.

The major cities of the Islamic and Arab world include each of the capital cities of the nations of the Maghrib (North Africa), the Levant (Lebanon and Syria), southwest Asia and the Arabian peninsula where Mecca and Medina in Saudi Arabia are the cities of Muslim pilgrimage, and central Asia. With 17 million inhabitants, Cairo is the largest of the Middle Eastern cities. The major languages spoken include Arabic predominantly, Turkish, and Persian (Farsi). Minority languages include Berber (Amazigh), Nubian (Rotana), Aramaic, Hebrew, Armenian, and Kurdish.

The major contours of the book are taken from an anthropologist's perspective, derived from my nearly six years of residence and research in three Muslim countries and visits over the years to ten Middle Eastern nations and

Fig. 1. Layers of history: Egyptian obelisk (in foreground) and Blue mosque in Istanbul, Turkey.

Uzbekistan in central Asia during the Soviet era. The book is intended as an introductory text or for a popular audience—it is popular in the sense that it derives from people, from the grass roots, from lives lived and observed. I am an American woman whose view spans three decades. I first lived in the Sudan with my husband and older daughter, and later resided and researched in Egypt with our two daughters, and in the Maghrib nation of Tunisia. Our younger daughter, Nichola, studied at the American University in Cairo during the fall of 2001. Many visits to the region have been interspersed with the longer stays. I began my formal research in 1970. The subsequent three decades have seen dynamic change for the Arab and Muslim worlds and self-examination and critical evaluation of the West's role in these regions. These decades took me from my mid-twenties as a graduate student to my mid-fifties as a senior anthropology professor.

Anthropological studies of the Middle East and North Africa, as Ernest Gellner observed, are generally approached "from below"; they are generally not rooted in texts and the analysis of records and documents. They may occasionally utilize textual sources, but these are often supplemental to what has been experienced firsthand. The basic anthropological method of participant observation presupposes long-term stays, the ability to conduct research in the local language or dialect, and residence with the people studied. Research is often not predictable, and the best insights can occur in the interstices, where they are least expected. There is not the comfort or security of texts, of documents viewed and reviewed, or perhaps photocopied for later viewing, in libraries or research institutes; there is not the certainty of the written word that can be quoted and cited. There is only the uncertainty of self and of self in relation to others, of life lived and observed in its untidy, ever-changing, day-to-day dynamic.

I recall with some embarrassment even today an exchange that took place early in my fieldwork in the Sudan when I was still learning conversational Arabic. Several young Sudanese women were questioning me about American culture and religion, when one of them broke in with the question, "Do you eat pork?" I replied, "Oh, not very often," proud that I could express a degree of frequency between always and not at all. A hushed silence replaced the banter that had been under way. I realized that I had made a terrible error in revealing this unclean, unacceptable pork-eating behavior to them. Red-faced, I tried to turn the conversation to another subject, but I was unsuccessful as they looked at me now not just as an oddity but as an unhygienic one. It is this sort of experience which makes an indelible impression about the deep feelings associated with a food taboo in society, feelings that are not replicable for a researcher working with a text or document.

Orientalism

Orientalism is an important body of literature in the West that has been associated with the study of the Islamic faith and its textual sources. It can be defined most simply as the study of the East (the Orient) by the West. Orientalist scholars have examined the holy books of Islam: the Qur'an, the books of Hadith concerning the Prophet's sayings and doings, the books interpreting the religious law called the Shari'a, and the opinions of many of the famous Muslim scholars on religious subjects. Orientalism as a scholarly body of literature dates from the time of Napoleon in Egypt, 1798–1803. He brought teams of scholars with his military expedition to inaugurate this Western study of the East in the early European encounter, but the heyday of Orientalism was during the European colonial rule, c. 1850–1960.

While the Orientalists served to introduce Islam to the West, they also introduced or carried forward a number of misconceptions about Islam and Muslims. One of the most fundamental errors made was the reference to the religion of Islam as Mohammedanism. In doing so they elevated the Prophet Muhammad to the status of deity, like Jesus Christ, for whom the religion of Christianity is named. Muhammad was a man and the Messenger of Islam (al-Rasul Allah), last of the great prophets of the Abrahamic tradition in the Middle East, but not God or a son of God. The term *Mohammedanism* came into the West and became a standard reference for the religion in English throughout the colonial period. Orientalist painters, such as Jean-Leon Gerome, Eugene Delacroix, Pierre-Auguste Renoir, J. F. Lewis, and David Roberts, created beautiful, romanticized paintings of mosques, bazaars, and "Arab" festivals, and they were especially fascinated by the harem and by conditions of "Oriental" slavery, certainly different from the images of plantation slavery in the New World. Whereas no Muslim would call himself or herself a "Mohammedan," the use of the term reflects the Orientalist approach that relied on relatively superficial contacts with people and was occupied with its own construction of Oriental reality. These images directly affected photographic and later cinematic representation of the "Arab" male and female and the "Orient" as exotic and erotic that can be studied in highly popular films from *The Sheik* in the 1920s to Disney's *Aladdin* in the 1980s.

Another Orientalist view that created an offense against the religion of Islam was the idea that the Qur'an, which Muslims believe to be the revealed word of God, was written by Muhammad. This assertion has often been posed as a great puzzle by the Orientalists, since Muhammad was not literate enough to produce a work that set the standard for the rich and complex Arabic language. It is perhaps this "puzzle" that Salman Rushdie's *Satanic Verses* attempted to resolve. This work of fiction said that the Qur'an was dictated to Muhammad by Satan, instead of by God. Highly controversial, this work was defended in the West as artistic freedom, but was condemned and reviled in the Muslim world as the latest example of the West's ignorance and intolerance of Islam. In Iran only, anger was expressed to the point of a sentence of death in a *fatwa* (religious opinion) issued by Ayatollah Khomenei and renewed by his successors. This fatwa was not supported by the larger Muslim community of scholars.

Noted Western scholars, from Karl Marx to Max Weber, relied on Orientalist stereotypes as they theorized about "Oriental despotism" or "Kadi justice." While there has been a systematic effort in the West to ignore or dismiss much of what Marx wrote, Weber's writings on "the Orient" have had an enduring impact upon Western discourse concerning Islamic law and Muslim societies. Kadi justice, according to Weber, not only operated without precedent but also was responsible for the failure of a rational capitalism to develop in the Muslim world (Peletz 2002, 67).

Orientalism began to disappear after the independence of Arab and Muslim nations of Africa and Asia and has been critiqued in postcolonial literature. Revision of earlier Orientalist views has fallen to Arab critics of the Orientalists, A. L. Tibawi, Anour Abdel Malik, and Edward Said. Others have joined this critical scholarship to note the errors, the arrogance, and the subjectivity of this unique Western viewpoint known as Orientalism (Hussain, Olson & Qureshi 1984). This critique, popularized by Edward Said, has entered mainstream Western discourse and is a point of view that is more recognized and is increasingly taught in courses that take a critical view of Western colonialism and the dominance of its views of the world.

Newer studies by Western, post-Orientalist historians and social scientists have sought to comprehend the development of Arab and Muslim society more on its own terms than as a consequence of or a reaction to events in Western history (Hourani 1991). Likewise, an increasing number of first-hand anthropological accounts of life as lived by Arabs and Muslims in various geographical and historical contexts have helped to correct the literature regarding previous Orientalist inventions of Islamic society. The interpretations presented in many of these works are incorporated into this present text, which seeks to present an alternative to Orientalist views.

More formal studies of the Islamic faith by Muslims in English, such as works by Fazlur Rahman and Sayed Hossein Nasr, are valued aids in studying Islam, as are various introductions to the religion intended for a general Western audience (see "Suggestions for Further Reading"). In sum, these works constitute a body of knowledge that permits us in the West to have access to a more objective understanding of the religion of Islam and the society it invokes and promotes.

The Experience of Fieldwork, 1970–1990

Anthropologists employ participant observation, which presumes long-term residence and language acquisition in the culture being studied. Familiarity with everyday life is a given, and anthropologists quickly learn that they often have unusual mobility in other peoples' societies. Our older daughter, Josina, is an outdoor experiential educator, and she says she learned about experiential education as the daughter of anthropologists with nearly four years of her life spent in Muslim or Arab societies.

Learning Arabic in 1968 and 1969 in the United States, in our case in Chicago, was not easy. Only a generation ago, most universities did not teach conversational Arabic (al-daraji) or literary modern standard Arabic (al-fusha). This has changed greatly today due to increased interest in Arab-Muslim societies, but three decades ago the formal study of the Arabic language was available mainly to the linguist and the religious specialist. My husband, Richard Lobban, and I realized that this skill would have to be acquired in the field.

Sudan and Egypt, 1970–1984

When we arrived in Khartoum in 1970, we had a basic training in Arabic letters and sounds, but little Arabic conversational ability. Since so much information in anthropological fieldwork is acquired by listening and observing, learning Arabic by ear became a natural extension of that process. There are obvious advantages to learning a language in its natural setting, and the assuredness about the contextual use of expressions and phrases that this conveys is one that has served many an anthropological insight. Often recalling a phrase or word as being used in a particular mood to convey a special meaning is an excellent means of analyzing cultural values. *'Ayb* (shame) is a powerful word-expression with many contextual uses. It can be used to reprimand a child or to criticize a politician; it can be used by a judge to reproach some shameful adult behavior, and it is a type of divorce due to impotence in a man. Absorbing the contextual use of language aids us in understanding the nuances of language and culture.

The disadvantage of learning a language by ear is that literacy in the language lags behind, and the act of conversation and human interaction surpasses the desire or ability to read the newspaper, for example. We frequently took in the news of the world by ear, as conversational use of the language overtook its literary usage.

After some initial study of Arabic grammar and linguistic structure, Richard and I settled into a life where we spoke English at home and Arabic in public. This was a process, we soon realized, that was much like that of a baby learning to make linguistic sense of its world. Thus we made many silly mistakes in the initial phase of learning conversational, colloquial Sudanese Arabic. For example, the Arabic words for liver (*kibda*), cheese (*jibna*), and butter (*zibda*) presented a special challenge because of their similarity to our relatively untutored ears. So we often mistakenly asked for one when we meant the other. Likewise, the different forms of a word, from the singular to the dual or to the plural were a challenge and an amusement to us. *Finjan* (one cup) becomes *finjanain* (two cups) and is then altered further to *fanajin* for three or more cups, only to revert to the singular *finjan* after ten cups. *Bayt* (one house) was easily transformed to *baytain* (two houses), but we frequently had to guess what the proper plural form would be, in this case, *bayoot*. Occasionally, the roles of teacher and student were exchanged. If an English-speaking Sudanese would mispronounce the word *port* as "bort" or Pepsi as "Bepsi," due to the lack of the consonant *p* in Arabic, we could make the gentle correction. Generally, our language acquisition was accomplished in pleasant company with good times, due to the patience and hospitality of our hosts. After six months, when we had the occasion to meet the then president of the Sudan, Ja'afar Numeiri, we were pleased to have been able to conduct that brief conversation entirely in Arabic. By this time we had been given Sudanese names, which never failed to make an impression and helped people to remember us by a familiar name. My name, Mihera bint Abboud, was selected from nineteenth-century history, the name of a Shayqiya woman who exhorted the hesitating men of her group to resist the invading Turco-Egyptian armies by riding ahead of them on camel back and ululating, what Sudanese call the "zagharoot," "ayoo-yoo-yooo." This story never failed to excite me and stir my imagination, and I was proud to bear the name of this genuine Sudanese heroine. I have since examined Mihera's story as a part of a larger "Lady of Victory" cult that is historically present in other Arab and North African societies. Richard was given the name of one of the great nationalist leaders of the 1924 "White Flag" rebellion against British imperialism, 'Abd al-Fadil Al-Maz, a name that was symbolically important, since this fallen hero was a southern patriot from the days when northerners and southerners fought together against the common foe of colonialism, rather than fighting each other.

In the Sudan, as well as in Egypt and Tunisia, words and phrases have developed in the local dialect as a special way of expressing cultural values. The Egyptians have a more formal and hierarchical approach to casual contact with strangers or foreigners, and the special Turkish-derived "Effendum, Effendi" (Madam and Sir) is common. Much of my own language acquisition has been in the company of women with whom I have spent the greatest amount of social time. I thus learned to greet another woman with the more familiar "Izzayik?" or "Kaf al-hal?" (How are you? How are things?) rather than the more formal "assalaam alaykum" (Peace be upon you) that men would use. More recently, within the context of a revival of Islamic culture, both sexes use the more formal, universal Muslim greeting—"assalaam alaykum," with the response "wa alaykum assalaam" (and upon you peace). Both the greeting and response employ the plural you, referring not only to the individual being addressed but the individual's family as well.

In terms of housing arrangements, over the years we have tried to be a part of community life. That approach has taken us from life on a houseboat on the Blue Nile in Khartoum, to residence with families in Omdurman, Sudan, when accommodation was problematical, to renting apartments in the suburbs or within the city's bustling market area, to living near the main transportation lines in the cities of Tunis and Cairo, since we mainly relied on public transportation. The advantage to this, with research conducted within communities, is that of being in daily touch with life as lived by people. Conversations overheard on the tram, train, or bus into town, complaints about government corruption or inefficiency, working women discussing their problems at the butcher's, waiting in line at 5 A.M. for bread, all add up to powerful and lasting impressions, an immensely rich and constantly stimulating experience.

Although it may have been difficult at times to be American nationals, as during the Vietnam War in the early 1970s in Sudan or just before the Gulf War in Tunisia, we rarely experienced any direct anti-Americanism. Perhaps our language ability in Arabic offset the potential critical remark, but more often we were praised, far beyond our real ability, for our fluency in Arabic. The fact is that few Westerners speak Arabic, although they have long come to parts of the Arabic-speaking world as travelers, tourists, or even as long-term residents. And the amazement with which we would be greeted was frequently followed by a barrage of questions as to whether we were of Arabic origin, or very clever at languages, or employed as spies. Why else would one bother to learn to speak Arabic, a language they believe is devalued by Westerners, and in Tunisia is even devalued by many of the Westernized Tunisian business and professional class? The possibility that we were merely curious people with a genuine interest in their culture and history was sometimes difficult to convey at first meeting.

Having children in the field has been a great benefit. At first we were just a couple as graduate students in Sudan in 1970–1972, and returning to the Sudan in 1975 still childless added fuel to the serious doubts, apparently, that many had about our being married. But returning in 1979 with a lovely, redheaded two-year-old daughter was greeted with joy and a newfound legitimacy for us as a family. The experience of a young child in a predominantly Muslim society added a fresh perspective for us. First, on the matter of language, Josina was just beginning to speak English when we took her to Khartoum. So when we began to use Arabic on a regular basis, she took understandable offense. This came of some necessity since we were unable at the time to find separate accommodation and needed to live with a friend's family. While we used English among ourselves, most daily conversation was in Arabic, so in defense our daughter invented her own gibberish language that only she and her stuffed animals could understand.

Once we were established in our own flat in the central Suq al-Arabi area,

Josina became adept at mimicking particular details of everyday life that she had observed on the street from our balcony or as she traveled about with her parents. She would imitate Sudanese women's clothing, the tobe, by placing her blanket over her head with a corner held between her teeth, as she had seen women do when riding on public transportation. One day she amazed us by bringing out to the living room a bath towel, arranging it carefully and performing perfectly all of the motions of Muslim prayer, without the words. Where had she learned this? Apparently she had observed from our balcony the local merchants praying together in the late afternoon before the shops opened for the evening.

She absorbed a great deal more about the practice of Islam in daily life without special instruction just by being a child trying to understand her surroundings. Hearing the call to prayer early each morning at sunrise and drifting back to sleep for a little while longer, hearing it another four times during the day from home or while out walking made an impression, and our daughter would cup her ears, in the manner of the muezzin she had seen on television, and call out, "Allahu hapgar." "No, no," we would say, "Allahu akbar, God is great," and she would repeat her first version, which she had learned to say by herself.

The generosity that an egalitarian society like Sudan engenders is a value that is highly recognized and praised in Islamic society as well. Sharing is an expected part of being Muslim, especially with the less fortunate. The growing number of homeless on the streets of major cities is made more shameful and pitiable due to the continued strength of the value of extended familial bonds. A homeless person suggests no family to help out and makes a sad situation even worse. Offering some spare money to such persons is a good act, and Josina would beg us to give her some coins to give to the street people. Her small act of generosity was often met with approving smiles or outright verbal praise from strangers and passersby. Frequently, when making a small purchase, such as candy or chewing gum, Josina would offer a piece of the newly purchased item to the salesperson with the usual invitation, "Itfadl," thinking that she was doing the right thing culturally, and most salespeople would accept with a broad appreciative smile.

Josina had already assimilated enough American culture before coming to Sudan that she experienced a certain amount of culture shock. She did not accept the sexual segregation of her parents when visiting friends and initially tried to get me to sit with Daddy and his friends. After repeated failures, she learned the rules of this cultural tradition, almost too well, and would enforce the rule strictly when guests came to call at our flat. Women, she would insist, must go into the bedroom to visit, while the men should stay in the living room.

She also resisted learning the language that her parents had suddenly shifted to just as she was beginning to master some basic English. Although she could follow a conversation pretty well, she often refused to perform on command to say hello or good-bye in Arabic. Her hidden talent was displayed one day when, having refused to greet some strangers on the street who had stopped to admire her red hair, and who remarked that she was as sweet as sugar, she shot back in perfect Arabic, "Ana mish sukara. Ana fil fil," meaning "I'm not sugar. I'm hot pepper!"

Two years later, we brought our two daughters to Cairo. Nichola, being just one year old at the time, was just beginning to learn language and culture. Rather than experiencing some measure of culture shock, which her sister had earlier in Sudan presuming a foundation of prior cultural learning, we had a child with basic motor skills ready and eager for language and behavioral training. This space was filled with everyday speech and mannerisms of the Egyptians with whom we lived and the grandfatherly cook, Hafez, who took a special interest in her nutrition and proper education. She began to speak Arabic at the same time as English and did not make much differentiation between the two. "No!" seemed to have twice the impact if uttered in both languages, and the first full sentences were peppered with Arabic nouns and English verbs. Some important words started in Arabic and remained as a basic part of her vocabulary for a long time after our return, emotion-laden words, like "futa" for her special blanket and the personal pronoun "Ana" for self-identification.

It was Hafez who first noted that Nichola regularly sang after a meal once her stomach was full, a personal trait that continues to this day. It was with Hafez in the kitchen that she was able to observe the boys' elementary school, with its three sessions daily, and the more devout among them praying in the small mosque just below our window. She too learned the basic motions of prayer in this fashion and would try to mimic the call to prayer, only this time she had a native speaker to correct her and train her properly to say, "Allahu akbar." Years later, when Nichola entered the great Blue Mosque on a trip to Istanbul, she pleaded to stay longer after the tour, to sit and be quiet, to watch the faithful at prayer, and to absorb the serene ambience. A spiritual sense was awakened in her, perhaps evoked by a distant memory of her early childhood in Cairo.

Nichola and her sister were taught to use Arabic on the street for every little treasure that they wanted to purchase. "Ana owza bassassa," meaning "I want a lollipop," was Nichola's first and perhaps most frequently used sentence. She would also beg for candy from our neighbor downstairs, greeting Umm Mohammed with "Hellawa" (something sweet) instead of a more proper "Hello." Thus her language learning seemed utterly opportunistic.

Her name, Nichola, is similar to a Greek boy's name, Nicola, so our little daughter was often taken for a little boy, since she did not have the customary ear piercing at an early age. Upon meeting her and learning her name, most Egyptians would remark what a handsome boy, to which Nichola learned a number of choice retorts. "No, I'm a girl" (Bint, mush welad!) Appropriate hand gestures went along with the words, hand upraised, palm outward, moving it back and forth as in the American wave good-bye, but signaling no, absolutely not a boy! This particularly undesired form of public attention was an excellent inducement to wear a dress or child's *jellabiya* out-of-doors, instead of the more comfortable American overalls.

Josina spent her kindergarten and first grade school years at Cairo American College, an international school. There they taught Arabic twice a week and took field trips to mosques, which are open to the general public and to non-Muslims in Egypt, unlike our experiences in Tunisia and Sudan. Josina also went to the Pyramids for field trips and learned that there is no riddle to the Sphinx except how to save it from the devastating effects of pollution. Almost two decades later, Nichola attended the American University in Cairo for her collegiate study abroad experience.

Tunisia, 1990

Our next opportunity to travel and live in northern Africa came when the girls were thirteen and nine. By this time they were seasoned travelers, having sailed around the world with their parents on the University of Pittsburgh Semester at Sea program, and were accustomed to the culture, language, and food differences. But they were also more established American culture bearers, having spent seven years back home in Rhode Island. They added to their knowledge of Arabic quite a bit of French, since Tunisia is strongly bilingual, especially in the urban areas. We had continued to teach courses dealing with the Middle East and Islam and derived the benefit of working with sincere students eager to fill gaps in their traditional learning. Over the years we have benefited enormously from our students' interest. They have shown great enthusiasm not only in stories and slides but also in physical, tactile, and sensual objects from the region, such as clothing, perfumes, Arabic calligraphy, music, children's books and Arabic learning boards (*loh*), local money, good luck amulets, such as the "hand of Fatima" and "evil eye" symbols, and a host of other ephemera associated with daily life. This has encouraged us over the years to bring more such items back for use in the classroom. Also, more subtly, our own understanding and insight into the culture of "the other" and our own culture was deepening in this process of living abroad and returning and then reflecting upon the experience for the purpose of teaching and communicating with Americans. The result is more one of interpretation than direct translation of cultural ideas

Fig. 2. Author's daughters, Josina and Nichola, in Tunisia, 1990.

and practice. This sincere interest displayed by our students and the general public, motivated by an effort to correct the lack of general education about the region and its peoples, is inspiration for writing this book.

Living near a local market and public transportation made our comings and goings frequent and much observed, so that within a short time we were known as the Americans who can speak Arabic and French (Richard and Josina possess some conversational fluency). Few American families visit Tunisia or live there, except for diplomatic personnel, so we were something of a curiosity. The fact that I had to rely on Arabic and could not use French for everyday affairs puzzled many salespeople. Why would a "European" know Arabic and not French? The Islamist activists that I came to know later were pleased that I used only Arabic, and they made exceptions for my

Sudanese-Egyptian accent while they assisted me with the local Tunisian dialect. This was, for me, an important lesson in the powerful legacy of French colonialism, as language is a critical shaper of worldview, and contextually in Tunisia, French is the language of discourse and the educated, while Arabic is the common language spoken by poorly educated people. This made public reaction to me complex, and I was frequently taken for an Egyptian or Syrian woman. People heard my colloquial Eastern dialect of Arabic as classical Arabic, which gave me praise far beyond my ability. I came to understand that the Islamic revival sweeping Tunisia and other parts of the Maghrib reflects also a desire for the restoration of the Arabic language, as well as the recovery and strengthening of Islamic traditions.

The girls, already addicted to American malls, rediscovered the pleasures of the original indoor shopping mall, the Middle Eastern bazaar (*suq* or *medina*, literally city, as the Tunisians refer to it). The jewelry, perfumes, inlaid boxes, leather handbags, and Tunisian specialties such as ceramic tiles and items carved of olive wood were a constant source of delight and diversion. They remained shy about the bargaining essential to every purchase, but did not hesitate to enlist my efforts when spending their money. A favorite game to play with the eager merchants, especially during the slower winter months, was to have them try to guess our national identity. They would begin with French, and the girls would respond in either French or Arabic. Then "Deutsch?" "Nein," they would reply. "Spanish?" "No, señor." The last guess, typically, would be English, meaning from England? "Yes, for the language." "You are American?" "American, Bush, America?" (the year was 1990; also works after 2001). "Yes, yes," with broad smiles, and not a hint of anti-Americanism, only genuine curiosity and the omnipresent word for welcome, "Marhaba!"

This was at the time of the buildup to the Gulf War when several hundred thousand American troops had been deployed to the Arabian peninsula. We were in the city where the Palestine Liberation Organization had its international headquarters and where there was tremendous public sympathy for the Palestinians, with a strong antiwar sentiment. Yet we, as an American family, were not subjected to a single unkind word. I could not help but reflect upon this as Arabs and Muslims across the United States became targets for harassment during the several months of the Gulf War.

Islam in America

Islam has become America's second most practiced faith with an estimated 8–10 million Muslims in the United States, about 40 percent of whom are American converts, and the rest who are Muslims born in the United States

Fig. 3. The U.S. Army's first Muslim cleric and family.

or those who have come to America as migrants from Asia, Africa, and elsewhere. The first mosque in America was built by Lebanese immigrants in Cedar Rapids, Iowa, and today there are thousands of mosques throughout the country, with the largest concentration of Muslims in Detroit, and in large cities of the Northeast and West Coast.

It is often overlooked that a significant percentage, perhaps as much as one-fifth, of enslaved Africans brought to the United States during three centuries of the transatlantic slave trade were Muslims, especially from the west African regions of Senegambia and the Gulf of Guinea, and from the interior of what is today Ghana and Nigeria (Austin 1984). The popular televised series *Roots*, a signal event in African American history, began with Alex Haley's ancestor Kunta Kinte being captured from the Gambia River and later portrayed him praying to Allah at the bottom of a Christian slave ship. Many contemporary African American converts to Islam speak of their "reversion" to Islam, rather than conversion.

Increased enrollment of Muslim children in American public schools has led to some accommodation of school routines with Muslim practice. Some high schools have acknowledged fasting teenagers by offering alternative space to the cafeteria during lunch in the month of Ramadan. Others provide quiet rooms for prayer or permit students to leave school to attend mosques for Friday prayer, while a few school districts permit students to take off the Muslim holidays without penalty. Young Muslim women choosing to cover themselves with the *hijab*, headscarf and long dress, generally have been supported. However, many Muslim women in America report that their employers have forced them to remove the hijab. Often education for the employer remedies this type of job discrimination, but otherwise legal or quasi-legal remedies must be sought.

American recognition of Muslim holidays has progressed but is far from the accommodation made to Christian and Jewish belief. Although in the United States separation of church and state is lawful in many domains, Christmas, Chanukah, Good Friday, Easter, Passover, Rosh Hashanah, and other religious holidays are recognized by school districts and by many states. Americans do not recognize the 'Eid al-Fitr, celebrating the end of the month of fasting, nor the 'Eid al-Adha, commemorating Abraham's willingness to sacrifice his son, although today America's practicing Muslims outnumber its professing Jews. The Clinton administration was the first to acknowledge Islamic holidays by inviting Muslim leaders into the White House on these occasions. In 2001 the 'Eid Mubarak (blessed holiday) stamp was issued to acknowledge American Islam at the time of the 'Eid al-Fitr, which for that year fell close to Christmas and Chanukah. Since the Islamic calendar is based on a lunar system, Muslim holidays occur about eleven days earlier during each solar calendar year. This historic first "Muslim" stamp (figure 6) had been planned before September 11, 2001, and in that year it turned out to be an excellent opportunity for America to show in one way that its war was not with Islam or Muslims.

The Nation of Islam has had greater notoriety and visibility in the United States due to prominent and charismatic figures such as Malcolm X and Louis Farrakhan. Historically, the Nation of Islam projected an image of militant and racial exclusion for black people only, an idea contrary to the teachings of Islam. Also, its founder, Elijah Muhammad, was regarded by some followers as an American prophet, also anathema to Islam's message of Muhammad as the final prophet. The Nation of Islam has been both feared and admired in America—feared for its militance and admired for the upright image and discipline exhibited by its followers. Malcolm X made the pilgrimage to Mecca and visited the Arab-Muslim world, where he experienced genuine racial harmony with Muslims, perhaps for the first time in his life. With a changed heart and mind he returned home as al-Hajj Malik al-Shabazz and repudiated the racial attitudes of the Nation of Islam. Many believe that this was the reason for his assassination in 1963. Warith Deen Muhammad later led many Nation of Islam members to mainstream Sunni Islam.

Louis Farrakhan assumed the leadership of the movement after the death of Elijah Muhammad and again drew fear and praise from the media with his Million Man March in May 1998 in Washington, D.C., which attracted nearly that number of predominantly African American men to a renewed sense of commitment to God, family, and community. Many non-Muslim men and women attended this historic rally, and a woman's march was organized the following year. The ability of religion, in this case Islam, to mobilize people in the United States may be used as an analogous example for understanding the mass mobilization of people for various social and political causes throughout the Muslim world.

Stereotypes of Arabs and Muslims

Cultural stereotypes are typically rooted in some familiarity with the subject, but as the truism goes, a little knowledge can be a dangerous thing. Ignorance of the faith of Islam, combined with a lack of knowledge of Middle Eastern history or direct experience with Arabs and Muslims, can result in simplistic generalizations. In the aftermath of the World Trade Center bombing in 1993 and the collapse of the towers in September 2001, racial profiling of Arab and Muslim-looking people was common, and there were many cases of mistaken identity, notably Indians and Sikhs being harassed as "Arabs." Regrettably, some argued that this was an acceptable form of prejudice, denying civil rights or civil liberties to persons who appear suspicious to the untutored eye.

Relations between the West and the Middle East have been forged through unwelcome or hostile historic encounters. Beginning in the seventh century with the spread of Islam into former Christian states and continuing through two centuries of Christian Crusades in an attempt to reverse Muslim reign, it has culminated in the approximately 150 years of European colonial and American neocolonial control and influence in the Middle East. The current Western preoccupation is with Middle East politics, due to the importance of oil, the strategic value of the region, and the immediate fear of terrorism. Add to this the U.S. support of Israel and its fear of the Arab and Muslim backlash, most obvious with the rise of Islamic militancy, and a broad cultural groundwork is laid for stereotyping.

The mass media reflects this deep history of hostility. "Terrorist" is often the first word association I receive from students in my class in response to my question "What do you know about Arabs or Muslims?" "Arab-Islamic Culture and the West" is one of many courses students can take in our core curriculum in general education that balances the study of the West with the non-Western world. In this class and another, entitled "The West and Its Others," I perform an exercise whereby I create a bipolar continuum with the United States at one end and "the others" at the opposite end. I ask students to name countries or regions that, relatively speaking, are closer to or farther away from "us" in terms of culture and values. Canada and Europe are always the closest; Australia is often next, followed by Japan, South America, Russia, and China. Almost invariably the "Arab world" and Islamic cultures are placed farthest away from the United States. I remind students that our Western cultural and religious heritage comes from this region and that the great Asian civilizations they place closer to "us" are really more culturally remote, but they remain adamant that Arabs and Muslims are least like us.

When I ask what else students associate with Arab men, they respond that Arabs are dark with shifty eyes, dirty, scary, lecherous, wearing long robes and turbans.

"Anything good?" I ask.

"Yeah, they're rich."

"What about Muslim men?"

"They're the same, aren't they?"

Indeed, it is true that many lump Eastern peoples together, whether Arab, Muslim, or Hindu. One of our study abroad posters was defaced because it advertised a music program in India and featured a dark man with a turban playing a small sitar. The graffiti read, "Get the explosives, the Americans are coming!"

Students often describe Arab women as veiled, passive, always walking behind their husbands, having no rights. Some associate Arab women with belly dancers. When I point out that veiling (Islam) and unveiling (belly dancing) are contradictory and that there is little social middle ground in this stereotypical view, the students begin to think, yes, where are the housewives and mothers, and from here their hearts and minds begin to open.

The "Hollywood Arab," as Jack Shaheen has revealed, is an unabashed bad guy stereotype played out in innumerable films from *Iron Eagle* to *State of Siege*. The hugely popular Disney cartoon *Aladdin* was criticized for its anti-Arab opening song lyrics:

Oh, I come from a land, from a faraway place
Where the caravans and camels roam
Where they cut off your ear if they don't like your face
It's barbaric, but, hey, it's home.

Protest from Arab-American antidefamation groups brought about the following change to the third line: "Where the desert's immense and the heat is intense" but leaving in the presumably less offensive lyric, "It's barbaric, but, hey, it's home."

Plenty of profit has been made in the stereotypical film portrayals of Arabs and Muslims. What has been lacking has been the range of humanity that one would expect of any religion or culture that encompasses over a billion people. Has terror been used as a weapon by Arabs and Muslims?

Yes, and it has been used by many other cultural groups as well, including the Irish Republican Army, the Tamil Tigers, and the Americans. Terrorism can never be justified by any faith, and the foregoing is certainly not meant as an apology for terrorism. But as a wise Sudanese once told us, "Remember that every time you point a finger at someone else, think of the three fingers that are pointing back at you."

The Aftermath of 9/11 and the Future of American and Arab-Muslim Relations

Since the Iranian Islamic Revolution in 1979 and the taking of American hostages in Teheran, and then the bombing of the American embassies in Nairobi and Dar As-Salaam, and finally the events of September 11, 2001, the American people have come to fear militancy in Islam and perhaps Islam itself. Extremist Muslims like Osama bin Laden and al-Qaeda members are no more typical of Islam than are KKK terrorists who burn black churches typical of Christianity. Rather than focus on the Islamic faith and Muslims as the source of the problems, Americans might examine American and Western policies that may have provided the background to these attacks. While attacks against the United States loom large in our consciousness, Americans have little knowledge of acts committed by the United States against Arab or Muslim nations considered acts of aggression, such as the U.S. bombing during the Reagan era of Muammar Qaddafi's home in 1988 in which his daughter was killed; the bombing of the Shifa Pharmaceutical plant in Sudan in 1998 during Clinton's Monica affair; and the seemingly uncritical support of the Israeli occupation of Palestinian territories. The U.S. "war on terrorism" targets an amorphous, transnational group of men whose movement can be traced to U.S. support of the "mujahideen" fighters in Afghanistan whose Muslim and nationalist zeal was mobilized in the cold war against the Soviet occupation in the 1980s. Emboldened by their success after the Soviet withdrawal, they sought new recruits among disaffected youth in secular Arab and Muslim countries, while they found safe havens in weak Islamist states, such as Sudan, and later Afghanistan under the Taliban. The Gulf War in 1991 was a turning point, with major U.S. military presence in the Holy Lands of the Arabian peninsula; this coupled with the imbalanced support of Israel over Palestinians and U.S. intervention perceived in the region to control all of its oil constitute some of the main reasons that recruitment and support of groups like al-Qaeda exist in the Arab and Muslim worlds. It stands to reason that the overwhelming majority of the world's Muslims reject acts of terror that resulted in the loss of innocent lives, such as in the World Trade Center attacks and those on the

U.S. embassies in Nairobi and Dar al-Salaam, and they do. It is vital that the U.S. "war on terrorism" not be seen as a war against Muslims. On the streets in Arab and Muslim capitals, it is widely believed to be just that.

In the quest for a new relationship with the Arab and Islamic worlds, it is vital that knowledge and familiarity replace ignorance and stereotyping. To incorporate a worldview shared by Muslims should not threaten our own, nor does knowledge mean conversion or blurring of difference. Imagine a U.S. president or secretary of state opening a meeting with an Arab or Muslim head of state with the universal Muslim greeting, "assalaam alaykum," as an elementary beginning. Life in the twenty-first century calls for acknowledgment and reassessment of the prejudice that is as ancient as the Crusades and as modern as the present revival of Islam. The Muslim "other" needs to be redefined as fellow human, rather than simplistically as enemy or one not to be trusted.

Ignorance and stereotyping must be replaced with corrective knowledge. We have so little experience with Islam or Muslims in the United States that we typically are not even aware of the important holidays. We hear little of the hajj unless there is a disaster or some political unrest, as in the heyday of the Iranian Revolution. Political reporting of the latest violence from the Middle East by Western media frequently is filmed with the correspondent standing in front of a mosque, and it is considered better if the call to prayer can be heard in the background. This lends an air of authenticity, it is no doubt believed, but it also sends a subliminal message that politics (often of a violent nature, which attracts the media) is associated with the mosque and Islam. So strong is the association between Islam and terrorism in the United States that when news broke of the bombing of the Murra Federal Building in Oklahoma City, the first and strongest suspicion fell upon Arabs and Muslims until it was revealed that the terrorism was homegrown. After September 11, there is little doubt that Arabs or Muslims are involved in such acts, although the FBI reportedly believes that the perpetrator of the anthrax scare immediately after 9/11 was an American.

Since the first edition of this book in 1994, my husband and I have made almost annual trips to Egypt. However, after the Islamist regime seized power in 1989, we did not return to Sudan until 2004. Our younger daughter, Nicki, returned to Egypt in the fateful fall of 2001 to study at the American University in Cairo as an exchange student from the University of Denver. Only weeks after her arrival, the attacks on the World Trade Center and the Pentagon took place. She reported that Egyptians were generally sympathetic about the loss of lives but nonetheless critical of U.S. policies in the Middle East that foment such intense anger and extreme actions. She had no negative or unpleasant experiences. About a quarter of the American students at the American University went home, but Nicki expressed a strong desire to remain. The American students were instructed by the U.S. embassy staff not to travel together in large groups and only to move about with Egyptian friends. Nicki traveled alone, often to the Sinai Red Sea resorts, without incident.

As the fall wore on and the U.S. war in Afghanistan began, the simultaneous dropping of bombs and food provoked a good deal of cynical comment. Often taken as Russian (she has strong Ukrainian features from my mother's side), she did not reveal her American nationality. Had she been living in some of Cairo's poorer neighborhoods where Islamist activism is strong, her experience might not have been so uneventful. In my public lectures, I often contrast her positive experience in Cairo during this stressful period of Arab and American relations with the discrimination and prejudice that many Arabs, Muslims, and those mistaken for them experienced in the wake of September 11, 2001. Only days after 9/11, an employee at the college announced that a terrorist had been caught in Providence. I asked, "How do you know?" Her response was that the person apprehended wore a turban and had a beard, to which I replied that not all men with turbans and beards were terrorists. The "terrorist" turned out to be an Indian Sikh who was taken off a train from Boston in Providence and charged with carrying a concealed weapon, the *kirpan,* a religious symbol ritually required to be worn by all Sikh males. It took weeks of political agitation before the city of Providence dropped the charges, doing so without apology to a victim of cultural ignorance and prejudice.

We remain involved with Sudanese studies through the academic association we helped to found in 1980 and through friends in Egypt and in the United States, among the many who have sought political refuge in the wake of the persistent civil war and numerous violations of civil and human rights under the National Islamic Front. From these recent visits to the region it can be said that the reserve of goodwill toward Americans is faltering under the influence of our unbalanced foreign policies in the region and Islamist propaganda that views the West as both the unshakeable ally of Israel and a country that is ignorant and hostile to Islam. Patience is limited, while visible and audible anger expressed toward the United States has become more apparent. The need for a more knowledgeable and engaged presence of America is more urgent than it was nearly a decade ago when the first edition was written. There is simply no substitute for accurate information, sensitivity, and a basic knowledge of the faith of Islam as a part of the Abrahamic tradition that includes Judaism and Christianity. Coupled with an interest in the region's history and culture—its story—as well as an appreciation of life as it is lived in the regions where Islam predominates, the West can develop new and more equitable relations with Middle Eastern and Muslim people.

Before and after September 11, I made a habit of inviting students in my

Fig. 4. Colgate University students visiting the Islamic Center of Central New York in Syracuse.

classes on the Middle East, Africa, and Islamic societies to local mosques to observe Friday prayers. I have never made this compulsory, preferring that students actively decide to enter this space. Typically a few choose to do so. We are invariably welcomed, at times having our presence favorably mentioned in the Friday sermon in Rhode Island, and in the case of the Islamic Center of New York in Syracuse, the students were treated to pizza and soft drinks by the imam, who sat with them and answered their questions. From these visits I have learned that there is a keen desire on the part of Muslims and non-Muslims for improved communication. These simple experiences of meeting face to face can be transformative.

As the West engages more with the regions of Islam—and interest has never been higher since 9/11, as any Middle East or Islamic studies expert will testify—it is well to be aware of the complex dynamic that is occurring in Muslim societies that have been shaken to their core by the very same events. Intense reflection is taking place about the internal and external politics that have given rise to such acts of violence carried out by Muslims. Critical examination is also occurring of how the holy sources of the faith of Islam—a religion founded in tolerance, mercy, and compassion—could be so misused as to justify these acts of violence. This dialogue, which is internal to Islam, is as important as the West's need for knowledge and engagement with the world of Islam and Muslims.

Ironically, this complex set of reactions following September 11 has produced a sharp awakening of the American public regarding its ignorance of the Middle East and Islamic society. There is rising interest in Islamic historical culture and civilization, as well as in the contemporary music of North Africa, the popular Rai (meaning opinion, or speaking out) music that combines rock, hip hop, and traditional Berber and *ghanawa* (West African roots from Ghana) rhythms. Rai groups that performed in France are now in demand in the United States. Various humanities forums have enlisted my services, from working with the Rhode Island and Massachusetts Committees on the Humanities, each of which devoted yearlong series to "Understanding Islam," to my being appointed NEH humanities professor at Colgate University in the spring of 2003 to teach courses about anthropology and Islam. In these and other forums I have met Americans and Muslims living in the United States eager to learn more, to discuss the sensitive issues that seem to divide us, and to find peace and reconciliation through such dialogue. It is to these sincere learners that this book is dedicated.

2

Islam and the Five Pillars as Observed by Muslims

The faith of Islam was the last of the great prophetic traditions to emerge from the Middle East, and the revelations made to the prophet Muhammad and recorded in the Holy Qur'an are seen as continuous from the time of Abraham, through Moses, to Jesus Christ. Each of the previous prophets is recognized and revered by the religion of Islam.

Islam is derived from *salaama*, Arabic for peace, and means the personal peace derived from submission to the one God known as Allah in the Arabic language, the one and only deity in an uncompromising monotheistic faith. The person who submits is known as a Muslim.

The special inner and personal peace that comes to a Muslim who has submitted to God is reflected in the greeting "Assalaam alaykum." The beauty and simplicity of this greeting is such that it conveys greeting to the individual addressed, while the use of the plural *kum* extends the greeting to all of your kin and beloved, as well as the entire world community of believers. "Assalaam alaykum" is a Muslim greeting used throughout the world, irrespective of language. The response is "Wa alaykum assalaam," meaning "and upon you and yours peace."

The religion of Islam is rooted in the spiritual and cultural traditions of the Arabian peninsula and the Middle East. The time of ignorance, the period before the introduction of Islam, is known as the *jahiliyya,* after which came revelation from God of the new religion: reason, enlightenment, and reform. The reference to a time of jahiliyya resonates today, as many inspired by contemporary Islamic revival see the dominance of secular ideology or Western culture as another "time of ignorance"; thus they see the triumph of an Islamist approach as one which can stem the tide and prevent the return of darkness.

Islam is uncompromising in its monotheism with the concept of a single indivisible God, Allah. The principle that there is no other divinity or trinity to compromise God's oneness is known theologically as *tawheed*. Saints are prohibited, as are any images of God or the prophet Muhammad that might promote the idolatry found in pre-Islamic times. Tawheed is a fundamental principle that can be applied in many religious and social contexts to understand Islamic beliefs and practice.

The Islamic calendar begins with the date of the flight of the early community of Muslims from Mecca to Medina in 622, known as the Hegira (flight), when refuge and security were sought and expansion beyond the small group of followers at Mecca was possible. Underscoring the fact that Muhammad is not revered as a divine person, the year of his birth, 570, does not begin the Islamic calendar, as Christ's birth begins the Christian calendar. The appropriateness of flight from danger or tactical withdrawal is thus viewed as entirely legitimate from the standpoint of the protection of the Umma, the world community of Muslims.

The Muslim Calendar

The Islamic calendar follows a lunar cycle, with twelve months of 29 or 30 days forming a 354-day year. The Islamic calendar months are Muharram, Safar, Rabi al-Awaal, Rabi al-Tahni, Gomada al-Awal, Gomada al-Thani, Rajab, Shabaan, Ramadan, Shawwal, Zu al-Qada, and Zu al-Hijja. This makes the Muslim calendar 11 days shorter than the solar Gregorian calendar employed in the West since 1582 C.E., when history was divided into two eras: before Christ, B.C., and "in the year of [our] Lord," anno Domini, A.D. There is not a simple 622 years difference between the Muslim lunar and the Western Gregorian solar due to the annual 11 days difference. For example, 1991–92 A.D. is 1411–12 A.H. (anno Hegirae), making a difference of 580 years. To complicate matters a bit more, the Persian-Iranian tradition follows a solar Muslim calendar, making 2003 A.D. the year 1381 A.H., while the Sunni recognize the date as 1423 A.H. on the lunar calendar.

The months of the Muslim calendar reflect the annual observance of the faith, such as the month of Ramadan (known as Farvadin in the Persian language) or the period following Ramadan known as Dhu al-Hijja, when pilgrims make the hajj, or the month of Muharram, when the important 'Eid al-Adha (Feast of Sacrifice) takes place. However, in 1970 when we learned Arabic in a decidedly more secular Sudan, we learned the months as Shahr Wahid, "the first month" (January), Shahr Ithnain, "the second month" (February), and so forth. Today, in the context of revived Islam, the Muslim names of the month are being used again in print and in daily conversation, and one diagnostic feature of an Islamist publication is the use of the Muslim calendar month and year, alone or together with the Western version.

Sources of the Faith, Foundations of the Community

The Qur'an, the revealed word of God, is the fundamental source of the Islamic faith. Its texts, revealed between 610 and 632 C.E., expound matters of belief and practice. More than 1 billion Muslims from diverse cultures belong to the Umma.

After the Qur'an is the Sunna of the Prophet, understood as the words and the example of Muhammad and his companions. The belief that the Messenger was inspired by God established the basis that his life and teachings could be a source of the religion (Esposito 1988, 81). The preserved sayings of the Prophet are known as Hadith and constitute the recorded and accepted Sunna of God's Messenger. These fundamental sources of Islam are authoritative and immutable, although they are subject to study and interpretation, as has been the case over the fourteen centuries of the faith. The ones who study and interpret the holy sources are known by various names: ʿalim (ʿulama, pl.), meaning "learned one"; mujahid, meaning "one who interprets"; and feki or faqih (foqaha, pl.), "ones knowledgeable in al-Fiqh," the religious laws. The common reference to the religious scholars in Western literature on Islam is ʿulama, so I have used this general term throughout this book, except in specific cultural circumstances where another term is preferred.

The formal interpretation of the holy sources has occurred with the development of Islamic theology, jurisprudence, and law. Islamic jurisprudence (al-Fiqh) has interpreted the sources and devised laws of Muslim religious practice and social behavior that apply to all Muslims, laws which are enforced in Islamic courts by Muslim judges known as qadis. Four schools of legal interpretation have developed in the Sunni Muslim tradition: the Hanafi, Maliki, Shafiʿi, and Hanbali schools. However, they do not differ significantly with respect to the sources, and their differences are neither doctrinal nor dogmatic.

The Arabic word for "correct path" is Shariʿa, and this has become the common referent for the religious law, since following God's law guarantees that a Muslim will adhere to the straight path and enter paradise after the Final Judgment. Legal theory and social practice of the Shariʿa are discussed more extensively in chapter 6.

Sunni and Shiʿa Branches of Islam

The religion of Islam is divided into two branches, the Sunni and the Shiʿa, with Sunni constituting over 90 percent of Umma. Shiʿa Islam has always been a minority movement. Unlike the great divide created in Christianity by the break between Eastern Orthodox and Western Roman Christianity, or the Protestant Reformation, and unlike the differences between Orthodox and Reform Judaism, the split between Sunni and Shi'a Islam has more to do with succession, governance, and leadership of the community of Muslims than with differences in theology.

When Muhammad died in 632 C.E., he had appointed no successor, thus leaving to the early Muslim community the decision as to who would be the rightful successor and deputy of God on earth, the caliph. The first caliphate fell to Muhammad's friend Abu Bakr and then to two other companions, 'Umar I and Uthman ibn 'Affan, during the first twenty-four years of succession. This was a golden period consisting of rule by men who had known Muhammad, and they are regarded as the Rightly Guided Caliphs from whom inspiration is still derived.

At the time of the accession of the fourth caliph, 'Ali, in 656, the matter of the rightful succession of caliphs came into question. 'Ali, a cousin of the Prophet, had married Fatima, the daughter of Muhammad and Khadijah, and they had two sons, Hasan and Husayn. With the appointment of a member of the Prophet's family as caliph, the whole matter of genealogical and dynastic succession was raised. This disagreement led to warfare between Muslims, with supporters of the families of the Prophet and first three caliphs against 'Ali, his sons, and his partisans, known as Shi'at 'Ali. Five years later, in 661, Mu'awiyah laid claim to the caliphate, establishing the Ummayad dynasty in Damascus, and 'Ali was assassinated by former followers disappointed that he had failed to prevent Mu'awiyah's succession. The Islamic caliphate shifted geographically from the more isolated Arabian peninsula to Syria, closer to the center of world events, and the subsequent spread of Islam was remarkable and dramatic.

However, when Mu'awiyah's son, Yazid I, succeeded his father in 680, the anger of 'Ali's son could not be contained, and Husayn mounted a rebellion in Kufa, Iraq. His relatively small band of followers was easily defeated, and Husayn was murdered at Karbala, Iraq. This martyrdom of both 'Ali and Husayn, from the perspective of the Shiites, represents an injustice that influences their distinctive view of religious leadership and governance. Many special Shi'a rites commemorate the murders of 'Ali and Husayn, some of which are quite passionate. Battlegrounds are sacred places of special pilgrimage. Ashura occurs on the tenth day of the first month (Muharram) of the lunar year—just after Ramadan and the 'Eid al-Fitr—and it has been historically associated with many auspicious events, such as the landing of Noah's Ark. However, after 680, when Husayn was brutally murdered, decapitated, and mutilated on the day of Ashura, it became a particular observance of the Shiites as a day of mourning and remembrance of the suffering and death of 'Ali's son and Muhammad's grandson. It has been revived in the current era, especially in places where Shiites are minorities, such as Lebanon. In Shi'a Islam, public processions recount the battle of Karbala and Husayn's martyrdom. In Iran where Shi'a Islam is the state religion, the emphasis is on lamentation through recitation of verses with open displays of mourning. India and Pakistan follow the Iranian norms. Ashura rites have been compared to the passion plays that reenact the Crucifixion of Christ. The Ashura processions served as models for the demonstrations against the shah during the 1978–79 Iranian Revolution with one of the most popular slogans being "Every day is Ashura; every place is Karbala" (Chelkowski 1995, 141–43).

The Sunni majority and Shi'a minority branches of Islam disagree only over the legitimate method of succession to caliphs, whether by a method of selection or election as in Sunni principle or by divine succession to imam through the family of the Prophet. The former view won out among the dominant Sunni Muslims in the first century of Islam, and the Shi'a faction has remained a relatively isolated minority living primarily in Iran—where they are a 94 percent majority—and Iraq—where Shi'a Muslims at 49 percent outnumber the 46 percent Sunni Muslims, but the latter dominate Iraqi politics over Shi'a Muslims and the small Christian minority. In Lebanon Sunni and Shi'a Muslims are about evenly divided, and together they form about half the Lebanese, although the Shi'a sector has been more militant as a political force dominating the Islamist Hezb Allah (Party of God). In Syria Shi'a Muslims make up about 15 percent of the 90 percent dominant Muslim population, while in Egypt Shi'a Muslims are only 5 percent of the population, mainly of Asian origin. Over the centuries Shi'a Muslims have at times hidden their special practice of Islam, revering their martyrs, to escape majority Sunni persecution, making the recent public displays of devotion all the more significant.

During the first century of Islam, not only was this difference of politics and succession resolved politically, but Islam also spread dramatically throughout the Middle East and North Africa into Spain, where Muslim rule dominated the Iberian Peninsula until the expulsion of the Moors in 1492. Islamic religious law, the Shari'a, was also developed in the first century of Islam in four main schools of Islamic jurisprudence. With the caliphate in place and basic institutions established, Islamic society developed and began to assume a position on the world's stage where it became a force with which Western society would reckon.

The World of Islam and Muslims

Islam is the second most practiced religion in the world with 1.2 billion followers. The various branches of Christianity amount to perhaps 2 billion. Together with world Judaism, amounting to 8–10 million believers—mostly in Israel and the United States—the Abrahamic faiths originating in the Middle East constitute over 3 billion, more than 40 percent of the world's population.

Although stereotyped as Arab and Middle Eastern peoples, most of the world's Muslims are neither. Most are Asian, and only about 250 million are from the Middle East. The largest Muslim nations are outside the Near East and North Africa—Indonesia is the most populous at over 210 million, Malaysia at 25 million; Nigeria, as the African continent's most populous country at 110 million, is about 50 percent Muslim, making its size nearly that of Egypt's 65 million souls—10 percent of whom are Coptic Christian.

The world of Islam is truly global. It stretches from its founding core in the Middle East—the Arabian peninsula and southwest Asia—further to the east, to central, south, and southeast Asia. In these regions Pakistan, Afghanistan, and Bangladesh are almost entirely Muslim, while the central Asian areas of Azerbaijan, Turkmen, Uzbek, Kirgiz, and Tajik are 85 percent Muslim. Eleven percent of India's 1 billion people are Muslim. Heading south and west in the Indian Ocean to east Africa, Somalia is predominantly Muslim, Sudan is two-thirds Muslim, and Tanzania is one-third Muslim. Continuing west to North and West Africa, Islam is a majority faith in Guinea, the Gambia, Senegal, Mali, Niger, and Mauritania, ranging from 65 to 95 percent Muslim. The world of Islam also includes historical populations in southeast Europe and new migrant populations in western Europe and North America, where Muslims have increased their numbers in both Canada and the United States. In sheer numbers, Asians dominate the world presence of Islam.

The most dramatic spread of Islam occurred after its introduction in the seventh and eighth centuries A.D. in the Arabian peninsula—or in the first century A.H. in the Hijaz, the Arabic name for Arabia. After the first Ummayad caliphate was established in Damascus, Syria, the knights of early Islam spread the faith far and wide. Islam was established in Fustat (early Cairo) in Egypt by 640 C.E./13 A.H.; it was established in al-Maghrib (the place of the setting sun) at Karouan, Tunisia, by 661 C.E./39 A.H., and by the tenth century C.E./third century A.H. it had followed trans-Saharan trade routes from northwest Africa south to establish the earliest Islamic kingdoms in the continent in Ghana and Mali. Before the end of its first century, Islam was established in southern Spain with grand cities at Cordoba, Seville, and Granada with one of the greatest Muslim architectural attractions at the palace known as the Alhambra (al-Hamra, meaning red for its distinctive color). Many of Islamic Spain's great mosques were converted to Catholic churches after the 1492 expulsion of Muslims and Jews, and the ensuing Inquisition effectively cleansed the Iberian Peninsula of all faiths but Christianity.

Islam established itself in Iraq and Persia during the time of the early caliphs, and the decisive battles favoring Sunni Islam took place at Basra and Karbala in Iraq. Islam spread to India and flourished during the time of the great Moghul Empire by the twelfth century C.E./fifth century A.H. During the Moghul rule Shah Jehan built a marvelous tomb for his wife that is known to the world as the Taj Mahal—one of the greatest examples of Islamic architecture. Islam traveled along Indian Ocean trade routes to coastal India, Malaysia, and Indonesia. It traveled along the Silk Road from Venice to Istanbul to Bukhara and Samarkand, all the way to Urumqui in China, the terminus of the great trade route. Xian and other major cities west of Beijing welcomed Muslims into their midst. Chinese Muslims carried Islam with them into Vietnam, Burma, and Thailand where they established prosperous minority merchant communities.

The first mosque in America was founded in Cedar Rapids, Iowa, in 1938 by a Lebanese immigrant community. This follows the 1931 birth of the American Nation of Islam with the teachings of the predecessor of Elijah Muhammad, Wallace Fard Muhammad. However, the Nation of Islam has stood apart from Sunni Islam for its racial exclusion—Black Muslims—and its historical acceptance of Elijah Muhammad as a prophet, anathema to Muslim teaching that Muhammad was the last prophet of God.

The Five Pillars in Practice

The five pillars of the Islamic faith represent its most basic beliefs and practices. Formally, they are derived from the same immutable sources of the religion, Qur'an and Sunna. To the degree that they vary in expression from one Muslim community to another, they show the influence of the cultural and historical variation within the Islamic Umma. Variations along folk religious lines are often the result of syncretistic blends with preexisting religious trends, but they usually coexist and rarely violate the unchangeable tenets of the faith.

The Shahada (Testament of Belief)

The first of these, the *shahada,* or testament of belief, asserts the uncompromising monotheism of Islam, continuing the tradition of monotheism begun by Judaism and continued with Christianity. *Tawheed* is set forth in the first part of the testament, "la Allah ila Allah" (there is no deity but Allah). The second part of the shahada relates to the Prophet: "wa Muhammadun Rassoul Allah" (and Muhammad is His Messenger). Muhammad as the Messenger of God is the one to whom the Holy Book, the Qur'an, was revealed, and thus the prophet Muhammad exists in the realm of humanity, not of the divine, and is distinguished from Christ, who is believed by Christians to be divine.

Ideally, the shahada is the first thing that a child should have uttered in its ear and the last that a dying person should hear. Parents may begin to teach their children how to speak by repeating the shahada. Pressing the child close, a father may utter "Allahu akbar" (God is all great) and "Ashadu anu la Allah ila Allah" (I bear witness that there is no deity but Allah). Our own little daughters learned elements of the shahada by continuously hearing the call to prayer and watching the people around them respond by initiating prayer. The shahada is recalled with each of the five daily calls to prayer and is an ever-present reminder of the unity and oneness of God.

The invocation of the name of God, "bismiAllah," is an excellent way to begin things and can be heard in everyday speech from the start of meals, to the opening of a class lecture, to the starting of a car or the take-off of an airliner. Likewise, the expression "insha Allah" (God willing) is heard thousands of times daily in hundreds of contexts, ranging from greetings, to the making of appointments, to discussions of politics. The determining of one's fate or condition by God is discussed more fully in chapter 3, but it suffices to say that the name of God is called upon or invoked repeatedly in conversation and is a signature of the use of the Arabic language in many Muslim societies.

Within folk Islam there has been a tendency to revere local holy men, called sheikhs or *foqaha* in eastern North Africa and the Middle East and *marabout* in northwest and West Africa. Such holy men are said to possess much *baraka* (blessings from God) and in some cases are believed to be able to perform miracles or bring about cures. Frequently, tombs erected at the burial site of such holy men become the objects of worship, veneration, and even pilgrimage, a tendency contrary to tawheed and the unwavering monotheism of Islam. Official Islam frowns on such veneration, but these tombs of holy men are very popular with the masses in their everyday religious practice and are especially invoked in times of crisis. However, this practice falls short of saint worship in Christianity.

Salat (Prayer)

Prayer in Islam repeats the basic elements of the testimony of belief which is repeated in the call to prayer by the muezzin who historically stood atop the minaret of the local mosque calling the faithful to prayer five times daily. The minaret and mosque are inseparable in Islamic architecture and religious practice, representing the call to prayer (*adhan*) and the place of prayer and prostration (*masjid* is Arabic for mosque, meaning "place of prostration"). Many newly built American mosques have minarets, although they are more for symbolic purpose, for the call to prayer could not be heard by the widely dispersed communities they serve. "Allahu akbar, Allahu akbar" begins the call. "Ashadu anu la Allah ila Allah" (I bear witness that there is no God but Allah). "Ashadu anu Muhammadan Rassoul Allah" (I bear witness that Muhammad is His Messenger). Prayer is at the heart of the Sufi rites that commemorate or remember God with music, dance, and recitations chanted from the Qur'an.

Prayer in a mosque in the direction (*qiblah*) of Mecca began among the earliest Muslim communities in Arabia. It became ritualized around the following necessary steps: ablution (*wudu* or *taharah,* meaning purification); intention (*niyah*); bowing or bending forward (*raku*); and prostration (*sujud*). Purification before prayer involves first the cleansing of the mind and then the washing of specified body parts including the face, hands, mouth (unless fasting), feet, and forehead (Abu Rabi' 1995, 470). The motions of Muslim prayer are distinctive and define Muslims in a unique way.

Prayer belongs to the religious realm of *ibadat,* personal obligations of Muslims. Prayer is obligatory for all Muslims who have reached puberty; of course, many younger children begin praying well before the age of puberty. Ritual cleansing takes place at home if that is where the act of prayer takes place, or outside the mosque or the prayer hall where there are fountains and running water for this purpose. Prayer is performed respectfully without shoes, facing in the direction of Mecca (not always to the east, depending upon the geographical location of the Muslim), bowing with the hands at the knees, bowing and prostrating oneself, with the forehead touching the ground. The prayer consists of two to four prostrations depending upon the time of day. Prayer can be performed anywhere, and small prayer rugs can be used for the purpose, stored in a special place or carried with the traveler. The words of the Muslim prayer repeat the shahada, reflect upon the revelation of the Qur'an, and emphasize the glory and oneness of God. At the end of prayer, the Muslim looks to the right and to the left in symbolic greeting of the Umma.

Typically, no dwelling or place of work is far from a mosque, and in many of the more densely populated neighborhoods where I have lived with my family, there were several mosques within audible distance of the call to prayer. Thus the call often has the effect of surrounding you, enveloping you, reminding you of the time of day, or even awakening you at dawn. There are five prescribed times for the call: at daybreak, noon, afternoon, sunset, and evening. Pious Muslims respond to each of the five daily calls to prayer, but for many the demands of daily living make this impractical. Women with whom I was familiar and who were not salaried employees outside of the home would usually pray at home at sunrise and in the evening. Religious

Fig. 5. The call to prayer is within earshot of majority Muslim communities; minarets dot the skyline of this Tunis suburb.

men may stop by the local mosque on the way to or from work, but often they pray at dawn and in the evenings, like their wives. Prayer in the mosque is not a necessity, as the Muslim approaches God directly without any need of an intermediary person or place. Women in many Muslim societies do not pray regularly in the mosque; if they do, there are separate areas provided for them, since males and females praying together is considered a distraction from the intended singular focus on God. Mosques in America observe this pattern as well with separate entrances and prayer areas reserved for women and men.

Communal prayer in the mosque is considered a higher form of prayer because it is collective and involves the broader Islamic community. Friday prayer is congregational and is led by an imam who faces the *mihrab*, a niche in the architecture of the mosque indicating the direction, *qiblah*, of Mecca. The Arabic word for group, *jama'a*, is used in reference to the mosque (*jami'*); it is also the root from which the word for university (*jami'a*) is derived, since the earliest universities were religious and were attached to great mosques. Thus, the famous Jami'at al-Azhar in Cairo refers to both Al-Azhar University and Al-Azhar Mosque, adjacent buildings but with separate identities. Likewise, Jami'al Zeitouna in Tunis refers both to the famous Zeitouna Mosque and to the historic university of religious studies before it was closed by the secularist leader Habib Bourgiba and then reopened in the 1990s under popular and Islamist pressure.

Friday prayers are the largest gatherings of the practicing Muslims and are often led by the imam of the mosque and accompanied by a sermon that focuses on religious, social, or political subjects. In these days of increased Islamic consciousness and observance, attendance at Friday prayers is impressive, with overflow crowds quite typical. Accommodation for the faithful to pray in the courtyard or even in the streets surrounding the mosque is not uncommon, with mats or rugs placed on the ground for this purpose. Collective prayer is performed in unison and is a powerful expression of solidarity with one's fellow Muslims. For some people in the West, who may not understand this or who may have been influenced by anti-Muslim sentiments, this practice appears to be a robotic, unthinking performance of fanatics and radicals made by adherents of a faith that promotes terrorism. Western journalists have reinforced this impression by using the mosque-Muslim prayer motif as background to reports of explosive events in the Middle East.

Increasingly, with the gathering strength of Islamist forces, the sermon (*khutba*) at the Friday service has taken on more overtly political issues, and it may end in exhortations to political action, with demonstrations following the weekly ritual. This was certainly the case during the height of the Islamic revolution in Iran, and postprayer demonstrations have been a part of the Palestinian intifadas and Muslim resistance to Israeli rule in the occupied territories. In predominantly secular countries currently experiencing Islamist revival, such as Egypt and Tunisia, Friday prayer and the mosque have become associated with democratic opposition or Islamist agitation. Some of the central downtown mosques may be under government surveillance, and overt expressions of government force, such as the presence of police or army troops, may be a regular part of Friday prayer. This is not a militarist extension of the Islamic faith but an expression of the secular government's fear of politicized Islam.

In these days of Muslim awakening and revival, the call to prayer has taken on heightened symbolic meaning. For example, many of the Islamist groups use the name *Da'wa* (the call) for their organizations and publications. Furthermore, responding to public pressure from Islamist sympathizers, the call to prayer is often broadcast interrupting daily radio and television programming, even in a highly secularized nation such as Tunisia. The evening broadcast of the call to prayer (*al-maghrib* prayer) is special because most family members are at home. On television, pictures of the holy places of Mecca and Medina, the Ka'ba, or a famous sheikh chanting the call to prayer may be shown as part of this inspirational moment, the traditional pause that signals the end of the daytime and beginning of the evening's activities.

Sawm (Fasting)

Although the observance of Islam is intensely personal and individual, its rituals are highly public and collective. The observance of the annual fast during the month of Ramadan, the ninth month of the Islamic calendar, begins when the new moon is seen. In the Islamic calendar, the Ramadan fast moves forward eleven days each year. The month of fasting commemorates God's revelation of the Qur'an to Muhammad.

Fasting for an entire lunar month (about twenty-nine days) is a test and trial for Muslims and is viewed as a form of personal *jihad*, one of the more difficult inner struggles with the flesh and worldly appetites. Avoiding food and drink from sunrise to sunset for one lunar month is obligatory for adult Muslim men and women, with only the young, the infirm, pregnant women, and travelers exempted. One mark of the maturing adolescent is the decision to begin to fast, the timing of which is a matter of personal choice.

Fasting promotes a sense of personal religious discipline. When the month of fasting falls during the hot summer months, it is especially challenging. Some zealous Muslims observe a devout form of fasting, refusing even to swallow their own spittle; others may add extra days of fasting. Travelers are expected to make up the days missed, but this is strictly a matter of personal religious observance.

Those fasting usually rise well before the sun, prepare a light meal (in Egypt and the Sudan, this typically consists of seasoned beans with bread and sweet tea), and begin their day with the morning prayer. They refrain from consuming anything by mouth, including cigarettes or chewing gum, throughout the day until sunset, which is usually between 5 and 6 p.m. By the time of the setting sun, food has been prepared and the family gathers for the Ramadan "breakfast," literally "breaking the fast." In Khartoum and Cairo, traditionally a cannon was fired at this time, with the sound reverberating throughout the whole of the metropolitan area. Lanterns became an important symbol of Ramadan, as they were used to light the procession that went to view the moon and announce the beginning and end of each day's fast. Lanterns are still hung over the streets, in people's houses, and are given to children as presents. Nowadays people rely on radio and television to announce the time of the day's passing so that the fast can be started and broken.

Ramadan is a time of trial and sacrifice, but it is also a time of reflection and growing inner peace. It reminds the Muslim of the privation of those less fortunate and serves as a powerful unifier of the Umma, who are fasting at the same time. It is likewise a time of celebration and reunion with family, friends, and neighbors. Some of the Ramadan greetings and customs are illustrative. Although a time of denial, a typical greeting, "Ramadan kareem," translates as "Ramadan is abundant" or "Ramadan is generous." Although it is a time of fasting, it is also an occasion for feasting, and special foods are prepared for the nightly guests. The lavishness of such breakfasts varies considerably by class and may appear in stark contrast to the daytime period of denial. Wealthier families may entertain large gatherings of business associates and their families, who use the occasion to display their latest fashions and jewelry. Such conspicuous displays of consumption are contrary to the intended simplicity and reflection associated with the fast, and their "waste and inefficiency" were used as a justification by Habib Bourgiba of Tunisia when he recommended the end of fasting during Ramadan. However, his controversial suggestion was never implemented because of the multiple religious and social functions that fasting during Ramadan represents for Muslims.

While some breakfasts are more elaborate than others, all are characterized by a spirit of generosity, and a simple workman breaking his fast on the street with a meal of bread and beans might invite passersby to join him, as has happened to us on numerous occasions. At least one Ramadan invitation and reciprocal invitation are expected from neighbors and from work and business associates, although multiple family invitations are the norm.

The typical middle-class breakfast is more elaborate than the ordinary main meal, and it may include many special foods, such as a drink made from apricot paste called *qummereddine* or *mish mish* that is popular in Syria, Egypt, and the Sudan. Meat dishes of *kebab, kofta,* and vegetarian falafel are popular, as are sweetened macaroni dishes. In the Sudan and Egyptian Nubia, a special drink made from dried sorghum, called *abrey,* is served. Sesame candies and other sweets are offered after the main meal with Arabic coffee or sweetened mint tea. Tunisians prepare a sweet sorghum custard that is served with nuts. In short, all of the best and most highly prized foods are served during Ramadan. A simpler light meal called *sohour* is the last meal eaten before sleeping and awaking at dawn.

Those who are fasting often describe the first week of Ramadan as the most difficult physically. However, after the first week many Muslims describe a spiritual peace and sense of balance and contentment derived from succeeding in the internal jihad and from being part of a vast collective ritual. This euphoria seems to carry most people right through to the end of the fast, although some are naturally quite tired and become irritable. Businesses, schools, government offices, shops, and services all slow down and have lighter hours because workers have come to the job with perhaps only three or four hours of sleep, after entertaining late into the night and arising before dawn. Western businesspersons and diplomats with long experience in the region have learned to expect that appointments may be delayed during Ramadan.

Today, with the increased vitality of Islamic practice, the degree of stigma on public eating has intensified, even to the point of formal bans. In fact, the power of this stigma is an excellent measure of the new influence of Islamist movements. In Tunisia, which underwent the most dramatic revisions of Islamic institutions in the Arab world after it gained independence in 1956, fasting is still viewed as a matter of personal conscience, and some eating establishments are open for business during the fast between sunrise and sunset. A growing Islamist movement in Tunisia condemns this public insult to the majority Muslim community, but so far there has been no militant action to close these restaurants.

When we first lived in Khartoum during the early 1970s, the Ramadan fast was viewed as a matter of personal practice that most Muslims performed, but those who declined were not chastised. Since about one-third of Sudan's residents are non-Muslim southerners, many of whom live and work in northern Muslim areas, at that time it was considered a courtesy to them and to others not fasting for some restaurants to remain open. Many of our friends at the University of Khartoum did not fast, and the university's Staff Club was open for lunch as much to serve the Sudanese faculty and staff as to feed the foreign staff. An associate with a guilty conscience might ask my husband or me to bring back a beverage when we went to refresh ourselves during the hot days, but little was made of this quiet conspiracy. Some foreigners and non-Muslims we knew also fasted during Ramadan, and we refrained from eating or drinking in their presence.

With the Islamist surge in Egypt and the Sudan has come social and political pressure to conform to the standard of performing the fast. When we lived in Egypt during the mid-1980s, increasing numbers of restaurants were closed during the fasting hours, opening only in the evening. This trend intensified in the 1990s. Complaints were raised by Coptic Christians who owned certain centrally located eateries, but apart from the five-star hotels and restaurants frequented by tourists, it was difficult to find places to eat in downtown Cairo between sunrise and sunset. Under the Islamist regime in power in the Sudan since 1989, any public eating during Ramadan is banned and strictly enforced. McDonald's fast-food restaurants have innovated "McFast Breakfasts" for their predominantly Muslim clientele in Cairo and presumably elsewhere in the Muslim world where they operate.

For Sunni Muslims, authoritative word regarding the beginning and the end of Ramadan comes from Saudi Arabia, where the religious sheikhs make this determination. When the end of Ramadan is announced, the great ʿEid al-Fitr (Feast of the Breaking of the Fast) begins a three- or four-day celebration, one of the largest and most joyous of the Muslim holidays. New clothes are sewn or purchased for children, streets are decorated with bright lights, and children in Egypt carry lanterns as they go about the streets wishing

Fig. 6. ʿEid Mubarak (Blessed holiday greetings), a U.S. stamp issued in October 2001.

people "ʿEid Mubarak!" meaning "Happy ʿEid." Adults greet each other with similar expressions of good wishes, "ʿEid Saʿeed" (happy holidays) or "Sana Jadida Saʿeeda" (happy new year). The U.S. Post Office introduced the first American stamp commemorating the ʿEid al-Fitr in 2001, just after the attacks on the World Trade Center.

Traditionally, a sheep or goat was purchased by the family and slaughtered for the holiday; however, with rising inflation and the increased cost of living, the purchase of an entire animal has become prohibitively expensive for many middle-class families. They may settle for a portion of meat from the butcher or share with the extended family in the purchase of an animal for slaughter. The killing of the animal must be carried out by a skilled Muslim butcher, who cuts the animal's throat and allows it to bleed to death in the prescribed Islamic fashion. The animal is then butchered by the same specialist, who performs the service for a fee or for a portion of the meat. Other portions of the meat are set aside as gifts for family, neighbors, and the poor as a traditional form of charitable behavior. We were frequent recipients of such gifts of meat in honor of the ʿEid al-Fitr, perhaps because we were perceived as being needy since we were only a small nuclear family with no larger extended family to look after us. The more meat we received, the more we were able to participate in the honor of sharing, often ending up at the central mosque downtown where we could share our bounty with the poor who gathered in anticipation of such gifts.

The 'Eid al-Fitr is one of the national holidays in predominantly Muslim countries during which intense socializing and celebration take place. It is probably the closest thing socially to the Christmas holiday in the West, although its religious meaning is unrelated to either the birth of the Prophet or the materialism we have come to associate with Christmas. Socially it is a time of great coming together and marks the culmination of one of Islam's great annual collective rituals.

The birth of the prophet Muhammad, the Mawlid al-Nabi, is celebrated but not as a centerpiece of the Islamic faith. It may or may not be a national holiday, and although it may be commemorated with reverence, it does not have the same significance as the birth of the Christ does for Christians because Muhammad is not held as divine. In Egypt sweet sugar dolls are sold for the Mawlid, whereas the Tunisians prepare a special pudding of sweetened sorghum, which is shared with relatives and neighbors.

After the end of 'Eid al-Fitr, life returns to its normal routine, unless it is interrupted by a member of one's family who is preparing to make the pilgrimage to the holy places (the hajj) in the recommended time after Ramadan.

Zakat (Almsgiving)

Zakat is the religious responsibility of every Muslim to share with Muslims in need through charitable offerings. Zakat as an alms tax has been mandated in government law in certain Islamic republics, such as Sudan, Pakistan, and Iran, and thus has become a reliable index of successful Islamist politicization.

Zakat is worship of God, as well as an act of thanksgiving and service to the community. As a religious tax (usually about 2–3 percent) on one's accumulated wealth or assets, it is not comparable to secular notions of an income tax. It is predicated upon the recognition of the injustice of economic inequity and the responsibility of Muslims everywhere to assist one another and the faith in a material way. Clearly the issue of economic inequality between the oil-rich and poorer nations has some political potential. Centuries ago, zakat was collected and redistributed by the government treasury. The issue of zakat has been raised recently by Islamists as a legitimate activity for a Muslim government to pursue. Pious Muslims have historically performed zakat irrespective of the state's official position.

Zakat offerings are most frequent during Muslim holidays, but the poor can be found throughout the year near the central mosques of major cities where charitable offerings can be made at any time. One of the purest forms of zakat is that given anonymously to someone in need. One of my most pious students, Musa Balla Gaye, a Muslim from the Gambia, worked an extra job in Rhode Island in order to save money for a favorite uncle to make the hajj. The uncle had helped him as child, and he could think of no better way to express his gratitude to his aging relative. The uncle made hajj and died only a few months after his return from Mecca, thus multiplying the religious meaning of this gift of zakat.

Zakat not only embraces the immediate community in the present time. It also extends to the larger Muslim society for time immemorial. Certain charitable gifts can be made in the form of bequests offered in the name of God; such a bequest is known as a *waqf* (*awqaf,* pl.). Awqaf constitute a special category of Muslim giving and have been administered separately by Islamic states over the centuries, as well as recorded and regulated by agents of secular governments, such as the minister of awqaf of the Ottoman Empire. In addition, awqaf have been subject to interpretation and regulation by the Islamic courts. For example, jurists in the twentieth century ruled that individual bequests of waqf cannot be used to disinherit heirs prescribed by Islamic law.

The idea of this particular form of zakat is that it is a gift, made in the name of God, to be held in perpetuity. Awqaf can be bequests of land or funds to establish or maintain mosques, hospitals, and religious schools. Anything that supports or acts on behalf of the Muslim community can be nominated as a waqf. Substantial gifts of property or sums of money have been subject to regulation, since awqaf cannot be sold or transferred as private property, except according to the original intent of the donor. Waqfs made in the past to increase the share of family heirs have been regulated or eliminated, so as not to violate the spirit and intent of God's laws of inheritance.

Under the influence of the Islamic revival, countries such as Iran, Pakistan, and the Sudan have formally instituted payment of zakat by legislative mandate; however, enforcement is problematical because zakat has been seen as a personal duty and not as a matter of state imposition for many centuries before the current wave of Islamist activity. Generosity (*karam*) is a basic Arab and Muslim value that is fostered in many ways in Islamic society, and a sense of the responsibility to share is certainly reinforced by the Islamic precept of zakat.

Performance of the Hajj

The pilgrimage to the Muslim holy places of Mecca and Medina, in contemporary Saudi Arabia, is the final religious duty that every Muslim is asked to perform at least once. The focus of the pilgrimage is the Ka'ba, the small stone building in which one finds the black stone that the angel Gabriel gave to Abraham as a symbol of God's covenant with Abraham's son, Ismail, and by extension with the Muslim community. The Ka'ba was already a place of pilgrimage in pre-Islamic times, and tradition tells that one of the first things Muhammad did, upon triumphantly entering Mecca, was to cleanse the Ka'ba of its polytheistic idols and restore it to the worship and veneration of the one true God (Esposito 1988, 93).

The pilgrimage follows Ramadan and is held annually between the eighth and thirteenth days of Dhu al-Hijja, the twelfth month of the Muslim lunar calendar. Its first rite is the donning of the *ihram*, a seamless white garment worn by men and a simple white dress and head covering for women. Many men shave their heads; it is essential that men's heads be uncovered. As they don the ihram, the primary invocation of the hajj is recited ("Here I am, O God, at Thy Command! Thou art without associate"), thus reiterating tawheed, the fundamental unity and oneness of God. They then proceed to the Great Mosque where the Ka'ba is located and circle it seven times, symbolizing the unity of God and humans and that human activity must have God at its center. When making the circumambulations of the Ka'ba, pilgrims may touch or kiss the black stone, as did the Prophet in his pilgrimages. According to some traditions, the black stone is the sole remnant of the original place of worship built by Abraham and Ismail. The stone has no devotional significance and is not an object of worship itself, consistent with the uncompromising monotheism of Islam (Nawwab 1992, 30). During the days of the hajj pilgrims pray at the place where Abraham, the father of monotheism, stood; they run between Safa and Marwa commemorating Hagar's search for water for her son, Ismail; they stone three pillars symbolizing evil and Satan; they visit the Plain of Arafat, where they stand from noon to sunset in repentance before God and pray for forgiveness for themselves and for all Muslims (Esposito 1988, 94).

On the third day of the hajj, many pilgrims slaughter a sheep, goat, or other animal to commemorate Abraham's willingness to sacrifice his son to God (a belief shared by Jews, Christians, and Muslims) and to symbolize Islam's basic tenet of submission to God's will. Muslims all over the world share in this joyous and symbolic remembrance by performing their own sacrifice of animals, the 'Eid al-Adha (Festival of Sacrifice). Known also as the 'Eid al-Kabir (the Great Feast), it is the completion of the Muslim year and the culmination of the celebration that began with the end of Ramadan fasting. Again a portion of the meat from the slaughtered animal is set aside for the poor, as a traditional form of charity. The 'Eid al-Adha, like the 'Eid al-Fitr, is usually a national holiday in predominantly Muslim countries across the globe, and it represents another dimension of the shared religious and cultural ties that bind the Umma together.

Usually pilgrims precede or follow the hajj, the greater pilgrimage, with

Fig. 7. Egyptian home decoration commemorating performance of the hajj.

the 'Umra (the lesser pilgrimage), which takes place only in Mecca and can be performed at any time of the year. The 'Umra shares many features of the hajj, but it venerates the sacred character of Mecca.

Before the age of air transportation, the journey to the Hijaz was undertaken on foot, by caravan, and by sea; the hajj might take months or even years to complete. Pilgrims from West Africa were known to take five to ten years to complete the journey, often settling down for a time to earn some money to continue. The three great caravan routes of the past led from Cairo, Baghdad, and Istanbul. Pilgrim routes and trade routes were coexistent, and this great tradition of journeying reinforced knowledge of the other and contributed to the spread of Islam (Eickelman and Piscatori 1990).

Typically the pilgrimage is performed only once and after the prime of life has passed, so it is not uncommon to hear the terms of address Hajj or Hajja (masculine and feminine references to those who have made the pilgrimage) in association with older people. The terms are also used in a generic respectful form of address for older persons; for example, when passing in a crowded bus or train, you might say, "Excuse me, ya Hajj."

Over the centuries the obligation to perform the hajj has meant that Muslim peoples of widely disparate geographical and cultural backgrounds mingled in the course of the journey and the actual rituals associated with the pilgrimage. The powerful concept of the Umma becomes real during the hajj. The elimination of linguistic, cultural, and racial barriers to contact and communication has had a profound effect on many individual Muslims, especially from lands where racism or cultural discrimination has been a

Fig. 8. Former Sudanese president Jaʿafar al-Numeiri in prayer after attempted coup d'état in 1971. Reproduced by permission of the Sudanese Ministry of Information.

part of their socialization. The personal and political transformation of the African American Muslim leader Malcolm X is well documented in his autobiography and on film, with the performance of the hajj as a critical life experience leading to his renunciation of racism. In an extraordinary deviation from past practice, non-Muslim director Spike Lee was permitted to travel to the holy places to film the parts of the movie *Malcolm X*. After the hajj, Malcolm X changed his name to el-Hajj (the one who has completed the pilgrimage) Malik al-Shabazz.

Performance of the hajj has the power to heal as well as to renew the faith of the Muslim. Those who have suffered a tremendous loss, such as the death of a spouse or a child, often return more at peace. It is common for older people, upon completion of the hajj, to declare that they are now ready to die. The hajj can be both a culmination and a new beginning in life. For those who make it only once, it is the spiritual journey of a lifetime.

Others may use the performance of the hajj opportunistically, such as a secularist politician making the pilgrimage to prove that he is not anti-Islamic or that he has found new meaning and purpose in religion. Jaʿafar al-Numeiri of the Sudan marked his political shift from secularist socialism to Islamist orientation by undertaking the hajj. Others, such as the secularist successor to Habib Bourgiba in Tunisia, Zein Abdine Ben Ali, may make the ʿUmra to signify publicly their continuing commitment to religion.

The pilgrimage season is notorious for delays in air transportation that result from the sheer numbers of travelers en route to Saudi Arabia. It is a logistical problem that has been solved by chartered flights for the hajj and special terminals at international airports. To the Westerner, there is a remarkable lack of rancor or public display of anger at the inevitable delays that are part of the hajj travel season, but the relative peace is attributable both to the point of the journey and to a more general acceptance of one's fate as part of God's plan, a value discussed more fully in chapter 3. Recently I returned to the United States from Cairo on a plane with a number of American Muslims, mostly foreign born, who were carrying plastic containers filled with water from the wells of Zam Zam. One of the containers in an overhead cabin broke, and water spilled onto the leather luggage of an American. Angry and threatening to sue the Muslim and/or airline for damage, the passenger relented when other Muslims explained that the water had holy significance and that this was a time for peace, not anger.

Folk and Popular Observance of Islam

A good Muslim can observe the five pillars and also follow religious practices that are not strictly Islamic, as long as they do not violate basic principles or practice of the faith. There is an important distinction between official interpretations of Islam and folk beliefs and practices. Islamic states, whether in the great days of empire and the caliphates or in contemporary times, have fostered and utilized the group of religious scholars known as the 'ulama from whom official opinions have emanated. As the state interpreters of the basic sources of the faith, the Qur'an and Sunna, they have shaped the religious law, Shari'a, and have held power and given authoritative opinions by virtue of their official association with the state. A religious judge or the state's *mufti*—literally "one who opens the way," in this case to official interpretation—could issue a *fatwa* giving the official religious view on any subject. A fatwa was issued in the early Muslim Sudanese state on the permissibility of consuming the new drink, coffee, and a fatwa was issued in Saudi Arabia on the legitimacy of the presence of non-Muslim troops in the holy places during the 1991 Gulf War. Given what we know of history and politics, it is not difficult to surmise the positions taken in these fatwas. Fatwas have offered official opinions on controversial matters, such as the practice of female circumcision in Egypt and Sudan, and these views have differed over time. During colonial days the 'ulama of Sudan declared the practice to be in a neutral zone of custom, neither commanded nor condemned by Islam (Fluehr-Lobban 1987, 96–97). In 1998 the Grand Sheikh at Al-Azhar University in Cairo opined that female circumcision was "recommended" because it helps to promote the good conduct of girls and women. Such opinions have had the force of law with the power of the state behind them, but their impact has been felt largely in the centers of power, in the cities. Rural folk have generally continued their own particular synthesis of Islam and other religious traditions. Some folk practices may even be thought of by Muslim officials as un-Islamic.

The Sufi Way, the Spiritual Path

Perhaps the most powerful folk traditions associated with the spread of Islam are the mystical orders, the Sufi brotherhoods known as *tariqah* (pl. *turuq*). The Sufi designation probably derives from the word for wool, *suf*, referring to the type of garment many early Sufis wore, thus displaying their lack of concern for worldly comforts. These mystical brotherhoods date back to the early centuries of the spread of Islam, originating in Turkey or Iraq, as the famous Qadiriyah tariqah founded by ʿAbd al-Qadir al-Jilani, who died in Baghdad in 1166.

Perhaps the best known of the Sufi poets and teachers was Jalal al-Din al-Rúmi, known in Sufi circles as Mawlana, who founded the mystical order of the Mawlawiyah ("Mevlevis" in Turkish), known to the West as the whirling dervishes. The Mawlawiyah utilized the words and worldview of simple villagers, without using technical theological vocabulary, and thus they made divine truths accessible to those who were not literate or formally educated in theological Arabic or Persian. The kind of Islam they invoked was considered by the orthodox urban theologians to be "folkish" and "primitive" (Schimmel 1984, 128). Rúmi's place of worship is Konya in central Turkey, where the famous dervish dancers perform their *dhikr* (remembrance) and whirl to bring about an ecstatic religious state and spiritual union with God. From the standpoint of orthodoxy, there is nothing wrong with the veneration of God. But in his thirteenth-century evangelism for converts to the pursuit of the mystical path to God, Rúmi called all to Konya, not only believers: "Come, come, even if ye be an idolater or fire worshipper, come to Konya"! Rúmi's eldest son, Sultan Walad, became the organizer of the tariqah. Konya is a site of Sufi pilgrimage to this day, maintaining its universalism with pilgrims of all faiths and from many lands seeking its spiritual power. Rúmi's poetic words reveal this worldview:

> What is the solution, O Muslims:
> For I do not know myself.
> Neither Christian, Jew, Zoroastrian nor Muslim am I;
> I am not an Easterner or a Westerner, or of land or sea:
> Not of Nature nor of Heaven: Not of India, China, Bulgaria, Saqsin;
> Not of the Iraqs, nor of the land of Khorasan.

My place is placelessness: my sign is no sign.
I have no body or life: for I am the Life of Life.
I have put away duality: I have seen the Two worlds as one:
I desire One, I know One, I see One, I call One.
(from Rúmi 1979, xvi–xvii)

Music, dancing, and the exploration and cultivation of the spirit mark the Sufi tradition, which has sprung from the deepest heart and soul of Islam but has grown at the periphery of the state and has had a sometimes uneasy relationship with official Islam. I recall being warned by a Shari'a judge and a member of the Sudanese 'ulama in 1979 to stay away from the performances of the dervish dance that my husband and I used to frequent on Friday afternoons: "That is not Islam," he would say, "and you are here to study proper Islam." We continued to attend these popular Sufi dhikrs, feeling the same attraction as the first time we were drawn to them at a spontaneous dhikr we happened upon in the Khartoum market.

Sufism has nothing to do with the Sunni/Shi'a division in Islam, nor is it associated with any school of jurisprudence. It is not tied to any geographical area, family, lineage, or ethnic group. Sufi followers can be found irrespective of gender or age, although public performance is mostly male. It is all of these and none of these; it is everywhere and nowhere; it has no formal history of itself, yet Sufi orders are embedded in the historical spread of Islam.

The Sufi Brotherhoods

Sufi brotherhoods represent one of the most important forms of personal piety and social organization in the Islamic world (Voll 1995, 109). They have flourished in Persia, Iraq, Turkey, Egypt, and Morocco. They began using the term *tariqah* by the eleventh century for the rites of spiritual training, and they came to be associated with brotherhood and the community under a special master, often a monastery. They have founders or spiritual leaders, from the great Rúmi and the Mawlawiyas, to 'Abd al-Qadir al-Jilani in whose name the largest tariqah, the Qadiriya, was founded. During the twelfth and thirteenth centuries C.E., tariqahs spread throughout southwest Asia, North Africa, and the Iberian Peninsula, including Qadiriyah and Shadhiliya orders. Other more localized tariqahs developed later with the spread of Islam into West Africa and the Sahel, including branches of Qadiriyah and new orders, the Tijaniya, Sanusiya, and Khatmiya. In central and south Asia, the Ghawthiya branch of Qadiriya developed in the sixteenth century.

Sufi orders have been a significant part of the social fabric throughout the Islamic world. They provided outlets for the expression of faith for urban elites and rural farmers alike; they served as networks for regional travel and interaction; they provided an institutional structure for the spread of Islam; and they formed the basis for the later puritanical reform or spiritual revival movements that took shape after the colonial encounter (Voll 1995, 12). Tariqahs also helped to shape modern Islam in terms of popular piety and devotional life among the masses. The Sufi orders, for example, were a key part of indigenous resistance to colonialism.

Being a Sufi

The appeal of the Sufi orders is magnetic and undeniable, and it is a primary means by which Islam spread into the rural lands in the early formative centuries of the new faith and thereafter. The Sufis' approach is informal and humanistic. Asceticism, denial, and sacrifice are all important parts of being a Sufi.

Although the Sufis are mystics and ascetics, they are not like members of Christian monastic orders. Sufism does not espouse celibacy, because as the Prophet said, "There is no monkery in Islam" and "Marriage is my way" (Schimmel 1984, 122). Individual Sufis may travel, and they figure prominently in local folk and literary traditions about the stranger who comes to the village from the desert carrying only his staff. However, Sufi orders are based in local areas and find their adherents among local believers. Their adherence to the Sufi way and performance of dhikr are entirely parallel and do not replace their observance of the five pillars of Islam.

Stages of the Spiritual Path

The transcendental knowledge that Sufis seek is the opposite of science and is obtained through spiritual teaching, abandonment of the self, and the seeking of a oneness with the universal love. The spiritual journey begins with withdrawal from the material world. The end of the journey is the return to God. In between are seven degrees or states of the soul on the journey from the world of humanity to the world of the Divine. In the end everything depends upon love.

Ritual Remembrance

Purification of the self is accomplished through dhikr. To pray is to remember God. Dhikr, like prayer, can be individual or collective. Although the "prayers" or recitations are different in each brotherhood, the rituals are similar. Recitation from the Qur'an, beginning with the opening verses of the Fatiha, and chanting selections of the ninety-nine names of God. The dhikr is totally absorbing and the participant is separated from everything else and may enter a trancelike state. Music and dance aid this loss of self and heightened awareness of God. Self-denial of food or drink and physical motion may also assist the journey.

Whirling Dervishes

The most original custom of the Mawlawiya tariqah founded by Rúmi's son is the whirling dance, the *sama'*, which has made this Sufi brotherhood the most recognized among Muslim and non-Muslims alike. Dervish life was built upon a monastic stay of three years, originally at Konya, during which the devotee would lead an austere life dedicated to prayer and fasting. Over the centuries of Ottoman rule, the turuq were at times supported by the sultans' courts, while at other times they were feared as centers of opposition and were repressed. In 1925, Kemal Ataturk suppressed all turuq in Turkey, and they remain officially banned, although still popular with the masses.

Sufism has been more open than official Islam to women practitioners and leaders. Some of the original mystics and poets were women. Some Mawlawiya women guided disciples along the Sufi path. In the past, women's performance of the dance was private. The "Contemporary Lovers of Mevlana" recruits followers from non-Muslim countries. Founded in Istanbul by Sheikh Hasan Çikar, this "new age" tariqah has eighty-three members, seven men and seventy-six women, since "the sexes are equal in the eyes of God." Men and women wear the same flowing robes and whirl for an hour or more in their dhikr recalling the oneness of God and universe (*Providence Journal,* December 12, 2000).

The sama' is the cosmic dance of the whirling dervishes. "There are many roads which lead to God," Rúmi said. "I have chosen the one of dance and music." Every moment and element of the sama' has symbolic meaning (Vitray-Meyerovitch 1987, 43). The dance expresses great emotion, joy, ecstatic religious love, pain, and sorrow. Rúmi's son recounts that after the death of his beloved teacher Shams of Tabriz, which had plunged the master into despair, his father would not stop dancing and whirling; any strong emotion could incite the dance. Tradition says that the sama' would take place in the streets coming home from Friday prayers.

There are many legends as to why the dervishes continue to dance the sama'. One is the obvious imitation of the practice of the Master Rúmi. Another is that the sama' repeats and reflects the cosmic dance as these words from the *Rubaiyat* reveal:

Oh daylight, rise! atoms are dancing
The souls, lost in ecstasy, are dancing
To your ear, I will tell you where the dance will
take you
All the atoms in the air and in the desert,
Let it be known, are like madmen,
Each atom, happy or miserable,

Is in love with the Sun of which we can say
Nothing

(Vitray-Meyerovitch 1987)

Or, for another explanation, consider the response I received when I queried the direct descendant of Rúmi in Istanbul in 1972 as to why the dervishes whirl in their dhikr. He recalled the legend that in the days of the prophet Muhammad, a new Muslim convert approached the Prophet and asked him if God was pleased with him. The Messenger of Islam replied that God wanted to know whether the convert was pleased with Him. As the story goes, this simple retort produced an ecstatic state in the new convert, who began to whirl in joy and happiness at God's response to his conversion.

On the use of music in Sufi ritual, some strict interpretations of the Holy Sources say that the only permissible music is the call to prayer or Qur'anic chanting. It is reported that Rúmi was listening with great pleasure to the music of a violin one afternoon when a friend entered and said the music should stop, for they were announcing the afternoon call to prayer. Rúmi responded that they both talk to God, one for his service, the other for His Love and Knowledge (Vitray-Meyerovitch 1987, 43).

The sama' ceremony is highly ritualized. The white robe represents the shroud, over which a black coat is worn representing the tomb, and the high felt fez represents the tombstone. The sheikh who enters last is the mediator between earth and the heavens. He salutes the dervishes, and they return the greeting. The Prophet is praised, the playing of the flute and drums begins, and the dervishes begin three turns around the dance floor, symbolic of the three stages taking one closer to God—the path of science, the path to vision, and the path toward union with God. The dervishes then shed their black coats, born or reborn with their full white robes flowing. They ask the sheikh for permission to dance and then start whirling slowly with arms outstretched like wings, the right palm turned upward toward the sky and the left palm turned downward toward the earth. Their movements represent universal motion, planets turning around the sun and around their own center. The sheikh enters at the fourth turn and begins turning in the dance circle, representing the sun's rays, and the rhythm quickens and the flute player improvises. This is the high point of the desired union sought in the sama'; when the sheikh leaves the circle, the sama' is over. With the last salutations, God's name is evoked—"Allah, Allah"—with "It is toward Him that this adoration has ascended" (Vitray-Meyerovitch 1987, 43–47).

Shrine Dhikrs

My husband and I used to attend the weekly dhikr of the Qadiriyah tariqah, held on Friday afternoons at the tomb of a local holy man, Sheikh Hamad al-

Nil, in Omdurman. The performance of this dhikr is exclusively by men, but women attend to receive the blessings of the remembrance of God. In Cairo today, women have become participants as well as observers of Sufi dhikrs. For the dhikr in Omdurman, members of the order dress in white jellabiyas (loose, ankle-length robes). However, the leader and "dervishes" may be dressed in green jellabiyas or in jibbas, patchwork quilted shirts and pants, signifying disavowal of worldly possessions and recalling the garb of the followers of the Sudanese Mahdi Muhammad Ahmad. For about two hours before sunset, the dervishes form a circular procession to drum, dance, and sing the praises of God and His Messenger, Muhammad. They chant the shahada—"la Allah ila Allah, wa Muhammadun Rasoul Allah" (There is no God but God and Muhammad is His Messenger) and repeat God's name—"Allah, Allah, Allah"—as the celebrants move around the circle of attendees and worshipers. The dervishes whirl in rapid bursts of energy using the same formula as the Turkish dervishes with right hand and palm raised toward the heavenly sky and left hand palm extended down toward the earth. In the heat of the afternoon sun, such intense dancing and whirling can bring about an ecstatic trancelike state. The dancers are left alone to recover while the others continue the dhikr until sunset, when the ritual stops and the followers depart with the farewell, "Assalaamu alaykum." Although recognized as non-Muslims, we were always greeted and welcomed at the dhikrs by the sheikhs of the tariqah, and my husband was often exhorted to join in the dancing in the true nonsectarian spirit of the Sufis, while I learned how to ululate in the company of the believing women.

Annual festivals in Egypt, *mulids*, are pre-Islamic and date to the pharaonic concept of pilgrimages to the tombs of revered figures (Sonbol and Atia 1999, 7). The festival of the Prophet's birthday (Mawlid al-Nabi) is widely observed in Egypt, Pakistan, and elsewhere in the Muslim world, although purist Islamists disapprove of this saintlike holiday, which might be confused with Christmas. The mulids also involve processions around the town, with flutes, drums, and dancing that begin or end at the saint's shrine or tomb. A mulid may last from one to four days and has all the earmarks of a carnival. The biggest night involves a grand procession of all the Sufi turuq, each led by its own sheikh, who may be a descendant of the revered holy man, or in the case of Christians, the Virgin Mary. At mulids, Muslims and Coptic Christians gather together. Folk tales are recited, such as the stories of the conqueror of conquerors, Abu-Zayd al-Hilali. Whirling dervishes entertain or inspire. Joy, brotherhood, release, and God's blessings abound. Women attend as frequently as men and have become sufis participating in the rhythmic swaying and holy chanting. Open to visitors as well as devotees, these festivals are expected to bring blessings to all those who participate.

Fig. 9. Qadariya Sufi order gathering at tomb of Sheikh Hamad al-Nil, Omdurman, Sudan.

Many villages and towns have their own legendary sheikhs or patrons for whom mulids are annual celebrations. Habib Swela is a newly venerated holy man in the Swahili culture of Lamu (an island off the Kenyan coast), observed there by both Sunni and Shi'a Muslims. During a visit to the island of Lamu in 1996, traveling there from Mombasa, Kenya (one of the stops on the Semester at Sea educational voyage around the world), I had the unique opportunity to witness a dhikr within Swahili culture devoted to this holy man, who had died only about twenty years before my visit. Habib Swela was a pious man renowned as a teacher and endower of schools and mosques, who was popular with both Sunni and Shi'a Muslims, who are equally divided among the island's population. "Remembering" the island's holy man and his good deeds involves men and boys of the island's mosques, who parade, drumming and dancing, while non-tariqah women and men observe the procession and seek blessings. Swahili culture on the island dates from the fifteenth-century introduction of Islam into East Africa through contact with sailors from Oman and other south Arabian ports along the Indian Ocean trade winds in their *dhows,* which still ply these trade routes. Swahili culture on the island is relatively conservative, with women facially veiled in public and segregation of the sexes socially enforced. However, the mulid is both a religious and social outlet as it binds men of different generations and unites Sunni and Shi'a Muslims in the spirit of Sufi universalism.

Tension between Folk and Official Islam

The tension between folk expressions of Islam, such as the Sufi brotherhoods, and orthodoxy is most apparent in the practice of veneration of local holy men. Revered in life and worshiped after death, they are often regarded as miracle workers and persons from whom one can obtain blessings. Frequently tombs are erected at their burial site and may become places where dhikrs are held, or they may be sites of local or regional pilgrimage. The marabout tradition in the Maghrib and Franco-phone West Africa is part of this folk expression of Islam, and tombs of local holy men dot the North and West African landscape. In eighteenth-century Arabia, Muhammad ibn ʿAbd al-Wahhab (d. 1791) condemned Sufism and saint worship. The Wahhabis took control of the Hijaz in 1804, including Mecca and Medina, so that the holiest places of Islam were purified and Sufi folk Islam was eradicated by demolishing saints' shrines. This condemnation of saint veneration has been maintained in conservative Saudi Arabia to this day (Voll 1995, 122).

Clearly this veneration of men is contrary to the fundamental principle of tawheed, and any special veneration of the Prophet of Islam has been greatly curtailed in Islamic practice. Some Muslim scholars object to the special observation of the Prophet's birthday, for fear that this leads away from the worship of God alone. Visitation of the burial site and associated mosque of Muhammad is not mandatory in the performance of the hajj and may only be added at the beginning or end of the pilgrimage, or it may be performed as a part of the lesser pilgrimage. However, the attraction of these Sufi holy sheikhs is more powerful than are the warnings and constraints of theological Islam. Rural women especially, and others, perhaps illiterate farmers, visit the local tombs with supplications for cures, for solutions to problems, or for fulfillment of deep desires. They may bring children to receive blessings from the sheikh, and they may leave small gifts or tie a brightly colored piece of cloth nearby as a remembrance of their visit.

Yet the power of the Sufis to attract and entrance Muslims endures even as its appeal to non-Muslims continues, some of whom may eventually embrace Islam as a result of their mystical experience with Sufism. Open to all who are seekers of the divine through mysticism, and dealing with the fundamentals of human existence, such as one's mortality, the power and the mystery of the Sufi way will continue to be popular.

Other Folk Traditions and Local Practice of Islam

There are other practices commonly found in Muslim societies that belong distinctly to the realm of folk belief and are not associated with Islam. Perhaps the best known of these are the set of beliefs associated with the evil eye, which are found across a broad spectrum of countries and cultures. Found in Mediterranean Muslim culture as well as in non-Muslim cultures, the evil eye probably can be traced to Pharaonic Egypt and the powerful Eye of Horus. Beliefs surrounding the evil eye emphasize the need for protection, especially for small children. Amulets with the familiar bright blue stone with the yellow eye are pinned on children's clothing or hung over cribs; evil eye amulets may be found at the doorways or entrances to Egyptian homes, perhaps alongside beautiful works of Islamic calligraphy. Men may carry evil-eye amulets in their pockets with their car keys or pocket change, and women may wear jewelry with the evil-eye symbol.

It is thought to be a dangerous solicitation of the power of the evil eye to compliment a child on its beauty or attractiveness, and some rural women may dress their children in less attractive clothes so as not to attract the attention of the evil eye. Likewise, it is considered imprudent to compliment a family too much on its possessions or to give excessive praise to a woman's jewelry or clothing. Jealousy is thus held in check and humility is promoted. Social scientists have suggested that the social control imposed by the limitation on ostentatious displays of wealth explains the continuation of evil-eye beliefs and practices.

Another practice rooted in Islamic traditions but definitely belonging to the arena of folk belief is the supernatural power of the written religious word, as found among many Sahelian African Muslims. Reading and writing are strongly promoted in Islam because of the powerful motive for studying the Qur'an. The Islamic schools, known as the *kuttab, madrasa,* or *khalwa,* focused exclusively on learning to read and write the Qur'an. Islamic art, with its ban on representational art, has developed an elaborate tradition of religious calligraphy. The calligraphy adorning mosques is a graphic portrayal of the word of Allah. Illiterate Muslims were thus impressed with the writing of God's words, which led to the belief that the words themselves can cure or bring about the desired solution to a problem.

A supplicant might visit a local religious feki or sheikh and ask him to recommend a Qur'anic verse to suit his or her problem. The holy man will write the appropriate verse on a piece of paper and place it in a *hijab,* a covering made of leather or silver, and the hijab is then worn until the desired end has been achieved, or it may never be removed. Likewise the sheikh may write passages from the Qur'an or Hadith on a *loh,* a wooden writing board used in Islamic schools, and then wash the ink from the board. The supplicant drinks the inky water with the belief that a solution to the problem will be found.

Within the realm of Islam but inhabiting the domain of the spirit world are the *jinn,* beings that have been part of Middle Eastern folk culture for millennia, and they have even entered Western culture in the form of the "genie" stories. There is a story that when the Messenger of Islam first began to hear the call of the angel Gabriel to recite the words later compiled as the Qur'an, he was reluctant, fearing that people would think him possessed or inspired by jinn (Esposito 1988, 9).

Fig. 10a and b. Qur'anic writing board, *Loh*, and *sibha* beads used in religious schools; teacher and students in *kuttab*, Fez, Morocco.

Belief in the jinn is widely held, forming a broadly expressed system of ideas regarding the visitation of spirits, especially at night, and their influence on human activities and endeavors. Jinn visit with the howling winds, or they surprise humans by making appearances in ordinary places, along a road or in and about the house. They can be simply mischievous, or they can determine the fate of a human, as in the well-known story of the genie and the three wishes. They are a part of the supernatural world, a world that commonly intrudes upon human experience and is troublesome, but a world that is respected and to a degree placated. On a recent visit to the westernmost Egyptian oasis of Siwa, I was shown the particular places outside the oasis where the jinn reside and can be heard as travelers return from the desert roads to the town.

A well-documented but non-Islamic type of supernatural activity is that associated with Zar spirit possession, which is found in the Nile Valley and Ethiopia as well as in Sahelian western and north Africa, where it is sometimes known as Bori cult. It is a form of spirit possession practiced by Muslims and non-Muslims alike and is the special province of women—rural and urban—who are both the possessed and the exorcists who drive out the spirits causing the illness or depression. Women who are possessed claim that some illness, personal difficulty, or unfulfilled desire is responsible for the spirit possession. Such women host their own Zar parties, where a *sheikha* presides, animals are slaughtered, and drumming, dancing, and spiritual possession of attendees and the afflicted woman take place. Various spirits appear and possess susceptible women. My attendance at Zar parties was valued by the other attendees, given the exotic nature of the spirits who visit. After these spirits have spoken, sometimes intelligibly and directly addressing the problem at hand, the possessed woman collapses and some catharsis appears to have taken place. At Zar parties women act in ways otherwise unacceptable in Islamic society, such as smoking or using crude language. Zar has been analyzed as psychodrama (Kennedy 1967) and as a type of spiritual feminism (Boddy 1989). However one interprets it, it operates outside the framework of Islam, although many good Muslim women are fervent believers and practitioners.

There are also popular folk festivals that are not rooted in either Islam or Arabic culture, such as the springtime secular Sham al-Nessim holiday in Egypt and Nouruz in Iran. Sham al-Nessim is popular with Christians, Muslims, and foreigners alike. This spring festival occurs on the Monday following the Coptic Easter Sunday, whose calendar is based on that of ancient Egypt. This is a day for family picnics and for the renewal of ancient customs like smelling green onions first thing in the morning and hanging them at the door to ward off disease, or playing games with hardboiled eggs to see which player cracks an egg first.

3

Arab-Islamic Values and Social Practice

Perhaps if the recent history of the world were different and Western society did not have the imperial advantage that it has inherited from the legacy of colonialism and economic domination, we might have studies of American culture by non-Western social scientists. A chapter entitled "Western Values and Social Practice" in such a study might include sections on individualism, self-sufficiency, entrepreneurial spirit and materialism, male supremacy, or optimism. The treatise, written in Arabic, might be read in translation by some "natives" who think it is reductionist and a simplification of their multifaceted social reality. Others, desiring a basic knowledge of the "other" (i.e., the Westerner), might find the study helpful as an introduction to some of the values underpinning Western society. Turning back to world realities today, the truth is that very little is known or understood in the West about basic values underlying Arab and Muslim society, and in this chapter I offer that kind of basic introduction.

Arab and Muslim

Islam originated in Arabia, the Hijaz, in the seventh century of the common era and was founded upon the existing Arab culture there. The Arabs occupied Arabia for at least three millennia before the introduction of Islam. Between 1000 and 500 B.C.E. the camel was domesticated, enabling the Arabs to develop a distinctive way of life dependent upon it for food, drink, clothing, shelter, and transport. The culture the Arabs developed left no great buildings, but a rich worldview is embodied in their language and poetry.

Of the Bedouin it has been said that their one great monument is their poetry (Labid, Polk 1974, vii). It is a poetry born of solitude, privation, and social interdependence, and it is nurtured in the soul of a people. The poems of the ancient Bedouin extol the virtue of generosity and the bravery of the warrior. But the warrior must not be an uncouth barbarian; without diminishing his worth as a warrior, he must strive to be a poet, a man of beautiful and important words. The ancient ode (*qasida*) was composed to be sung; it typically evoked the importance of people and not places, and included praise of one's own people, and of bravery, yet of skill in the verbal arts of rhetoric and argument, as well as of generosity and hospitality among one's companions (ibid., xviii). The art of recitation was practiced by the *rawi*, of which there was at least one in every extended clan, whose task it was to memorize the poetry in order to entertain or educate fellow clan members. Such recitations would occur once the camp was settled at night, refreshed in the cool of the evening air. The audience was not passive, but broke in with commentary or recitations of their own, all to savor the art of the poet. Recitations by women and female poets were not uncommon in the pre-Islamic and early Muslim eras.

The tradition of recitation and storytelling—perhaps best known in the West through *The Thousand and One Nights*—stories that I read to my daughters, who begged me to read more than a single night's story due to their engaging cliffhanger plots—continues in a few cafes in Cairo and Damascus, although television threatens this age-old custom. The professional storyteller known as the *hakawati* (from *haka*, he spoke) can regale an audience with stories from the great age of Islamic empires that can last a year in the telling with nightly readings or recitations of an hour or more. These stories impart core values as depicted in heroic deeds of kings and commoners, distinguished by their Muslim virtues. The hakawati stops reading at a critical moment in a story to keep the suspense high and ensure his audience will return the next night to listen while they sip strong mint tea or smoke their water pipes (Ghattas 2000).

The images of the camel, the gazelle, the wild ass, and the desert itself still inspire Arab poets, even though they may be urbanites who have never known desert life directly. The powerful similes and metaphors of the poetic tradition have enriched everyday speech and have made Arab compliments all the sweeter and insults all the more devastating.

I have often been struck by the number of men one meets in the Arab world who, despite their chosen profession of law or engineering or even their limited education, proclaim as their deepest wish the desire to write poetry. In the same vein, the number of lower- and middle-class working people Richard and I have met over the years, while traveling long distances on trains or meeting regularly at a cafe, who proudly declare themselves to be poets is a phenomenon that at first amazed us, but then we came to admire them greatly. The power of the word in pre-Islamic Arabia was reinforced by the focus on the revealed word of God to the Prophet Muhammad, the Qur'an. It remains to this day the highest standard of literary achievement and the most classical form of the Arabic language. The point is stressed in an oft-recited Hadith from the Prophet that the ink of the writer is more precious than the blood of the warrior.

Although the Arabs developed their culture in a desert environment, by the time of the coming of Islam Arabia was well connected to the rest of the ancient world through a complex system of trade routes crisscrossing the Arabian peninsula and flourishing along the coast. Mecca was an established trade center when Muhammad was born in c. 570 C.E. But desert culture survives in the Arabic language and in many customs associated with Arab culture. The basic greeting in Arabic, "ahlan wa sahlan," is difficult to translate, but it means something like "hello" or "be at ease, you are safe here." The harsh environment of the desert meant that relatively scarce resources, such as water and pasturage, were carefully regulated. Strangers could be violators of such customary rights, but once welcomed, the stranger had no need to fear for his security. "Ahlan wa sahlan" is the secular Arab greeting, while "assalaam alaykum" is the universal Muslim greeting.

Generosity (*karim*) is one of the ninety-nine qualities of Allah and is referred to in the popular male name 'Abd al-Karim (literally, "slave or servant of God, the Most Generous") or in the female name Karima. Generosity is recognized as a quality of the spirit and soul. Its importance has not diminished over the centuries or been fundamentally transformed by urban life and empire, by class division and social stratification.

Personal dignity (*karama*) characterizes this sense of generosity and the moral integrity that is conveyed by it. Karama is one of the best of human attributes and is used liberally in discussing possible marriage partners, in referring to friends, and in describing the good acts of public figures.

The survival value of generosity within the context of the harsh and unpredictable desert life is obvious; in addition, sharing constructs an intricate web of relationships in the bonding and reciprocity between individuals and groups that has enabled desert families not only to survive but also to reproduce and flourish in their challenging environment. Where land is not private property and possessions are minimal and portable, sharing life's necessities is valued. The last draught of water, loaf of bread, or portion of meat is given to the guest over the family member without fanfare on the part of the donor and without great expression of appreciation on the part of the recipient. Words from "The Golden Ode," an ancient poem from pre-Islamic Arabia, speak to the antiquity of the practice of generosity amid desert want:

And the guest and the neighbors from afar are
treated as though
Descending to the lush meadows of Tabalah
Every diseased, exhausted, and famished woman came
seeking asylum at the tent ropes
Like the camel, tethered to starve over the grave
of her master, shrunken inside the folds of its
skin
And they fill to overflowing, when the winds howl
from all sides
[Bowls like] ditches to which the orphans descend
to drink
Ah, We, when the tribal hosts gather, there is
never lacking among us a champion, contentious in
great affairs, one ever ready to follow through in
painful matters. (Labid Ibn Rabiah 1977, lines 151–57)

Sharing and hospitality are so deeply engrained that to notice its expression would be an oddity to any but the outsider. Even a passing visitor, without particular need, offends the host if he or she refuses the cup of coffee or tea. For example, Richard and I quickly learned that in response to the question "Won't you have something to drink?" we should never say, "No, thanks, I'm not thirsty," for this is incorrect and socially unacceptable. Even if you have drunk tea or coffee at the offices of a half-dozen bureaucrats before this moment of invitation to drink, you should accept and drink again. To do otherwise implies disinterest in both the traditional hospitality and in the nature of the business you wish to transact.

As Americans we are trained to say "Thank you" for what might be viewed in other cultures as common courtesy or normal human behavior. We thank people for their time, for talking to us or remembering us, for their sympathy; the clerk and the customer thank each other; the parent and the child thank each other for their love. As Richard and I learned Arabic, we made the normal transpositions of English language usage into the new language we were learning. Thus we were thanking people for serving us tea or coffee, local scholars for the time they had spent with us, the bus driver, trying in our way to be polite. When people would smile wryly or not respond with the appropriate "You're welcome" to our repeated thanks, we began to see that our sense of gratitude reflected our cultural background, in which generosity is not commonplace and the anonymity of everyday life and exchange is, perhaps, eased by polite but not very meaningful expressions of thanks.

The sincerity of our generosity was tested one early December morning in

Khartoum when Muhammad Ahmad, the caretaker of the houseboat on the Blue Nile where we were living, came to our door. "How many sweaters do you have?" he asked.

Since we had learned many Arabic phrases and expressions from Muhammad Ahmad, we were pleased to respond correctly, "Three sweaters."

"Fine," he said, "give me one. Winter is coming, and I have no sweater."

Taken aback, we reviewed the request, commenting to ourselves that he had not even said "Please." To reject his request would be to place our good relationship in jeopardy, we thought, so it was best to offer him a sweater. A few minutes later, when we presented him with a sweater, he took it and did not say "Thank you." At the time we were miffed, but as the months passed, Muhammad Ahmad brought us many small items from the market—dates, sesame candies, and the like—and we continued to say "Thank you." He would walk away mumbling to himself, "Okay, thank you, thank you," as if he were just saying the words to please us. Genuine karama is in the deed and not in the words.

Some Westerners are suspicious of this hospitality, especially when it is encountered in a tourist shop, and repeated greetings, "ahlan wa sahlan" or "marhaba" (welcome in both Arabic and Turkish) along with offers of drinks are made in an effort to have you, the buyer, extend your stay a little longer in the shop. Staying longer and having something to drink meets the twin goals of extending a welcome and encouraging a closer look at the items for sale. Perhaps this distrust on the part of Westerners stems from the degree of alienation that exists in Western societies, or perhaps it comes from certain negative, preconceived notions about Arabs and Muslims. Whatever its cause, it can result in miscommunication, upset, and a reinforcement of negative stereotypes on both sides. Westerners are often seen as distant, aloof, and noninteractive. When pressed in a bazaar to "Come in, have a cup of tea, and see my shop," the Western tourist often declines with a certain measure of suspicion about the sincerity of the invitation. The Westerner usually does not understand that he or she could actually sit amicably and sip tea or Pepsi and visit with the storekeeper for nothing more than a pleasant chat without the obligation to buy. The hope is, of course, that you have had a pleasant respite, will return another time, and perhaps even bring a friend to enjoy this hospitality, but there is no specific obligation to do so. All such interactions are played out in an atmosphere of generalized hospitality that may or may not have some specific return.

Given the anonymous nature of buyer/seller interactions in the West, the same tourist is often surprised to find that the shopkeeper recalls his or her face and the conversation they shared, despite the fact that many days, weeks, or even longer periods of time have passed. This puzzle to the Westerner is readily explained by the close personal relations that pervade every activity, including commerce and trade. Cultural differences and potential misunderstandings between Western and Middle Eastern people are discussed further in chapter 5.

The twin values of generosity and hospitality are generalized throughout Arab and Muslim society and straddle class differences, although expressed in different ways. No matter what the class level, it is important to give the appearance of abundance. Preparing more food than can be consumed by guests and encouraging them to eat more and fill themselves beyond normal capacity is customary. Complimenting the delicious food and indicating that one is finished by praising God is usually not sufficient to end the meal. Hosts will encourage guests to continue, often implying that not to continue would be an insult, so that often the guest indulges in a bit more food consumption. Notions of hospitality extend to a social pattern of frequent visits between relatives and friends that often last late into the night, despite work schedules in the morning. The guest may have tried to leave several times, citing the lateness of the hour or commitments the next day, but the host will discourage such leave-taking with remonstrances such as "No, it is still too early." Having been in this situation ourselves many times and feeling a Western sense of frustration about time and logistics of transportation, Richard and I were often pleasantly surprised to find that our hosts had arranged and paid for our transportation home or that they were prepared to accompany us to a taxi stand and wait until we were safely on our way home.

Displays of generosity that we in the West would find incredulous are an everyday occurrence, so embedded are the values of generosity and hospitality in Arab and Muslim life. In addition to numerous free taxi rides because a friendly conversation had ensued, Richard and I have received free dental service because "You are a guest in our country." Likewise offers of assistance in the realm of automobile breakdowns and repairs (of which there have been many) added to an appreciation of the depth of these values. Sometimes, when our vehicle had broken down or had a flat tire, other motorists would stop and spend the better part of an afternoon getting the vehicle going again. When we realized that any offer of money as gratitude would be deeply insulting, we had to be creative about finding culturally appropriate ways to express our thanks. We would often obtain the name and address of the person and drop by the house for a visit with a gift of fruit or sweets, although this was never a necessity. Thus new relationships could be formed and continued, and the network of cooperative relations on both sides was expanded. What did people want from us? They wanted the external network, in the form of information and access to the West.

The contrast between American suspicion of generous acts and Middle Eastern hospitality is clear in a story related to me by a Sudanese friend living in the United States. He had stopped by an American roadside to help a stranded motorist with a flat tire. When he stepped out of his car to approach the woman with an offer of assistance, she rolled up her window, locked the car doors, and screamed for help. He tried to explain that he was only there to offer assistance, but to no avail.

Although the poorer members of a family may experience some shame because they cannot provide the same generous hospitality displayed by richer family members, such differences are usually overlooked in public, with the highest value placed on overall family solidarity. In recent years, economic difficulty for many in the relatively poor Arab and Muslim nations has become a source of shame and disgrace because hospitality cannot be extended in the ways that have been customary in the past. Families may be unable to offer meat as often as they would like to their guests, or they simply will make excuses for not getting together more often. Social visiting beyond the extended family becomes constrained, as it is shameful to invite guests to one's home without providing adequately for them. This is a contemporary social tension that symbolizes, for the average person, the cultural changes that are occurring as a result of economic hardship.

In the broader realm of social differences between the richer and poorer Muslim nations, much is related about the excesses and waste that can occur when engaging in conspicuous displays of hospitality and generosity. The most prosperous strata of Arab-Muslim society may engage in some notoriously wasteful examples of such consumption, which are witnessed and reported by servants from the poorer Muslim nations. For example, a whole sheep may be slaughtered and cooked for two or three guests, and the rest is discarded. Such practices have occurred within the context of recent acquisition of unprecedented wealth, and conspicuous consumption in this manner debases the essential qualities of these long-standing cultural patterns.

The Collective in Society and Religion

The idea of the group (*jama 'a*) in Islamic society is fundamental to the powerful collective consciousness that the religion of Islam promotes. It is expressed in the concept of Umma, that world community of believers from widely differing geographical and cultural backgrounds. The choice of words for the idea of the United Nations in Arabic opts for the use of al-Umam al-Muttahidah, rather than using the more common term for state or republic, Jamhuriyya. Umma is meant to be a powerful unified collective. It was upon

Fig. 11. Detail of Imam mosque in Isfahan, Iran. Courtesy of Mahmoud Khoja, mayor of Isfahan.

this concept that Julius Nyerere drew in his enunciation of *Ujamaa* as a political and social philosophy to unite Tanzanians in the common purpose of building the new nation-state.

On a more prosaic level, *jama'a* in colloquial Sudanese dialect can be used to refer to the group of one's friends or classmates (*majmu'ah* in modern standard Arabic). But it also is readily elevated to more significant group activity, such as groups which collect in the mosque. Although the term *masjid* may be used to designate a mosque, the term *jama'a* is the popular referent for the local community mosque where group prayer takes place.

From the earliest times of Muslim education, the place of learning—where the Qur'an and Sunna could be studied in conjunction with reading and writing Arabic—was the grand mosque, usually centrally located in a large city. These places of learning associated with mosques also became known as *jami'a*.

The sense of the group and the collective is so entwined with Islam, its rituals, and its society that it is difficult to discuss as a separate subject. I have already emphasized the importance of collective ritual in the practice of Islam through the five pillars. In addition, for the most part, the collective rituals are embedded in social practice where the cultural value of the extended family and group life is already well established. It is difficult for Muslims living in the West to maintain the integrity of the collectivity in their practice of Islam; for example, fasting during Ramadan is difficult in a society that often neither acknowledges nor appreciates the rites associated with Islam. But many Western converts to Islam find an attachment to a community and an enlarged sense of group identity when they embrace Islam. Others may reject an identity that Western society has placed upon them, as is the case with large numbers of African Americans who have converted to Islam.

The collective and group life are treated more thoroughly in chapter 4, where I examine matters of family, neighborhood, and community.

Honor

Honor (*sharaf*) is a fundamental value that is at once highly personal and individual and also utterly collective, rooted in family and group dignity and identity. Sharaf is a quality desired in all people. The man's name Sharif identifies an honorable man, and the desirable quality of the bride-to-be is signified by describing her as *sharifa* (an honorable woman). When guests arrive, the most elegant and formal greeting offered by the host is "Itsharafna," meaning "it honors us that you have come." The guest might respond, "Itsharafti ana," meaning "I am [likewise] honored."

Sharaf goes much deeper than good manners. Honor embodies the pride and dignity that a family possesses due to its long-standing good reputation in the community for producing upright men and women who behave themselves, marry well, raise proper children, and above all adhere to the principles and practice of the religion of Islam. A good Muslim family has its honor intact and produces sons who are sharifs and daughters who are sharifas.

Honor is understood in a complex way as the absence of shame, for honor and shame are bound to one another as complementary yet contradictory ideas. Shame (*'ayb*) falls upon a family when a member conducts herself or himself improperly or gives the appearance of improper conduct. Much of this misconduct is construed as being of a sexual nature. A dishonorable man is one who shirks his familial responsibilities, wastes his money on frivolities or drink, or conducts himself in a way that suggests loose morals. A woman's honor can be questioned for much less serious conduct. A woman who frequently goes out alone at night or wears clothing, adornments, or excessive perfume that draw the attention of men can be gossiped about and accused of being dishonorable. In more conservative societies, a woman who has spent time alone with a man classified as a stranger (not a kin relation) can be accused of dishonor. Women respond by dressing modestly and carrying themselves in a restrained way in public and thus are recognized as being above reproach.

Shame in the Rearing of Children and the Reproach of Adults

The entwined relationship of honor and shame has been long recognized in Arab and Muslim societies as well as in the generalized Mediterranean social complex (Gilmore 1987; Peristiany 1966). 'Ayb is a concept that is used liberally in the rearing of children and in the reproach of adults. 'Ayb, whose closest English equivalent is "Shame on you," is usually not applied in the training of very young children, because it implies a degree of prior knowledge and instruction that would have dictated a different course of action. Older children who have disobeyed or have behaved in a disrespectful manner often hear a lecture from a parent or close relative that begins and ends with the admonition "'Ayb."

As a collective society, it is not uncommon to hear neighbors reprimanding children, usually boys, who are misbehaving in the streets by saying, "'Ayb, 'ayb alaykum" (Shame, shame on all of you). What is most surprising to Western adults is that the boys usually listen to the reproach, modify their behavior, and do not respond with some curse, insult, or worse, as might happen in the United States.

The power of the use of the negative value of shame is that it reinforces the positive idea that one's behavior is a direct reflection on one's personal honor and dignity, and that one's personal behavior represents a part of the important whole of family honor. One's sense of honor is acquired in later childhood and remains with the person throughout life.

When arguing and trying to make a point, adults may invoke the concept of "'ayb," that somehow the behavior or words in question have brought about a diminution of honor and therefore represent something shameful. Foul language is undignified and shameful; losing one's temper and shouting insults is shameful; failing to come to the aid of a family member or neighbor when one is able is worthy of the reproach. Failing to support family members for whom one is responsible is dishonorable and shameful; gossip that potentially causes harm is improper and shameful. Anything that adversely and unfairly affects the dignity of another person is likely to draw the criticism "'ayb."

In a related vein, conditions of life that do not permit the normal course of events to prevail may also be described using the concept of "'ayb." A broadly accepted ground for the judicial divorce of a woman from her impotent husband is known as "talaq al-'ayb," in this instance a defect in the man that is shameful. The shame of impotence reveals a great deal about societal views of male dignity and honor. Impotence is legally determined by meeting a set of conditions whereby the couple cohabit in suitable privacy for a prescribed length of time during which the consummation of the marriage can occur; if it does not occur, the wife testifies or the husband admits his impotency and a divorce is granted.

Honor, Shame, and Homicide

Personal and familial honor is such a powerful cultural value that its breach can result in dire consequences, even violence and death. Insults between men or women sting most deeply when they impugn family or personal honor. They are the fighting words that can make tempers flare and portend an immediate response or deferred rage and revenge. In a study of more than four hundred cases of homicide in the Sudan that I conducted for my doctoral research, I found that the insults, often coupled with sexual jealousy or the suggestion of impropriety, were a major context in which homicide will occur. If the circumstances already mentioned are associated with drinking and inebriation and if weapons are present, the probability that violence and murder will occur increases markedly (Fluehr-Lobban 1976).

Direct insults between husband and wife, such as "You were not a virgin when we married!" or "You are impotent!" may be brought up in court as evidence of shameful behavior that makes life for the couple intolerable. Insults between men suggesting that their wives or sisters are whores or that their mothers were prostitutes and that they are consequently bastards are so provocative that threats or violence must necessarily follow. Insults that curse one's religion can also provoke violence. These examples suggest that a sense of personal dignity and honor stems from attitudes about good sexual conduct and self-esteem derived from religion. Insults impugning a lack of personal generosity or other forms of individualistic behavior are not as likely to result in aggression or violence.

Honor Killings

The traditional right, or cultural responsibility, of male kin to admonish, reproach, physically punish, or even kill a daughter, sister, or wife for improper conduct or alleged sexual impropriety has been challenged on human rights grounds. Female chastity is seen in Arab society as the boundary line between respect and shame. Reflecting a powerful double standard, an unchaste act by a woman is viewed as a collective offense affecting not simply herself but her family and lineage as well; a man's sexual impropriety is an individual act, little recognized, unpunished, and only mildly affecting his reputation. This right to execute a woman judged guilty by her kin of sexual misconduct is usually exercised by the father and/or brother. It is a cultural practice long upheld in Arab society that is not specifically rejected or condemned by Islamic interpretations thus far. Honor is restored to the family by "washing the shame with blood," and true to the double standard of patriarchal societies, the penalty falls on the accused woman and not on the man with whom she is alleged to have had sexual relations. In some conservative communities, the mere suggestion of impropriety can be punished with a beating, a clear warning to the woman to avoid more serious entanglements. This customary right has generally not been challenged in the applied law of Muslim societies, although several verses in the Qur'an would support lesser punishments, such as flogging, house confinement, or forgiveness after repentance (sura [verse] 4:15–18; sura 24:1–9). However, honor killings have been challenged by international human rights groups for violating the fundamental rights of women and girls to be free from the fear of punishment or death from male family members for the mere suggestion of a breach of family honor due to her personal behavior.

Basma al-Goul, a Palestinian woman of Resaifah, Jordan, ran away with a man after her husband suspected her of infidelity. Her husband divorced her, and while in hiding she married the other man. "We were the most prominent family with the best reputation," said Um Tayseer, her mother, who went looking for her daughter carrying a gun. In the end it was Basma's sixteen-year-old brother who pulled the trigger. "Now we can walk with our heads held high," said Amal, her eighteen-year-old sister (*New York Times,* June 20, 1999). As a result of cases like this one, Jordan has moved to criminalize honor killings and to inform the public that this "Arab" custom is no longer to be tolerated.

In Arab and Muslim societies, many feminists have written and lectured about the problem of honor killings as an indefensible relic of conservative attitudes toward women (Mernissi 1975; El-Saadawi 1980). Across the Arab world—in Jordan, Egypt, Syria, Lebanon, Yemen, among the Palestinians—young activists have begun to battle these honor killings. They argue that honor, construed as a set of values that confines the ambitions and restricts the mobility of women within a web of fear of possible allegation of sexual misconduct, is in need of modern reinterpretation and reformed law. "What is honor?" is a question raised by Egyptian journalist Abeer Allam, recalling how a high school biology teacher, sketching the female reproductive system and pointing to the vagina, said, "This is where the family honor lies!" (Jehl 1999). Like other social issues discussed in this book, the best method of social reform is initiated from within, by those desiring change possessing the necessary courage to seek and achieve it. Such killings are problematical in Jordan where the American-born Queen Noor, widow of King Hussein, has been an active opponent, and honor killings are opposed by human rights organizations in Egypt. The goal is to criminalize this behavior and eliminate cultural justification for it. I have written about this subject in regard to the limits on cultural relativism in anthropology. Cultural practices that cause harm, especially to vulnerable girls and women in harshly patriarchal societies, cannot be justified on the ground of cultural relativism (Fluehr-Lobban 1995, 1998).

Patriarchy and Reform Movements

Muslim theologians argue that Islam is not patriarchal and that the Qur'an —the word of God—and Sunna—the words and deeds of the Prophet—are gender neutral and thus free of bias. Further, they argue that Islam reformed preexisting, more harshly patriarchal social traditions in the Arabian peninsula. This is a correct view of the Holy Sources. But it can also be said that the three great religions that have sprung from Middle Eastern roots—Judaism, Christianity, and Islam—all did so after the rise of the state, civilization, and patriarchy. It has been argued by feminist writers that interpretation of the Holy Sources has been exclusively in the hands of men (Mernissi 1975; Ahmed 1992) and that the institutions that have been constructed since the expansion of Islamic states and empire are patriarchal. This can also be said of Judaism and Christianity.

Like their unreformed Christian and Jewish counterparts, Muslim religious officials are overwhelmingly male. The imams, who are leaders of mosques, are universally male, like Catholic priests and orthodox rabbis. The ʿulama, the religious scholars, are male, as are the political-religious sheikhs who lead villages and Sufi brotherhoods. Overwhelmingly Islamic court judges are male, and some countries such as Saudi Arabia and until recently Egypt specifically ban the judicial appointment of women. Women themselves have responded to this history of patriarchy by forming groups studying the Qur'an and Sunna from a feminine perspective, and by organizing movements that specifically address the position of women in contemporary Islamic societies, addressing domestic violence or female circumcision and other harmful cultural practices that may be informed by Islamic interpretations. Despite the fact that more women have been heads of state in Muslim countries than in the West, "It's a man's world" still applies to the world in general as well as to the Arab and Islamic worlds. The subject of women and their changing roles is addressed more fully in chapter 6.

One's Personal Destiny or Fate Determined by God

A great deal has been written and alleged about Arab and Muslim fatalism. More superficial analyses have focused on the invocations "insha Allah" (if God wills it) and "al-Hamdulillah" (God be praised), by which virtually every action or condition of being is prefaced or concluded. "I will meet you at 10 a.m., God willing," which usually means that the appointment will be kept, but if my car breaks down or if I am sick, which I cannot foresee and only God knows, I will not be able to be there at 10 a.m. If I manage to keep the appointment despite illness or a breakdown in traffic, God be praised."

There are many jokes among Westerners who have spent long periods in Arab and Muslim society about the use of "insha Allah." These usually refer to the Westerner, trying to get something accomplished with a government bureaucrat or small businessman, who is told, "Come back tomorrow. Everything will be ready, if God wills it." Of course, the Westerner returns the next day and is told, "Come back tomorrow." The frustration and clash of worldviews are evident in a well-known Western parody and renaming of select Arab corporations as IBM, for "insha Allah" (God willing), bukra (tomorrow), and "ma' lesh" (never mind). In the short term, tempers have flared; in the long run, however, patience is always a virtue.

Everyday greetings and expressions of interest in the well-being of others are rooted in continual references to the influence of God: "How are you?" "I am well, praise God" or "I am not very well, praise God." Irrespective of one's physical condition, God is the defining force. "And how are your children?" As the conversation progresses with inquiries about family, job, and well-being, it is not necessary to describe the condition of each, but simply to reply "al-Hamdulillah" to each question. The formula for the opening of conversation between individuals is to begin with a rather lengthy (by Western standards) litany of inquiries that conveys interest in the other's individual and collective well-being and that reinforces the relationship between the two people. A Westerner might find this exchange cumbersome or even a waste of time, but it constitutes another way by which the fabric of collective society is knitted on a daily basis.

Does the continuous repetition of references to the influence of God over one's condition or actions reflect or shape a worldview that is fatalistic? Do people really believe that God determines every facet of their lives and every moment of the day? The answer is both yes and no. Perhaps a Muslim has received a kind and well-intentioned invitation that she or he knows is unlikely to be fulfilled. Instead of replying truthfully to the question "Will you please come tonight?" with "No, I cannot make it, I am sorry," the invited person may respond, "Insha Allah, I will try to come tonight." This is a softer, less direct way of saying no, but it is one that relies on the well-understood set of phrases and meanings that places ultimate determination with God and personal responsibility with the individual. Attendance at weddings, circumcision parties, and funerals is obligatory and is not subject to the nuance of "insha Allah." This is also understood.

When one is faced with a difficult situation, such as illness or financial trouble, friends will often comfort with the words "Allah kareem" (God will provide). This is a familiar phrase of comfort in the West as well, and it signals both resignation and an element of hope that the situation will improve. In the meantime, action should be taken, a child should go to the doctor, or funds should be sought to relieve the immediate financial emergency. Sometimes a situation is so grave that a friend will comfort by saying, "There is little we can do. These things are out of our hands."

A sense of acceptance of one's fate is greater in some societies than in others. Folk Egyptian beliefs are well documented as accepting that one's life is foreordained or "written," as in the common expression that such and such is *maktub*. Falling into the category of maktub are such life events as one's marriage partner, or the number of children to be born and to survive, the death of family members and of oneself. There is little that is important in life that is accidental or not explained by a supernatural view of a grand plan. This is especially observed among Egyptian peasants who have endured for millennia a marginal economic existence controlled more by outside forces or government than by themselves. It is this context, not a surprising worldview, that is likewise found among peasants throughout the world and is identified in anthropological texts as peasants' "image of the limited good."

However, among more urbanized, educated groups, an attitude akin to fatalism is not usually expressed. Salma El-Jayussi, the great Palestinian poet and anthologist of contemporary Arabic poetry, once told me that the most important thing her mother told her was that she controlled her own fate. Likewise, activist political movements—nationalist, feminist, and even Islamist—today believe that social change requires human agency. Although it can certainly be an advantage to claim God as an ally, such movements do not rely on the philosophy that God will provide but are proactive, urgent, and very much of the moment.

Proverbs and Folk Wisdom

The Arabic language and Islamic culture are rich with proverbs that convey a sense of values that belongs to the realm of oral and folk traditions. People comment on the universal human condition and the particular irony of the specialized craftsman going without the service he provides: From the Sudan

Fig. 12. Contemporary secular Arabic calligraphy. Top example translation: "Ignorance is the essence of tranquility."

and throughout the Arab world comes "The door of the carpenter is always broken" (Bab al-najjar makhalla), and in Tunisia, "The shoemaker goes barefoot" (Kul iskafi hafi). These proverbs recognize the importance of the service provided and the continuous labor necessary to make a living, such that one's own needs are neglected.

In the area of consumer protection, to put a modern phrase to a bit of ancient wisdom, there is "Cheap becomes expensive and expensive is cheap" (Rakhis ghali wa ghali rakhis). In America we say, "You get what you pay for." Using the consumer idiom to talk about what you might buy in the butcher's market also has resonance in the challenges of everyday life: "In every piece of tender meat there is the bone" (Kul lahma fiha adma). In English, "Take the bad with the good."

In the realm of the maintenance of good social relations is a very wise adage: "The most important thing about a house is its neighbors" (Shoof al-jar qabal al-dar), literally "look at the neighbors before the door of the house." This stresses the importance of neighbors and community in its very definition of a good place to live. Indeed, according to Islamic law, a "good" house that a husband is obliged to provide for his wife is one that is not isolated and that is near good neighbors.

"Jebahu feza'a biqa waja'a," which means "You bring someone to solve your problem and then they become the problem," is my favorite Sudanese proverb, used in our family to comment on a range of issues from the personal to the political. You call a computer specialist to correct your small e-mail problem, and he/she destroys your hard drive, or you support a politician to cure a problem of corruption, and he loots the campaign fund.

An appreciation of difference and of changing times is found in the sage saying "For every time has its knowledge" (Kul saa' wa'almha). Another interpretation might be that every period has its differing customs and ways, and it is wrong to judge by current standards.

Patience is a virtue extolled in Arabic and in Muslim life. The Shayqiya of northern Sudan advise that when you are losing your patience, try a little more patience—"Min ghalaba al-sabr, esubra schwiya." Patience, endurance, and even fatalism are contained in one of Egypt's most famous sayings, "And tomorrow there will be apricots" (Wa bukra fi mish-mish), cynically meaning, in whatever the context, "You're dreaming." Living in Muslim societies has taught me to practice patience in tedious and tense situations, and this is one of the greatest gifts I received from life in Muslim societies.

Contrasting Western and Arab-Muslim Values

I would place individualism and materialism at the top of any list comparing American values with those in Arab-Muslim cultures. Western individualism contrasts sharply with the collectivism that is found in more egalitarian communities that have not passed through or been transformed by industrialism and where the dominant ideology remains one of family in the extended sense, community solidarity, and a strong sense of common place and mutual ties. Such communities are still predominantly agrarian, and can be made accessible to a Western audience by recalling the West's recent agrarian past. Individualism is a good thing when the goal is the accumulation of private wealth, and the small, mobile nuclear family is necessary for the development and maturity of a capitalist society. The relatively small nuclear family is well adapted to capitalistic societies, but it isolates its members from the extended family and reinforces individualism. "Rugged individualism," especially among American males, is a particular cultural trait in which pride is taken that a man is never dependent and can always take care of himself. To be needy or to ask for help is considered weak or unmanly. American women also strive to be self-sufficient by "earning their own keep," while children are encouraged to strike out on their own as soon as they finish school. Younger children are taught to respect others' private property and may have difficulty in sharing with others, although that is also stressed in early childhood socialization. Older children living at home after they have graduated college or high school are considered a temporary aberration until they can support themselves and become independent. The elderly want to remain independent as long as they are able, and they fear dependency as they decline physically. Community is relatively insignificant, since individual and family mobility is high and institutions such as churches or other voluntary associations take on the role of community. Individualism is manifested ideologically and legally in individual "my rights" over a collectivist "our rights," and individual freedom is praised. Western courts have historically ruled in favor of individual civil liberties over the good of the community.

By contrast, in Muslim societies, individual identity is embedded in family and community. The extended family still prevails; family members tend to stay in one place; unmarried children remain at home supported by their parents until they marry; the elderly are incorporated as part of the extended family and are cared for at home until they die; community ties tend to be strong and enduring. Breakdowns in this basic picture stem more from political causes and realities than from social factors. Civil wars or repressive regimes forcing people into exile, civil uprisings among Palestinians, and interstate migrations due to political unrest have changed Muslim community and family patterns, whereas industrialism has altered European and American agrarian life.

These very human dimensions of family and community life are the subjects of frequent questions from my Middle Eastern friends. How can a single parent manage? How can so many mothers go to work without help at home or adequate daycare? The relatively high divorce rates in the West are also a subject of interest, especially the view in the West that divorce may be positive and a source of liberation for women. Divorce in the East is almost always viewed as the last resort in the breakdown of a marriage, while the apparent ease of divorce in the West reinforces the impression that personal responsibility and marriage are taken too lightly.

I have also been asked how elderly parents can be put into homes where they are cared for by strangers, and if it is true that Americans employ the services of other strangers, funeral directors, to care for their dead relatives.

They ask why Americans pay huge sums of money to strangers to wash the body and prepare it for burial, and why they may wait several days for interment of the body. Muslim burial, as in Judaic tradition, takes place on the same day as the death, before sundown, if possible, and the body is washed and prepared for burial by close relatives following gender and kinship rules. Forty days of mourning follow the burial, and families accept visiting mourners for this period, although most visits offering condolences occur in the first week. Of course, burial customs vary around the world, but the nature of the questions I have received has more to do with the impersonality of Western rituals of death than with the specific religious or cultural rites. These questions may appear naive to a jaded Westerner, but they reveal the deep communitarian values of the questioners, who have difficulty fathoming the degree to which family life has been constricted while individualism is pervasive as a value and as a real way of life.

Materialism is a close relation to individualism and is the clearest and most powerful indicator of the good life in America. The good life is calculated in individual terms—individual achievement, success, and wealth. One's personal worth and well-being are significantly measured by the quality and quantity of one's material possessions in the United States and in the West at large. The relative value in dollar terms of the car driven, the home and neighborhood resided in, the private or public school attended, and many more such indicators let Americans know how well they are doing in this highly competitive society. A friend from Muslim Africa who left the United States after years as a graduate student concluded that "America is not a place for losers." He pitied America's losers: the poor, the homeless, the personally defeated.

Certainly wealth and material goods are desirable throughout the world, including the Middle East and Islamic world, but the good life is conceived of more as a common good, expressed in the prosperity not so much of individuals but of an extended family. Private property is less individually expressed, as is individual ownership less obvious, whether from simple items of clothing to more expensive items such as cars, which can be generally shared. A fight between siblings over wearing the other's clothes or borrowing the car without permission would be ludicrous, as personal property is not strongly expressed as a value.

The acquisition of great personal wealth among elites of the oil-rich countries, as well as in relatively poor Arab and Muslim countries, has been dramatic in recent decades. Consumption—conspicuously displayed in the form of grand houses, expensive cars, gold, and other forms of precious jewelry and Rolex watches—is often the type of materialism manifested by this class of elites. The wasteful consumption of valued foods, such as an entire sheep or goat served to a small group of guests, has become the subject of gossip and legend in Middle Eastern cafes and living rooms in nations that are not so well-off, where families can no longer afford to purchase a sheep or goat for the 'Eid al-Fitr. Among the masses of these poorer nations, families having numerous children are still an expression of wealth, with an average number of children to women in Islamic Africa and in the Middle East double or triple that of women in the West. The trend toward smaller families and fewer children per woman in the West is a function of individualism and materialism, as is most dramatically demonstrated by the average of less than one child per woman in Italy and less than two children per woman in the United States. These figures show a paradoxical contrast— having fewer children in the West may represent a desire to enjoy material wealth without the expense of too many children, while Middle Easterners have larger families as a sign of wealth, strength, and optimism with the knowledge that the extended family structure can better support the children. Most women who asked me about my family said they thought two children were not enough.

The West has no doubt about its technological superiority, nor does the Arab-Islamic world doubt this. This explains why so many foreigners seek to study technical subjects, such as computer science and engineering, in the United States.

The East has little doubt about its family values as a superior way of life, yet the West has little interest in learning morals from cultures it has a habit of looking down upon, even those from which it is derived, like the Middle Eastern cultures. The British and Americans are known internationally for being monolingual, satisfied that others can learn English. An American friend and I were told a joke by a Moroccan, who was amazed and delighted to find we spoke Arabic.

Q. What do you call a person who speaks three languages?
A. A trilingual person.

Q. Okay, what do you call a person who speaks two languages?
A. A bilingual person.

Q. Fine, now what do you call a person who speaks one language?
A. An American! [adding that "British" would do just as well]

Monolingualism easily translates into monoculturalism or "McDonaldization" of the world. This has become the catchword for a process of cultural domination that much of the world fears and about which the West appears not to be concerned or self-critical. The monopoly that Hollywood has engineered ensures that American culture and values are imported into nearly every hamlet and city on earth, making Rambo and the Terminator into international cultural icons that the commercial film industry perhaps never intended them to be.

The West prides itself on its freedom as contrasted with the more repressive governments and societies of the Middle East and elsewhere. In the wake of the September 11, 2001, attacks on the World Trade Center and the Pentagon, as Americans struggled to understand the reasons for the anger directed against the United States, freedom was a key value cited—their envy of our freedom, their hatred of our freedom. It might surprise Americans to learn that many Muslims and Middle Easterners view Western societies as too free, as having placed no limits on freedom, resulting in sexual promiscuity, alcohol and drug addictions, irresponsible access to deadly weapons, and social decay and decadence. A large proportion of the world's drugs come from Turkey and Afghanistan, yet few Middle Easterners or Muslims are addicted to drugs. Westerners who hear these ideas tend to dismiss them as too religious or conservative. This is where the religious fundamentalists of the East and West meet, for the U.S. religious right has been making many of the same points.

Unlike much of the New World, including the United States, people in the Middle East have a strong sense of place, and they take pride in the antiquity of their cultures. Deep roots and attachment to the land of one's ancestors contrasts sharply with the relative rootlessness of the new societies of the Americas. The Egyptian idea that it is the *Umm al-Dunia* (Mother of the world) speaks to the cultural pride and self-image as an ancestral society to the West. Imagine the Egyptian reaction to the declaration of English colonial architect Lord Cromer that "England made Egypt." Iraqis, Syrians, and Lebanese have a similar pride in the Mesopotamian-derived civilizations of Sumer, Babylon, the Hittites, Assyrians, and Phoenicians. They know that the Greek and Roman states came later and were dependent upon their foundation. Islam, Christianity, and Judaism originated in lands still occupied by the descendants of these ancients, making Bethlehem, Jerusalem, Mecca, and Medina gifts of faith that the Middle East gave to the world. There is little in Europe or the United States to match this sense of place. The Crusaders, the European holy warriors who captured Jerusalem, are still a living memory, and stories from an Arab viewpoint are still told to children. Visits to the homes of rural and urban people, or to the farms that are still maintained by urbanites, reveal a sense of enduring attachment to the land that makes partition or sale of the land virtually unthinkable for lands held by families. The rootlessness of Americans with the easy transfer and sale of family land and property undermines that attachment to place which would impede key vertical mobility necessary to economic success. Businesses may move a nuclear family every two years, conveying the impression that family considerations are secondary. Family and genealogical ties come first in the East, perhaps to the exasperation of the aspiring businessman, but even in the cases where geographical mobility may be required by corporate demands, the family home base usually remains intact and the individual moves rather than the family.

A paradoxical fact is that the chief global power at this time possesses a remarkably provincial worldview. U.S. borders are so vast that one language and a common culture stretch from coast to coast, often alongside pockets of great cultural diversity and de facto bilingualism. The United States has been called "the nation of nations," yet its understanding of global affairs and cultural differences is naive at best, ignorant at worst. Students in the Middle East often begin to learn English or French in grade school. This is coupled with an outward-looking educational model in many of the historically secular Muslim countries that stresses the country's relationship to the rest of the world. Students know the names of foreign leaders, whereas Americans exhibit an embarrassing ignorance of even the most basic geography, history, and cultural and linguistic variety, not to mention not knowing the names of the presidents, kings, or prime ministers of Middle Eastern or Muslim nations. This ignorance is not easy to explain to Middle Easterners, and only those who have experienced America firsthand seem to understand. I am not sure I can adequately explain this beyond reference to our archaic Eurocentric and American curricula. I also have had difficulty explaining why youngsters carry guns into schools and go on shooting rampages. But the frequency and persistence of questions along these lines has made me realize that huge cultural canyons separate our experiences and worldviews.

It is equally important to point out the many areas of convergence of our shared humanity and heritage. The West tends to forget or gloss over the cultural debt that it owes to the Middle East. When Europe was in its dark age, the centers of learning and enlightenment were in the Moorish cities of Spain and in the Caliphate of Baghdad, where the knowledge of the ancient world was translated, transcribed, and transmitted to the West in Arabic, Greek, Hebrew, and Latin. This tradition can be a source of common pride, yet the history of the West and East is most often narrated with reference to enmity between the Crusaders on both sides and the expulsion of Islam and Muslims (as well as Jews) from the Iberian Peninsula after 1492 and at Tours in France in 732 C.E. Efforts to open the study of this rich exchange of cultures and knowledge from the eighth to fifteenth centuries C.E. would yield an appreciation and understanding of the encounter between East and West that would be less confrontational in content and spirit.

The core value of hospitality and generosity for which Arabs are famous is also shared in basic American values. Americans are generally well liked by Arabs and Muslims, and vice versa, when they have had the opportunity to know one another. This is generally true when people unfamiliar with one another become better acquainted, but the value most often mentioned by Arabs about Americans is their friendliness, warmth, and hospitality. What may not be appreciated is the extent to which Americans are a religious people, for belief and practice are less visible and more separated in the United States than in the Muslim world. The Hollywood stereotype of promiscuity, decadence, and all manner of personal excesses may overwhelm the realities of life in America.

There has been a great deal of global common dialogue that "fundamentalism" and extremism are found in all religions and that it is mistaken and unfair to focus on Islam and Muslims as religious fanatics. Likewise, there has been progress in dialogue about universal human rights, especially equalizing women's struggles toward ending domestic violence and promoting the rights of the child. These are signs for hope that familiarity and exchange of ideas about conflicting and converging values can be facilitated and that common ground can be achieved.

4

Women and Men in Muslim Societies

Family and Community Relations

The perceived low status of women and their presumed oppression by men and Islam in the Arab-Islamic world is a cherished theme in Western thought and in the media treatment of the region. It may give the West a sense of moral or social superiority to imagine their better status as compared with that of Arab and Muslim women. As with any simple sketch of reality, the truth is more complex. For example, the fact that more Muslim women than Western women have been heads of state in recent decades surprises most Westerners. This list includes the contemporary prime ministers of Bangladesh, Khalida Zia and Sheikha Hassina; Megawati Sukarnoputri, head of Indonesia, Benazir Bhutto, former head of Pakistan, and Tansu Çilar, former president of Turkey. This does not mean that all Muslims idealize women seeking careers in public office, or that theologians agree. Similar debates about women's abilities have occurred in the West, but the fact is that the United States has still not successfully elected a woman even as vice president.

Likewise, family values have received a great deal of attention in the United States, while comparisons of family life between the Arab-Islamic world and the West have been of interest to the Muslim world. In the space of a few decades the United States, along with much of Europe, has moved from a time when the nuclear family predominated to a situation in which subnuclear families, especially those composed of divorced women and their children, have become an accepted and expected variant of the family. The extended family that dominated in agrarian times has long since been undermined by the Industrial Revolution, with its emphasis on the more compact, efficient, and mobile nuclear family. Family mobility has reached extensive proportions in the United States for the nuclear family, such that it is common to find parents and adult children living hundreds of miles apart. Westerners have some of the highest rates of marital separation in the world, while remarriage and the blending of parts of former nuclear families after remarriage have presented new challenges to the definition of family structure.

Such dynamic reshaping of traditional concepts of gender and the family is fascinating, but to the outside world, especially to the Muslim world, it may appear as alarming evidence of breakdown and decay. This is not to say that change is not impacting many parts of the traditional Arab and Muslim world, altering family patterns, but that change is slowed by limited industrialization, even though rapid urbanization has occurred. Religious revival, likewise, has made an issue of "family values" Muslim-style and has served to reinforce traditional family patterns.

Patriarchal Traditions

Islam, Judaism, and Christianity all contain patriarchal traditions. Patrilineality was commonly found among pastoral peoples practicing the traditional economy of pre-Islamic Arabia. Patriarchy exists in many cultural settings and is based on the principle of male authority. With the growth of towns and the widening of trade networks, patrilineal kinship ties have been utilized to extend commercial linkages, and patriarchal ideas have been borrowed from neighboring societies or developed independently as an outgrowth of urban society and patrilineal descent.

Patriarchal social relations developed in the context of the formation of the state in pre-Semitic but regional Mesopotamian culture. The Babylonian Code of Hammurabi includes control of female sexuality and reproduction before and within marriage, which can be readily adjudged as the enforcement of patriarchal traditions already well established (Lerner 1986). A strong case can be made that Islam brought about a degree of reform improving the status of women within a long-standing patriarchal society (for example, making female inheritance legal, albeit only half that of a man, and ending female infanticide). Theological examples of the reformist tendency toward greater status of women in Islam include the Muslim view of God as neither male nor female, the Islamic telling of the story of Adam and Eve whereby both sin and sinners are forgiven by God, and the idea that men and women are spiritually equal. Contrast Eve's responsibility for the fall of mankind and the pervasive idea of God the Father in Christian teachings.

While the West finds it easy to condemn patriarchy in Arab and Islamic society, it rarely is able to see the patriarchal roots and continuing expressions of patriarchy in Christian and Judaic customs derived from the same roots. The controversies over the training and anointing of women as rabbis, priests, bishops, or other church officials are among many cases in point.

The Episcopal Church in the United States and the Church of England in the United Kingdom are divided over the ordination of women, while the Catholic Church refuses to consider the matter, and the Orthodox branch of Judaism does not permit women to become rabbis. Although all three religions stem from a common religious and cultural foundation in the Middle East, Islamic society has been singled out in the West as a worst-case example of the low status and poor treatment of women. Its women are held to be universally veiled, subordinated, and passive social nonparticipants who are to be pitied, whereas their male counterparts are to be feared (as potential terrorists) or reviled. The realities, like so much else in the story of Arab-Islamic society, are vastly different from the mythology.

Veiling

As the most visible sign of a Muslim woman's faith and modesty, the veil has become an icon for the way that the West perceives women in Islam. Whether veiling is associated with passivity or subjugation, seclusion or protection, the West has a fascination with it in Orientalist representation and modern media coverage.

Fig. 13a and b. Contrasting images of women: veiled women in Hijaz; Sudanese feminist Fatima Ahmed Ibrahim lecturing at Rhode Island College.

Muslim women are not compelled by Islam to veil. Rather, they are enjoined to dress and behave modestly. The Qur'an says, "And tell the believing women to lower their gaze and be modest, and to display of their adornment only that which is apparent, and to draw their veils over their bosoms and not to reveal their adornment save to their own husbands or fathers, or their sons" [and other close male blood kin are enumerated] (sura 24:31).

Hijab means to be covered or concealed, and Islamic dress need not include covering the head or face. Covering the body in today's terms may mean long dresses or pants that do not reveal the body in a way to be overtly sexually attractive in public. Often full body veiling in public is cultural, such as the *shador, milaya,* or *thobe,* which women have worn as public covering in the Arabian peninsula or North Africa, while the *burqa* with its attendant facial veiling was a part of the Taliban political culture in Afghanistan or conservative Wahbism in Saudi Arabia. Countries that have mandated wearing the hijab, such as Afghanistan under the Taliban or Iran just after the Islamic Revolution, are violating the basic tenet that there is no compulsion in Islam and that donning the veil should be a matter of personal piety and voluntary. Muslim women don Shari' or Islamic dress from a personal sense of devotion to the faith, and many in secular or western countries describe putting on hijab as a personal jihad whereby they actively deviate from the conventions of public dress and subject themselves to scrutiny, stares, and sometimes discrimination. Women have been voluntarily putting on hijab in increasing numbers throughout the Muslim world, and although this has occurred since the rise of societal Islamism, it is not mandated and reflects social change, not political ultimatums.

Muslim women and girls who veil view the hijab not as oppressive but as a tradition that liberates them from society's focus on the female body. There is no compulsory age at which girls begin to veil. They may begin to wear hijab as early as seven years of age, but in predominantly Muslim societies, it is usually a part of a girl's passage from childhood to womanhood, with the onset of menstruation. Muslim women in the West argue convincingly that with the hypersexuality of Western culture, hijab places the emphasis on a girl or woman's personhood, rather than on her sexuality. They point to the excesses of tight-fitting and revealing clothes that neither enhance freedom nor liberate women, making them vulnerable to sexual exploitation.

Veiling is for public dress. Inside the home, in the company of family, veiling generally is not practiced. When strangers visit or television cameras are brought into the home, veiling is assumed so that a woman wishing to veil is covered and protected. When women go to the mosque for Friday prayer or communal activities, they will cover their heads and dress modestly, as non-Muslim women visiting a mosque will also be expected to do.

States that have mandated the veil—making it illegal for women to appear in public without the veil—are Islamist, that is, they have adopted a course that politicizes religious choice. Further, they violate the Qur'anic injunction that there is no compulsion to wear veils (sura 22:256). States that have enforced this expression of veiling as public morality include the Islamic republics of Saudi Arabia, Iran, Afghanistan, and Sudan and societies undergoing Islamism such as northern Nigeria. In highly secular states, such as Turkey and Tunisia, the opposite is the case, where women have been banned (in the case of Turkey) or discouraged (in Tunisia) from veiling because the hijab is seen as an unmistakable sign of Islamism. When Merve Kavakçi was elected to the Turkish parliament in 1999, she was refused her seat because she wore a headscarf (Secor 2003).

Veiling the head and body is an ancient Middle Eastern tradition, common in Mesopotamia before the rise of monotheism, and deeply embedded in Judaic, Christian, and Muslim traditions. Mary, the mother of Jesus Christ, is always portrayed as modest and veiled, and orthodox Jewish women veil whether in New York City or Tel Aviv.

A number of interesting cases that test the core American value of religious freedom have involved American Muslim women's right to veil in public. Two Muslim students of mine were involved in cases where employers demanded that they remove their veils as a condition of employment, one in a restaurant and the other in a hospital. In both cases they were veiled at the time of the interview for the positions, and only after they began their employment were they asked to remove their veils. Both refused—the student employed temporarily at the restaurant left the job without complaining, while the Muslim nurse appealed to common sense that nurses cover their heads anyway, and that she would be willing to have her veil sterilized for sterile areas of the hospital and that she could wear her usual veil in nonsterile areas. A case of a Muslim woman in Florida who refused to take off her facial veil for a driver's license photograph received national attention as she took the case to court. The state of Florida argued that a full face photograph is necessary for identification, while the woman retorted that she views the photograph as a violation of her religion and that she would provide fingerprints, DNA, or other information for identification. She lost her case (Canedy 2002).

Patrilineal Kinship and the Extended Family

Patrilineality is descent and inheritance traced through males and is characteristic of Arab and Islamic society, as well as the majority of the world's societies. The core group of patrilineally related males is known collectively

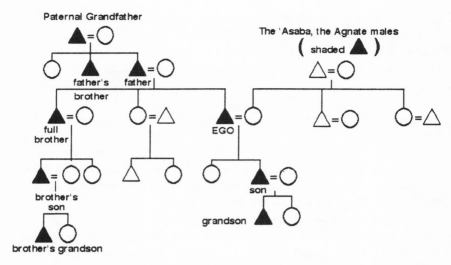

Fig. 14. Diagram of the 'Asaba, core group of males in patrilineal Arab Muslim society. From *Islamic Law and Society in the Sudan,* by Carolyn Fluehr-Lobban. London: Frank Cass, 1987. Reprinted by permission of the publisher.

Fig. 15. Grandfather and grandsons in Siwa oasis, Egypt.

as the *'asaba,* and they constitute the most prominent figures in the descent system and extended family. They also make the key family decisions. The *'asaba* includes the paternal grandfather, the father, the son, the paternal uncles, their sons, and so on. Following the logic of patrilineal descent, males both inherit and bestow patrilineal descent, whereas females inherit but do not convey patrilineal descent. It is important to recognize that females are not excluded from patrilineal descent.

The *'asaba* includes the real and symbolic heads of extended family segments and of the corporate family grouping that constitutes the lineage. These are men who, accordingly, receive a high degree of respect and deference from their family members, from women in general, and from younger males. As formal figures of authority, the *'asaba* are deferred to in making decisions for the family, particularly marriage and financial matters. While there is a great deal of informal decision making that goes on in families, the formal, public role falls to the father, as head of the household, or to a member of the *'asaba.* Younger males typically do not speak first in the presence of older men, or they wait until they are addressed; they do not smoke in the company of the *'asaba,* or they might ask permission before lighting a cigarette. One of the marks of a progressive family is the degree to which there is an open exchange of ideas, free of the traditional hierarchy of *'asaba,* younger men, and women.

A strong complement to patrilineal descent in many societies is a custom of patrilocal residence, in which the newly married couple takes up residence with or near the groom's family. It is the bride who leaves her home to join her husband. However, she does not join her husband's patrilineage. She remains a member of her father's patrilineal group, from which she will ultimately inherit land, property, or wealth. Her identity throughout life is that to which she was born, as in Fatima *bint* Mohammed, Fatima the daughter of Mohammed. At marriage she does not take her husband's name, but her children are born to their father's patrilineage and take the name of their father. In the event of divorce or death of her husband, or any other difficulty, she is always welcome, even expected, to return to the house of her father. Her young children are legally in her care and custody until they reach prescribed ages of majority at which time they are claimed by the patrilineal descent group into which they were born.

Family and lineage represent the largest measure of one's identity. Families are a part of lineages that comprise the lengthy history and genealogy of a people, known as *nasab.* A long line of upright and religious ancestors traced patrilineally is a source of pride in one's heritage and placement in the larger society. The right conduct and achievements of individuals are generalized to the level of the extended family and are a part of informal public knowledge and discussion. Even in large cities, the importance of family and lineage is not lost and is a part of everyday life affecting just about any institution from business to education to politics. As such many activities are carried out on a personal basis through contacts that are made between and through networks of extended families. Being a part of this complex network may ensure the best price in the purchase of an expensive appliance or car, admission to a university, less time or money spent in a legal matter or with a cumbersome bureaucracy, or access to otherwise unavailable services or purchases, such as desirable airline fares or tickets. Such favors again fall into the category of generalized reciprocity whereby family members and their friends do for each other, with a general expectation of return but without any specified cost accounting. In these ways and a thousand others, Arab and Muslim societies operate in a highly personalized context, making even the most urban setting less impersonal. It is frequently remarked of the world's Arab and Islamic cities that they are really clusters of villages, that is, groups of extended families concentrated in the city's neighborhoods.

High-status families are expected to perform in exceptional ways. Even their mediocre members are elevated. In contrast, individuals from low-status families may have to overachieve in order to receive equal recognition. These patterns, based in old class divisions and ideas about family honor, are quite conservative and resistant to change in brief periods such as a generation or two. The notion of rapid and unlimited social mobility, which is praised in America and believed to exist as a reward for hard work and merit, is not part of this worldview. As long as one has an attachment to family and lineage, one is secure; without it, life is in jeopardy.

Male-Female Relations

Within a society so shaped by patrilineal institutions and patriarchal traditions, it is not surprising that the most important gender relationships that have been constructed are between men and groups of men acting together. Male relatives, who may also be neighbors or live close by, possess strong bonds of kinship and friendship. The latter dimension often surprises Westerners, who may find that these kinsmen are often also the closest of friends. When these bonds are broken by offense, insult, or disloyalty, the hurt is great and efforts to mend relations go well beyond the feuding parties. Reconciliation may take place in the name of the family and for the good of the family.

Traditionally, the closest personal bonding takes place within the extended family along gender lines. Women who are related patrilineally as daughters and sisters and women who have married into the family—who may also be cousins—form a close network of associates. Because most women are not employed outside of the home (in most Arab and Muslim countries female employment is 25 percent or less), they spend their married lives in the domestic arena in the close company of other women.

Safeguarding the honor of families and the respectability of women is a continuous preoccupation in male-female relations, so there are settings where it is proper and generally permissible for males and females to mix and others that are more constrained. Public arenas may be mixed or sexually segregated, depending upon local traditions and rural-urban differences. Public transportation may be relaxed and mixed, as in Tunisia, or it may be sexually segregated, as in the Muslim Sudan, where women and men sit separately. In Saudi Arabia the movement of women outside the home is restricted, and travel outside of their local area is subject to legal regulation—supported by Saudi interpretations of Islamic law—requiring permission from male "guardians." In highly congested Cairo, where public transport is likely to be crowded, the close physical contact makes voluntary sexual separation a frequent choice. The new Cairo underground Metro provides separate women's cars to address the problem of crowding during rush hours. Dressing in conservative Islamic (Shari') fashion adds a measure of protection for women. In my own case, traveling with a child or another woman on the bus or train provided the additional protection that would offset possible curiosity or stereotyping of Western women. Travel with a male companion, assumed to be a husband, is the best guarantee for non-harassment. Rural areas are likely to be more relaxed about male-female interaction in public places than are semiurban or urban areas, and modest veiling of women has been less observed.

Education

Public education is usually sex-segregated in the elementary and secondary levels and coeducational at the university level. Male and female teachers are represented at each level. However, like the West, the teaching of younger children tends to be dominated by females. One of the major trends witnessed in twentieth-century education in the Muslim world was the increasing numbers of females represented, not only in elementary grades but also in secondary and postsecondary education. Many major universities, like Cairo University, now have about 50 percent female students. Saudi Arabia and some of the Gulf countries have opened women's universities to meet the twin demands of higher education for women and a nonthreatening sexually segregated learning environment. Some of these universities have adopted a system whereby male instructors teach their classes to women students by remote distance technology to avoid direct contact between the sexes. Ahfad University for Women in Omdurman, Sudan, the only university specifically dedicated to women's education in Africa, is a secular institution founded to promote female education and status, and it has one of the most active women's studies programs, with its own journal, in the Arab-Islamic world. Older universities for women are found historically in Lebanon, such as Beirut University College for Women, and as recent innovations in the Arabian Gulf countries to meet increasing demand for female education.

The university is a public place where males and females easily mix in classrooms, in the university environment in general, and in other public lecture sites. Outside the university a more conservative pattern prevails, although under the influence of Islamist activism, universities are experiencing a voluntary resegregation. Still, the university remains one of the few places outside of the family where respectable interaction between unrelated males and females can take place without fear of gossip or intimidation.

Social Mixing

At weddings, young women and men can converse, flirt, and, in some cultural traditions, dance together. They are under the watchful eyes of their adult relatives, but the relaxed and celebratory atmosphere of the wedding party provides a unique opportunity for unmarried people to socialize and be in closer contact than society normally permits. Weddings are thus very popular events and are typically large social affairs.

Male-female interactions that are improper or forbidden include all forms of dating before a couple has contracted marriage (or become engaged). Meeting at a cafe or a restaurant generally is not proper, and all but the most westernized couples avoid such a rendezvous. Even in the most westernized suburbs of major cities, discreet, secluded areas of a cafe may be reserved for mixed couples; only the tourist hotels catering almost exclusively to Westerners deviate from this pattern. Movies have always been a male-dominated recreation; however, engaged or married couples are increasingly in attendance. Movie theaters may provide sections for unescorted women, or women may attend the cinema during matinees when fewer men are present. Television soap operas dramatizing romantic encounters and love matches that oppose problematic arranged marriages are popular as nighttime viewing, as are more controversial dramas dealing with sensitive matters of interclass marriages and divorce. These dramas often originate in Cairo studios but are televised all over the Arab world.

Situations where unrelated men and women may be left alone together are also to be avoided, as the cultural presumption is that something of a sexual nature might occur between them. This prohibition is so strong that it is readily transferred to the West by immigrants. An unmarried girl should not go out at night alone and a married woman should not meet with men who are not relatives or close friends. This social pattern of chaperoning and protecting women was introduced into Spanish culture by the Moors and then into the New World such that it is recognizable and familiar to Latino cultures in the United States.

A male physician may not examine a woman without a third party present, usually a husband or close male relative or a nurse. The same prohibition prevails in the United States with gynecological exams. In the Arab and Muslim world this cultural tradition of protection and modesty is so strong that it alone constitutes a sufficient argument for training more female physicians.

Bonding

To the casual Western observer in Arab and Muslim countries, men are more visible in urban areas as they tend to congregate in coffeehouses and restaurants, and women are invisible. In reality, when large numbers of men are visible in the coffeehouses during the day, it suggests high unemployment, and the topic of conversation over endless cups of Arabic coffee is likely to be the job shortage or the possibility of emigration to a richer Arab country or to Europe. A high degree of mutual assistance and male solidarity is thus promoted where the focus is on male-male interaction without the distraction of women. Such coffeehouses have historically been places where political discussions flourished and activism naturally followed. It has flowed from this that the streets are public domain and thus more the province of men. When women have joined with men in the streets in public demonstrations around nationalist or more recently Islamist activism, their participation is that much more dramatic.

Fig. 16. Men celebrating *al-sebou'*, a child's seventh day of life, in Fez, Morocco.

Women's closest companions and friends throughout life are other women. Men and women do not marry to become each other's best friends, although genuine bonds of love and affinity do develop in many arranged marriages. Likewise, men's closest friends are men, and it is more often with men that their feelings flow with the recitation of poetry or the appreciation of a favorite singer or musician. In some cultural contexts, drinking alcoholic beverages has provided another context for male bonding, even though this behavior is anathema to Islam. Having friendships with unrelated females is quite rare, and when they exist it is often the result of a progressive ideology or some exposure to non-Muslim, often Western society. As a foreign woman I had more flexibility to develop friendships with men, but relations were always more restrained with me than with my husband. Close male-female bonding within the family may be more likely to exist between a brother and sister than between a husband and wife. Men and women do not marry for personal closeness and intimacy, as they do in the West. Husbands and wives will not walk down the street holding hands, but it is not uncommon to see two men walking hand-in-hand or to see men embrace and kiss one another several times on both cheeks if they meet on the street. To the casual Western observer this may appear unmasculine, as men in the West are socialized to be restrained in the company of other men and to shake hands rather than embrace and kiss. Although bravery and honor are extolled as male virtues, so also are poetry and expressive singing, which reveal another side of men.

Women, likewise, form their closest relationships with other women who are relatives, neighbors, or friends, as age-mates from school or other activities. Visiting, possibly in the *hareem,* or women's section of the home, is almost continuous. When life allows a more leisurely pace, women spend long hours together socializing in the context of simple visiting or working together in some domestic task, such as food preparation or sewing. Pure relaxation among women occurs in the context of some cosmetic rituals, such as lengthy sessions of hair-braiding or elaborate decorating of the hands and feet with henna. More often than not these sessions take place in preparation for a wedding or some other important occasion, such as the birth or circumcision of a child, and they have the double function of accomplishing a task and cementing female relationships. These informal sessions are lighthearted, open, and fair game for the discussion of any subject from sex and marriage, to birth control, to the economy, to the personal lives of those known to the group. It was in this sort of group setting that I learned the Arabic language and the multiple social meanings of many words and phrases. This intimacy takes place in the privacy of homes, and it is rare outside of the most cosmopolitan cities to see women out together socializing in public in a cafe or restaurant. The streets in the Arab-Muslim city generally are the province of men.

It is also in these group social settings where important information regarding women's rights in marriage and divorce is exchanged and where strategies are worked out. A woman whose family is experiencing economic difficulty may discuss possible ways of earning money without losing her respectability. Another, having marital problems, may seek advice as to who among her male relatives might intercede on her behalf with her husband or his relatives. Informal discussion of arranged marriages may take place first among women before it is approached or negotiated by the male 'asaba. Determining that a young woman is interested in a suggested marriage and would give her consent to it often takes place in the hareem before any public announcement occurs.

Women rely on one another for social support in public and prefer to go out together for shopping or other errands in small groups. Like men, women can be seen walking together arm-in-arm occupying a closer physical space than is customary for Westerners. Women who are strangers may stand together waiting in line at a bank or office, or women may be waited on first as a courtesy and a means of avoiding public scrutiny of a woman alone. The increased participation of women in the formal and informal labor force has necessitated modification of traditional patterns of sex segregation. A woman may don a more conservative form of hijab when she is working in public, or a poor woman selling her wares in a public market may wear a facial veil.

Extended Family Life and Group Values

Despite rapid and widespread urbanization throughout the Arab and Muslim world, the extended family has not been fundamentally altered nor is it seriously in danger of being replaced by the nuclear family or subnuclear family, as has occurred in the industrialized countries. Even in the few examples that might be cited of shifting marriage and family patterns, the ideology of the extended family still predominates.

The Middle Eastern extended family has been aptly described as embracing both genealogical and physical closeness, a concept of family and nearness that is known in Arabic as *qaraba* (Eickelman 1989, 156–58). Typically, a traditional extended family occupies a part of a local neighborhood, known as a *hai,* and houses of extended families would be clustered together. The relationship between houses and families is patrilineal, according to Arab and Muslim custom, and a hai might include a grandfather or great-uncle, their wives and families, father and mother, brothers, their wives and families, and perhaps cousins and their families related through patrilineal ties. A local household may include a paternal grandparent, uncle or aunt, unmarried siblings, or even a married brother or sister (though less frequent), and one's parents. A typical extended household may contain several nuclear families. These days, with massive rural to urban migration, and expatriate migration for work, the extended family household is relied upon as a secure, stable place from which one may leave and to which one may always return. Urban extended households have become something of a way station for family migrants from rural homesteads as a means to become established in the city, as well as for ambitious urban migrants who come from poorer Muslim countries seeking lucrative jobs in richer Islamic countries. The social base from which these economic strategies can be launched has been and continues to be the extended family.

Qaraba, with its double meaning of physical nearness or intimacy and being related by kinship, can result in some confusion. I would often describe a person as being *qaribti,* or close to me, meaning that we were good friends; frequently I would be misinterpreted as describing a relative, so I would add the descriptive noun "friend" or the explanatory phrase "like a sister." Likewise, the powerful kinship idiom pervades society and sometimes serves to soften or embellish impersonal relations. As you ride the buses, trains, or other crowded vehicles of public transportation in Cairo, you hear riders refer to the ticket collector as "Uncle" or the conductor urging a crowd to make room for newcomers by referring to them as "my brothers." Older women may address younger women in informal conversation as "my daughter," and women of more or less the same age may sprinkle their conversation with frequent use of "my sister," as in "Am I not telling you the truth, my sister?"

For the anthropologist conducting research within an extended family, friendship or close association with one member of a family usually means that you meet all the relatives. You become an extension of the family and may be addressed as if you were a family member. The hospitality that is offered freely and openly to members of the extended family can also include outsiders. During one of our research trips to the Sudan, Richard and I found it difficult to secure housing in Khartoum and were invited to stay with friends in Omdurman for as long as we needed. Our stay lasted for two months, and it included recuperation from malaria and ended at our request once we had found a flat in Khartoum. The matter of offering payment for our stay would have been ridiculous and insulting, so the appropriate thanks was to bring specialty foods or gifts that would be enjoyed collectively. I noted that gifts that I had especially brought to individual friends were received collectively, so I eventually learned to present familial gifts that were nonessentials, which could be used by all.

The social condition of the extended family provides not only shelter, food, and physical space for its individual members. It also contains a broader ideology of mutual support and solidarity for the family group. The idea of family (*'ai'lah*) is so engrained and powerful that it is rarely invoked inside the family, as it might be in the West where a family member is called upon to do something "for the sake of the family" or family name. Family is everything; there is no need to stress its importance to those who are well aware of the fact. *'Ai'lah* then is a term that is used more outside of the family in reference to it, such as identifying family members to inquiring anthropologists, for example. One of the kindest and most endearing ways of bidding good-bye to a close friend in Egypt is to say, "You are from my family" (*Inta(i) min ahali*), and in Sudan, "We are as one family" (*Nehnah 'ai'lah wahda*). It is an extension of a powerful kinship idiom to one who has been afforded the status of being like a sister or brother.

With the support that the extended family provides to its members comes responsibility as well. A family that may have pooled its resources to send a talented member to university at home or abroad bestows upon the recipient family member a responsibility to return a measure of what he or she has received (recipients are likely to be male and the burden falls more heavily on them than on women). Returning from the city where one has studied, or from abroad where one has worked or studied, one carries extra suitcases full of gifts or goods that will be absorbed by the household. Items that are not readily available locally or are too expensive, such as kitchen appliances, household decorations, or portable radios and televisions, are commonly presented to the household. Long stays and successful careers mean that large items, such as refrigerators or VCRs, may be purchased and given to the household. Gifts brought to individuals are in another category of special affection and are not part of the generalized system of reciprocity that functions in the extended family.

Sometimes individuals from extended family backgrounds who have spent long periods away, or have made new homes in the West, may be apprehensive about returning home because of the strong family bonds that they may perceive as tying them down or that they feel burden them with a sense of responsibility that they may not be able to meet. Money may be loaned to family members with little expectation of return on either side. Often unrealistic images of material success, especially of one returning from a Western industrialized country, may make visits home awkward for the struggling student or immigrant worker. The point is that the extended family has provided the background for whatever success has been achieved, and there is a powerful understood value of reciprocity for sharing whatever success has been achieved.

Marriage Patterns

Marriage is the central institution around which all other social and kin institutions revolve, and it is guarded and protected by the ʿasaba and revered by the entire social group. It is never taken lightly, and elaborate formal negotiations precede its contracting. Its celebratory rituals form the centerpiece of music, dance, and folklore. Marriage is the single most important event in the life of a man or woman; the ties that are created through marriage are so important that, traditionally, decisions regarding choice of marriage partner were rarely, if ever, left to the future bride or groom alone.

Endogamy, or marriage within the larger extended family, is extremely common, with the preferred marriage partner being the male's first cousin on the father's side (*bint ʿamm*, or the father's brother's daughter). In some traditional communities, 40 percent of all marriages involve cousins (Lobban 1982); whether its frequency is high or low, bint ʿamm marriage has persisted, even in highly urbanized communities. In Cairo, for example, first-cousin marriage remains the most common marital form, whether the marriage partner is father's brother's daughter or some other paternal first cousin or, failing this, a first cousin on the mother's side. Rugh (1984) notes that the preference for cousin marriage is still so powerful in Egypt that families may disguise the fact of noncousin marriage. In one sample of five hundred Sudanese women in Omdurman, 60 percent had married their first cousins (Grotberg and Washi 1991).

Explanations for this marriage preference are both economic and social. By keeping marriage within the extended family, wealth and property are thereby consolidated within the kin group. "Stranger" marriage, which is considered very risky, is controlled. By contrast, the more traditional bint ʿamm marriage is given strong support by extended family members, so that these marriages tend to be more stable and less likely to end in divorce or separation. The families, of course, know each other well, and trust in marriage negotiations and subsequent relations is high, unlike the situation with "stranger" marriage.

American students often ask about the possibility of genetic or biological abnormalities resulting from relatively close inbreeding. First-cousin marriage is prohibited by law in many states, although various states have differing laws regarding the marriage of second cousins. The study of the biological effects of this marriage-breeding pattern is sensitive in Arab society, and most research on the subject has been conducted in the United States and

Britain. A 1993 study of Pakistanis in Punjab Province found death rates of 21 percent among children of cousins but 16 percent in the general population, while a study of Mormons in Utah found that children of cousins were 70 percent more likely to die before age sixteen than offspring of unrelated parents. Researchers have challenged this idea of genetic risk of mating with close biological relatives. Pointing to mounting data that the risks are minimal, they have called for an end to the ban on first-cousin marriage (Grady 2002).

Nonetheless, authorities in some countries, such as the United Arab Emirates, are beginning to encourage public awareness of the genetic risks of first-cousin marriage. Cousin marriage has been strengthened by the oil wealth of the Gulf countries where the propertied and wealthy upper classes marry within their families. Inbreeding among the ruling families is said to result in high rates of diabetes and kidney disease (Demick 2000).

My personal observation of families in which the rate of bint ʿamm marriage is among the highest, for example among the Tuti Islanders of Khartoum, did not reveal any obvious problems or anomalies. Moreover, even if some genetic disadvantage in first cousin marriage were demonstrated, few families would make any dramatic change, because the perceived value of such marriages is so high. Indeed, in the recent period of accelerated class formation, endogamous marriage has been reinforced as a means of keeping newly acquired wealth within the family's control and governance. Also in conservative Muslim societies, such as in Sudan, the Gulf, and the Arabian peninsula, it is not only the concentration of family wealth that is reflected in this marriage pattern but also the custom of sexual segregation where men and women rarely mingle and the most likely place for romance and marriage proposals to occur is at family weddings.

Protecting the selection of a woman's husband is the responsibility of the marriage guardian (al-wali), who is most often the father or paternal uncle. In the past, women rarely contested the choice of spouse, but legal reform in the twentieth century that moved to ensure the consent of the bride to the marriage has offered interpretations of how, exactly, consent is given. In these more complex times, greater numbers of brides are protesting marriage proposals, persuading their fathers to favor their choices, or seeking legal remedies in court to prevent their fathers from forcing them into unwanted marriages.

Exogamous marriage, or marriage outside of the broadly interpreted patrilineal kin group, is thus defined as "stranger" marriage. Proposals of marriage that have not been negotiated by the natural marriage guardians, the ʿasaba, but have been initiated by the couple themselves are still relatively rare. The couple may have become acquainted at the university or at the place of employment. Such a couple must approach their elders for approval. Before permission is given, the family will gather relevant information about the background of the family with which they are about to be united. Relevant questions touch upon economic backgrounds and whether they are more or less equivalent in status, appropriate religious commonalities in piety and practice, the family's background, and other matters that place the two families on an equal footing in the proposed union. The appropriate match of families is known as "equality of standard in marriage" (*al-kafa'a fi al-zowaj*) and has been a powerful social tradition that has kept marriage not only within families but within class and religious community as well. Proposals of marriage between families who know one another due to business or community ties are considered less risky than marriage proposals made by individuals who have became acquainted by chance.

The Western idea of falling in love with someone you've met casually, for example, at a bus stop, at a cafe, or, perish the thought, at a singles bar, is considered reckless and dangerous. How can the couple possibly know what they are getting into without the appropriate social controls? "Stranger" marriage that has been opposed by one or both of the families represents the greatest challenge to the couple, who may have to resort to a Shari'a court judge to act as marriage guardian for the woman and approve the marriage. Without familial support, they face many financial and emotional difficulties, and statistically these are the least stable marriages.

Marriage is not legal without a negotiated dower and a contract. The dower, which can be compared to the institution of "bridewealth" in other patrilineal societies, is a large sum of money or wealth in property that is owed to the bride by the groom from the time the marriage contract is signed. Bridewealth payments involve an exchange of wealth from the groom's family to the bride's family, while the dower is a personal debt to the wife alone. The negotiated dower is usually large, in comparison with the family's status, so that the groom often negotiates payment in "prompt" and "deferred" amounts. The total amount of the dower may be thousands or tens of thousands of dollars for a middle-class marriage. Some of the Islamist resurgence movements in Tunisia, the Sudan, and elsewhere have criticized inflationary dower costs and have reformed the social practice to the negotiation of a symbolic one dinar or one pound (comparable to one dollar) dower.

In many locales the dower has become so high that men are forced to postpone marriage into their late twenties and thirties, until they have accumulated sufficient funds for the prompt payment, as well as for the house and furnishings they must also provide. A significant number of the young male laborers who migrate from the relatively poorer Arab countries to the oil-rich nations are temporary workers saving their money for marriage.

The Islamic dower is probably a reform of pre-Islamic patrilineal bride-wealth negotiations, whereby wealth was exchanged between families. Making the dower payable to the woman and the large amount of wealth it represents guarantees her economic security and protection in the marriage. It is likewise an insurance against divorce, since the full amount of the negotiated dower must be paid at the time of the husband's divorce from the wife. While the husband has the sole financial responsibility of the wife and children, the wife has the responsibility to bear and rear the children of the husband's patrilineage, and she owes her husband obedience, which is legally defined as cohabitation. The fathers and the paternal uncles of the groom occasionally help with the financial arrangements. The father of the bride sometimes receives part of her dower payment as a voluntary offering or as a matter of paternal authority. But to do so invites social criticism, because such behavior by a father may be considered unmanly.

The 'aqd, or contract signing, is the legal beginning of the marriage, but it usually precedes actual cohabitation by about six months or a year. Anything not contrary to Islam and mutually agreed upon can be put into the marriage contract. This might include a clause on monogamy, or a mutual agreement about child custody in the event of divorce or death. The contract signing ceremony is a simple affair that is a culmination of marriage negotiations. For all but the most conservative families, the period after the 'aqd is the time when the engaged couple can actually go out together and get to know each other better. If problems develop in this period before cohabitation, then a negotiated divorce can be effected with little permanent consequence to either party.

Dating, as we know it in the West, does not exist in most Arab and Muslim societies, nor do young people have the opportunities for sexual adventures. Controls on premarital sexuality are rigid, and the idea that a young person might live alone in an apartment is out of the question. Dormitories at universities are segregated by sex, or students live at home with their parents. There are few places where men and women mix freely and where it is socially acceptable to do so. Such mixed gatherings are in private homes under the watchful eyes of parents and guardians. Hotels are strict about seeing some proof of marriage before renting their rooms to couples, and many of the urban areas where prostitution once flourished have now been cleansed by Islamist activism. Young men who leave home to go to other countries for work or further education have greater freedom for sexual experimentation, which is dangerous and shameful for a young woman. Virginity is demanded of a woman at the time of her first marriage, but it is not unusual for the younger, less well-traveled groom also to be a virgin on his wedding night.

Elaborate weddings are the centerpiece of family and community life and folklore. Traditional weddings last for three to seven days, including rituals associated with dying the bride's hands and feet with henna, symbolic visits of the groom's kin to the bride's family and vice versa, feasting, music, and dancing, culminating in the final "night of entry" (*lailat al-dukhla*) when the groom and entourage come to the bride's house and, after much celebration and ritual symbolizing the union of the couple and the two families, the marriage is consummated. In some conservative families there may be the display of blood on a sheet indicating that the bride is a virgin and her family honor is intact, but this custom is considered old-fashioned and is dying out in many communities.

The urban version of the marriage celebration preceding cohabitation is the occasion for the large public gathering of family and friends, often in one of the major hotels equipped for large parties. This is an opportunity for a conspicuous display of wealth by middle- and upper-class families with lavish food, dancing, and music provided to the guests whose gifts of money to the bride and groom are welcomed. The contemporary bride often wears a white bridal gown of Western inspiration, but many Muslim couples are choosing to have less flamboyant weddings and simpler, more culturally authentic wedding costumes.

Some couples will spend a period away on a honeymoon, although the idea is clearly a Western import, as is the photograph in the white dress that some brides insist upon. Others use the wedding as an opportunity to begin a new life in a new place, perhaps outside of their city or country. By tradition, the couple takes up residence with the groom's family, where the young wife adapts to her new role as daughter-in-law. Very few couples live neolocally, that is, in their own place apart from either family. Nubians in Egypt and the Sudan vary this strictly patrilineal-patrilocal pattern with a period of matrilocal residence with the wife's family, from as little as forty days to the time of the birth of the first child, expected within the first year of marriage. This may be a remnant of the prior matrilineal descent that prevailed in Nubia until the introduction of Islam in the sixteenth century.

If the marriage ends, either by divorce or death, the wife must pass three monthly courses, if she is still menstruating, for a period of time known as the 'idda. This ensures that she is not pregnant and is therefore free to marry again. However, if she is pregnant, both she and the child are protected by law to ensure that the former husband will support the child until it is weaned. Many people in the Middle East are surprised to find that nothing like the 'idda is practiced in the West. They realize that, theoretically at least, non-Muslims can divorce on one day and remarry the next, but they worry about the possibility of pregnancy from the previous marriage impinging on the new marriage, as well as how the *nasab,* or legitimating genealogy, of the child will be protected.

Marriage is the normal state for men and women, and someone who has remained unmarried is either pitied or considered strange. Preference for the married state is clearly stated in the Qur'an, and there is no tradition of celibacy for Muslim religious figures, such as imams or members of the 'ulama. A few Sufis have abjured marriage as part of their religious self-denial, but this is a personal choice and may only be observed on a temporary basis. Marriage is a major preoccupation in Arab and Muslim society as the main vehicle by which families and communities are bound in all important networks of mutual interest.

A major difference between Sunni and Shi'a Islam is their respective views of "temporary marriage." A distinction between *al-nikah,* permanent, and *mut'a,* or "pleasure," marriage is not in the marriage contract itself, only in the length of the marriage contract to which the couple agree. Temporary marriage in Shi'a Islam is recognized as an arrangement for sexual pleasure and is considered "irregular" by most Sunni religious scholars. An amount of money is agreed upon between the man and woman, making the contract invalid without it (Haeri 1989, 53). "Divorce" takes place by the expiration of the contract period; however, Shi'a 'ulama have acknowledged the husband's right to terminate the marriage before the contractual period has ended. Such rights have led critics to refer to this marriage as legalized prostitution, and mut'a marriage remains a controversial subject in Islamic family law.

Polygamy

Polygamy occurs when someone has more than one spouse at the same time. Polyandry is the state of having more than one husband at one time, and polygyny is the state of having more than one wife. Polygyny was made lawful by the early religious leaders, based upon the following Qur'anic revelation, after the battle of Uhud created many widows:

> If you fear that you shall not be able to deal justly with the orphans, marry of the believing women, two, three, or four; but if you fear that you shall not be able to deal justly [with them], then marry only one ... to prevent you from doing injustice. (sura 4:3, Pickthall translation)

The clear Qur'anic injunction here is that polygyny should not be undertaken unless the man is prepared to treat each wife and family with equity and justice. This permission to marry more than one wife has never been viewed by the religious scholars as a license to be licentious or to marry motivated by lust. The marriage of widows, following the Sunna of the

Prophet, has historically been favored. Interpretation of the Muslim practice of polygyny has demonstrated the principle of equity. A husband having more than one wife must financially support each wife and family equitably with the same accommodation, preferably in a separate location, or minimally with bedroom and kitchen facilities. He must not only lodge but clothe and provide medical support for each wife and her children, and practice equitable nocturnal conjugal visits. Islamic legal traditions abound with the right choices that polygynous husbands must exercise to ensure this equity.

No historical assessment of the frequency of polygamy in Muslim societies has been conducted. In certain African societies where Islam spread, it may have had the effect of reducing it by keeping to a maximum of four wives where unlimited polygyny had prevailed.

Polyandry is rare, found primarily in south and southeast Asia; polygyny is more common among non-Muslims. In cases of non-Muslim polygyny, the number of wives is not limited to four. Joint households or family compounds where polygynous husbands live with their wives and children are found throughout Africa and Asia, with the only difference that the Muslim husband is bound by the Shariʿa to establish a separate household for each wife. In some cases junior and senior wives collaborate in household tasks; in others they are competitors. Many contemporary women reject the idea of polygynous marriage, while men either cannot afford a polygynous lifestyle or also reject polygamy as contrary to the standards of modern life. Even in conservative Saudi Arabia, polygamy is socially less acceptable today than in previous generations. More than one Muslim commentator has pointed out that the Islamic legal system of permitting a man to marry more than one wife is preferable to the disruptive pattern of Western serial monogamy where couples marry and divorce multiple times during their lives.

In my nearly six years of life in Islamic societies, I observed directly only one case of polygyny, that involving a man with businesses in two geographically distant locales. In another case, a male friend confided that he was considering marrying a second wife because of his dissatisfaction with the first marriage and because taking a second wife is preferred to divorcing the first wife, but he was not sure he could afford to carry out his plan. In the United States, an imam took a second wife, his congregation objected, and for this and other reasons the imam resigned. As yet there has been no test case in the United States for Muslim plural marriage comparable to that for the Church of the Latter Day Saints, which permitted Mormons to practice polygamy until the Supreme Court ruled that only monogamy is lawful. In Utah, the de facto practice of polygamy is still known. Polygamy is allowed in the United Kingdom as legal practice by a religious minority.

The case for reform or elimination of polygamy came with the feminist agendas set in virtually every Muslim nation that developed a nationalist movement. Because the foundation for permitting polygamy is Qur'anic, the resistance of the 'ulama to its abolition has been strong. Turkey and Tunisia have abolished polygamy in their path to secular reform; however, Islamist movements have sought to restore proper Shari'a in these countries. These events are examined in greater detail in chapter 6.

Divorce

According to one hadith of the Prophet, "divorce is the most hateful thing that God permits." Revelations in the Qur'an make divorce (*talaq*) permissible, and scholars have made it lawful according to the Shari'a: "And if they decide upon divorce (let them remember that) Allah is Hearer, Knower" (sura 2:227, Pickthall translation).

This stands in contrast with orthodox Judaism, all of Eastern Christianity, and Roman Catholic doctrines, which do not allow divorce. Divorce was made permissible after the Protestant Reformation, which relaxed many restrictions upon Christians, including not only the possibility of divorce but also the lifting of restrictions on usury and the eating of pork. I have cases of more than one opportunistic Eastern Rite Christian man in Sudan converting to Islam so that he might divorce his wife.

> Divorce must be pronounced twice and then [a woman] must be retained in honor or released in kindness. (sura 2:229)

> When you have divorced women, and they have reached their term ['*idda*], then retain them in kindness or release them in kindness. Retain them not to their hurt so that ye transgress [the limits]. He who doth that hath wronged his soul. (sura 2:231, Pickthall translation)

Divorce is always a last resort, and Islamic practice around it has made efforts to inhibit, slow, or defer the process of final divorce until every other option has been tried. For most of its history, talaq was interpreted as the unilateral right of the husband. Women seeking divorce would have to persuade their husbands to divorce them. Orthodox Jewish law in force today in Israel demands a similar act—that in order to divorce, women must obtain permission from their husbands. Divorce could be pronounced in the presence of two witnesses on three occasions, ideally separated by three-month periods of attempted reconciliation or arbitration. Divorce conducted in this way came to be known as *talaq talata,* or triple divorce, and it became notorious for its potential for abuse. Husbands could legally divorce their wives in fits of anger or drunkenness, or they could threaten divorce—"I divorce you once, twice, next time it will be the third and final divorce!" Such pronouncements of divorce, if made in the presence of two male witnesses, could effect divorce, or if two pronouncements were made, the wife would be bound to the marriage and only have been threatened with divorce. This practice was so widespread that threatening to divorce one's wife (*wilahi al-talaq,* by God, I will divorce my wife) is used in a joking way when a host exhorts a companion to eat or drink more in his home. However, significant reforms in the twentieth century interpreting Qur'an and Sunna regarding the rights of women to divorce revolutionized social and legal practice.

Ideally, unilateral divorce is never undertaken lightly; it should be conducted in a rational way with forethought and reservation before a husband proceeds to make pronouncements of divorce. The "first divorce" (*talaq awal rajia*) is a revocable divorce and is often called the "warning" divorce. Such a pronouncement in front of witnesses and registered with the *ma'adhun* (registrar of marriages and divorces) signals a "separation" within the house whereby the couple refrain from intercourse and they and family members attempt to discover the underlying problems that have brought the marriage to this crisis. A period of three months should pass before the husband contemplates pronouncing the second revocable divorce (*talaq tani rajia*), which should continue the sexual restraint and the efforts at reconciliation, especially by family members if this is an endogamous union of cousins. The third and final pronouncement (*talaq talata*) is a serious step, for it means that the couple may no longer cohabit and that the husband must marry and divorce another woman before he can remarry the divorced wife. Custody of children is determined by their age and gender. Children initially belong to the mother, and the father must continue to support them, but ultimately custody resides in patrilineal principles, and older children are guarded and cared for by their father's patrilineal kin. In my studies of Muslim family law in practice in Sudan, the overwhelming number of divorces of this type registered were the "first, warning" divorce. While my direct observation of divorce was mainly in courts, at the end of the process of attempted reconciliation, presumably the larger number of "first" divorces indicates that reconciliation or resignation to conditions of marriage has taken place. Because *talaq talata* became widely acknowledged as abusive to wives, or potentially so, it was recognized as a harm to women. In the early twentieth century, it was subjected to intense reform, first by the Ottomans and later by 'ulama in colonial settings following both the Turkish lead and approval by colonial authorities keen to pursue enlightened rule. The methods and sources for these reforms were entirely Muslim, using Qur'an and Sunna as well as Islamic legal thought developed in the four schools of jurisprudence.

Judicial divorce for women has been broadly applied since twentieth-century reforms throughout the Muslim world. The grounds for judicial divorce include evidence of harm or abuse; neglect and failure to maintain or support the wife and/or children; desertion or imprisonment of the husband. Meanwhile, court-mandated arbitration has inhibited any process of casual divorce. These reforms are detailed in chapter 6.

Divorce separates families, just as marriage unites them. Families mobilize to discern the problems of the couple and will formally or informally intervene to prevent their difficulties from worsening. So-called stranger marriages are more likely to end in divorce, perhaps because the family support and intervention system is not in place.

Inheritance Patterns

Inheritance follows a modified form of patrilineal transmission of wealth and property that is prescribed by Islam. The heirs in Muslim family law are outlined in the Qur'an, defined religiously, and not subject to very much in the way of human interpretation. These prescribed heirs include the father/mother, the grandfather/grandmother, the son/daughter, with the patrilineal kin generally being favored over relations through the mother's side, and blood or consanguineal relations being favored over relatives by marriage.

Again, the 'asaba is the core group through whom inheritance passes, although their role is as much one of guardian and protector of the family wealth and property as it is one of direct inheritance. Lineal relatives (parents, grandparents, children) are favored over collaterals (aunts, uncles, cousins) in inheritance, and males are favored over females. The rationale for the former principle is the strengthening of the lineal ties from father to son to grandson, while the reason for the latter principle is that females, who are supported by their male kin, have less financial need and no economic responsibilities toward their kin. Where males and females are in equal structural positions in the kinship system, such as with brothers and sisters, males are entitled to twice what their sisters inherit. Because women are also supported by their husbands, even when they have independent means of income, there has been little feminist objection to this apparent discrimination against women. Where Muslim family law is applied to non-Muslims, such as in Egypt where a significant Coptic minority is governed by general Egyptian law, there has been outspoken criticism of the inequitable treatment of males and females in inheritance law.

Family wealth that is controlled by the 'asaba often consists of its immoveable property, such as land, date trees, or houses. Although individual shares of this wealth may be inherited, there is a strong sense of corporate ownership among kinspeople, so immoveable property is rarely sold or transferred. Moveable wealth, such as money, animals, or jewelry, is less protected by the corporate responsibilities of the ʿasaba and is inherited more on an individual basis.

There can be differences of opinion among the ʿasaba regarding the disposition of land. Traditional family land may have increased greatly in value by virtue of its proximity to an urban area; what once was valuable agricultural land is now worth more due to real estate speculation. It may be difficult to achieve unanimity as to the future disposition of the inherited land among the corporate ʿasaba, and a conservative position to do nothing may prevail.

Individual gifts to family members can be made outside of the prerogatives and laws of Qur'anic inheritance. Such gifts, known as *hiba,* can be made for the disposition of valued and sentimental property, such as a family heirloom, or for a special purpose, such as on the occasion of the marriage of a daughter or son. They fall outside of the intent of the general principles of Islamic inheritance if such gifts favor inequitably one heir over another. Likewise, a religious charitable trust made in perpetuity for some social benefit may not be used as a way of disinheriting heirs, nor can it be used for increasing the share of an heir.

Islamic family law permits one to bequeath wealth and property to non-Qur'anic heirs and to increase the shares of Qur'anic heirs by means of a will, up to one-third of an estate. Two-thirds must be bequeathed to the entitled heirs, making it impossible to disinherit relatives entitled under Islamic prescriptions. This religiously based system of inheritance has had the effect of avoiding feuds and controlling disputes over the disposition of family wealth among kinspeople. Coming as I do from a Western family that has been divided for three generations over disagreements resulting from the distribution of inherited wealth, I can appreciate a system that has specific and predictable rules and makes illegal the disinheriting of legal and entitled heirs.

Bequests in the name of God (*waqf,* pl. *awqaf*), usually for communal religious purposes, have historically been an important part of Muslim inheritance. These bequests are typically made outside the immediate family, but generally serve to benefit the local community. A parcel of land set aside in holy trust for the construction of a mosque or school can be nominated as a waqf, or funds to maintain or expand a mosque or hospital can be similarly nominated. The intent of the donor must be clearly declared and recorded so that the heirs are informed and are not unfairly treated through this mechanism, intended for social good and not for family retribution through denial of inheritance.

Illegitimacy

To be without attachment to a patrilineage or a genealogy, without *nasab*, is virtually not to exist, and it is one of the worst conditions that can befall a Muslim. The social repercussions of illegitimacy are profound and so far-reaching as to haunt the mother, her family, and the child for their entire lives. The societal cost is so high that other mechanisms have intervened to mollify the effects on the children and to give the pregnant mother every benefit of the doubt. Maliki interpretation of the Muslim family law regarding legitimacy traditionally permitted four years to pass after death or divorce by a husband, during which legitimacy of the former husband's patrilineage would pass to a child born after their separation. Later interpretations, accepted by majority legal opinion, recognize a period of one year as sufficient to bestow legitimacy on any child born after separation, death, or divorce by the husband. This liberal interpretation of parentage, especially fatherhood, underscores the importance of *nasab*, of having a place in the social scheme of things defined as patrilineal ties.

The shame attached to illegitimacy is so great for the mother, as proof of her sexual misconduct, and for the child, born without legal tie to the father, that destruction of the infant may appear to be the only solution. This particular form of infanticide exists in conjunction with the idea of family honor and eliminating the shame of bearing an illegitimate child.

Cases that I have knowledge of where a woman has reared an illegitimate child alone are rare and often tragic. The social stigma is great and may be insurmountable. A woman may be driven from place to place, unable to keep long-term employment, or she may be forced to seek the anonymity of expatriation. Seeking the aid of kinspeople and raising the child with the mother's family is a solution, but one that makes the shame of the birth a constant reminder and may result in mistreatment of the child.

Beyond these facts, legal adoption is difficult and virtually impossible in Islamic courts of law. Legitimacy is only conveyed through nasab, and nasab is conferred through legitimate marriage or by an admission of paternity in a court of law, with its attendant responsibilities. There is no notion of adoptive paternity in Islamic law, and the fundamental criterion of legitimacy derives from the conception of a child during the lawful wedlock of its parents (Coulson 1971, 23).

For a childless couple, the "burden of proof" usually falls to the woman as the one responsible for infertility. Barrenness is one of the acceptable grounds for taking a second wife, even in today's reformed practice of polygyny.

While legal adoption is impossible in Islamic family law, informal fosterage is actually quite common. For an extended family, already a communal unit, to take in a child is not a serious logistical problem, as it would be where nuclear family norms prevail and individual privacy is a priority. The agreement to raise a child not biologically a member of the patrilineage is seen as a matter of convenience and human compassion and does not affect the patterns of inheritance. A child may be taken in because of some misfortune or death that has befallen its parents, perhaps in some other part of the country where the father of the extended family conducts business. The child raised as part of a sociological family does not enjoy the same rights as a legitimate child of the biological family but may inherit wealth or property if given as a special gift or bequest.

War and economic strife, such as the Sudan has experienced for decades, has created many economically stranded individuals or orphans; a few of these displaced children, Muslim or not, may be taken in and raised by a Muslim family. Naturally the child would then be socialized to Arab and Muslim ways, and in ethnically and religiously divided regions conversion under such circumstances is not desirable. While children raised in such a way do not acquire entitlement to patrilineal descent and inheritance, they do become associated with the household as part of its daily activities, work routines, and socializing. This inferior status may be exploited by other members of the family as the dependent child may be viewed as a kind of servant to the household. The child is often educated with the biological children, but may need a family protector to keep older siblings or others from temptations of verbal or physical abuse or demands for servile behavior. The lack of a mechanism for formal legal adoption creates an ambiguous status for the fostered child and might engender inequitable treatment.

Fosterage as a specialized topic in Islamic law deals with the legal ramifications of the relationship established between non-kin individuals where a woman has suckled a child who is not her own. According to Shari'a, the children of the mother who nursed such a child and her own biological children are as brothers and sisters. They are subject to the same incest and marriage taboos as brothers and sisters and cannot marry one another. This is the rather specialized meaning of fosterage in Islamic society.

The international aid association formerly known as Foster Parents Plan changed its name to Plan, International, primarily because of the difficulties it was having translating the concept of foster parents into a Muslim context. Having a specialized meaning for fosterage yet lacking a mechanism for adoption, the translation of the term *foster parents* became awkward and socially inept, and so the change was made in order to make the program viable in Muslim areas.

The whole subject of legitimacy is sensitive in Islamic society, and perhaps in its negation, it reflects the crucial importance of the patrilineal kin group and the sense of place it gives the individual in the grandest scheme of things.

Female Circumcision

Female circumcision has been a subject of great interest, fascination, horror, and feminist agitation in the West. There is little doubt that circumcising women is linked to control of female sexuality. Whether the genital cutting involves the "simple" excision of the clitoris, or the more severe type of circumcision known as infibulation, involving excision of the labia leaving only a small opening for the flow of both menses and urine, circumcision results in reduction of sexual pleasure and desire, and in the more severe form it can result in lifelong medical complications, including chronic infections and difficult childbirth.

Female circumcision, or female genital mutilation (FGM) as it has been described in the West, has been wrongly associated with Islam because circumcision of girls is predominantly found in Islamic Africa. Although the origins of excision of female genitalia are obscure, there is unanimous agreement that it is pre-Islamic and may have its beginnings in Pharaonic Egypt— "Pharaonic circumcision" is the reference still used in Sudan today—or in the customs of African pastoralists (Gruenbaum 2001; Hicks 1993). There is no reference to circumcision in the Qur'an, and it is only mentioned in the hadith where Muhammad is said to have advised Muslims to use the "sunna" method, not to destroy or mutilate, for this is better for the man and would make the woman's face glow. The right of a woman to sexual satisfaction in marriage is upheld in Muslim interpretations (Toubia 1995, 31–32), so it may be that "sunna" circumcision was intended to enhance sexual pleasure. This is not the usual interpretation; however, there is general agreement that female circumcision was customary in societies where Islam spread and that, since it was not prohibited by Islam, its continued practice was permitted.

The feminist campaign in the West has overshadowed the many activists in Africa and in Europe who have conducted education and public health campaigns to ameliorate or eradicate the practice since the time of colonialism (Passmore Sanderson 1981). However, most Muslims do not practice female circumcision, although male circumcision is required, as it is tradition in Judaism and Christianity. The prevalence of female circumcision is in the African continent—especially in northeast and eastern Africa and across the Sahel to West Africa—where it is also practiced by some Christian groups in Ethiopia and Egypt. The Islamic faith enjoins modesty and proper sexual conduct for males and females, but like the other faiths originating in the Middle East, the sexual double standard demands more protection and greater monitoring of women to guard their chastity. Female circumcision is a powerful ally, but it is not the only approach nor is it commanded by Islam. The *'ulama* in different Muslim countries have at different times interpreted the Shari'a as being either neutral to the practice (Sudan during colonial times) or in favor of female circumcision (Egypt under recent Islamist pressure). The grand sheikh of Al-Azhar, Gad al-Haq Ali Gad al-Haq, ruled in a 1995 fatwa that "female circumcision is a noble practice that does honor to a woman" and that medieval scholars had ruled that both male and female circumcision is mandated by Islamic law. Meanwhile, Egypt's grand mufti, Sayed Tantawi, argued that circumcising women is not part of Islamic teaching and is a matter best evaluated by medical professionals. The Egyptian Human Rights Organization filed suit against Sheikh Gad al-Haq in order to finance a public campaign to reduce or ameliorate the practice, which is estimated to be carried out on 95 percent of rural girls and 73 percent of urban girls (Sipress 1995).

Female circumcision is not practiced in some of the most patriarchal of Muslim countries, such as Saudi Arabia or Afghanistan, or in Jordan where there is an elevated number of "honor killings" of women.

None of the above is intended to rationalize or offer cultural justification for the practice of female circumcision. In recent years I have written about female circumcision as a cultural practice that results in harm to women and girls that can be seen as a violation of their human rights. The global women's rights movement has asserted that female circumcision belongs in a category with other human rights violations, such as domestic abuse and honor killings. These are found in many cultures and in my view cannot be justified by cultural relativism as morally acceptable. Anthropologists can inform such debates, but they must respect and affirm the right of individual cultures to advocate and implement social change.

Male Circumcision

Circumcision of males—cutting and removing the foreskin of the penis—is customary in the Judeo-Christian and Islamic religious traditions. Circumcision may be performed on infant or preadolescent males in Muslim societies depending upon local custom. Among young males circumcision is a major rite of passage full of great anticipation and family celebration of this religious rite of manhood. After circumcision a boy no longer spends much time in the *hareem* with his mother and sisters. He accompanies his father and other adult males to the mosque for Friday prayers.

Women and the Changing Dynamics of Gender in Society

For the professional woman or the political activist, of which there are many throughout the Middle East and Islamic worlds, her movements are shaped by this general framework described above. Her primary identity is with her family, her closest ties are often with other women, and her professional or activist life is protected by these associations. Major change affecting the status of women has occurred in virtually every Muslim and Arab nation and historically has been strongly associated with the nationalist movements and the first decades of independence. Women have achieved political positions at the highest levels, whether appointed as judges in Sudan, Tunisia, Iraq, or Indonesia, or elected president or prime minister of predominantly Muslim nations such as Pakistan, Turkey, Bangladesh, or Indonesia.

The Taliban of Afghanistan, the Islamic Revolution in Iran, and the Islamist movement in Egypt have focused on the proper status of women as a measure of their Muslim "purity." The West has focused on these Islamist extremist examples of the treatment of women that has masked some of the more revolutionary changes in the Muslim world. A Qur'anic passage—"Men are in charge of women, because they spend of their property"—has been interpreted differently in various countries to support both sides of the contemporary issue of women holding public office. Some scholars argue that this passage is confined to domestic matters and relates to the authority men derive from their obligation to economically support their female kin—following from this there is no ban on women serving the state in the public arena. Others argue for an absolutist interpretation that "men are in charge of women" in all spheres, public and private, and thus women cannot hold any public office, nor should they, for this exposes them to dangers that might compromise their honor and that of their family. Clearly, there is no consensus on this and many other points of religious interpretation affecting not only women but the daily practice of Islam.

In every instance in the Arab-Islamic world where colonialism was resisted and political movements shaped the new national identity, women played their part. Together with men they organized demonstrations for national self-determination in every former colony, with well-documented cases in Egypt and Algeria and among the Palestinians. Hoda Shar'awi and Ceza Nabarawi became internationally recognized symbols of the Arab-Muslim women's struggle when they returned from Europe and reentered Egypt as unveiled, emancipated women. Understanding the sensitive and complex set of values associated with veiling, they organized nationalist and feminist demonstrations of both veiled and unveiled women. To be sure, these pioneering Muslim feminists were highly educated and generally upper-class Egyptian women, but they forged an Arab-Muslim women's agenda that was intended to transform society once independence was achieved. That agenda included the promotion of female education at all levels, including the opening up of the professions to women; the acceptance of women participating in the public spheres of life; reform of certain of the family laws, especially the divorce laws; and suffrage for women.

In Algeria, where a war of national liberation against France was necessary to achieve independence, women collaborated in the armed struggle, carrying political leaflets and weapons under their veils. This heroic involvement of women is documented in a film, *The Battle of Algiers*. The French colonial authorities, seeking to undermine this political use of the veil and project themselves as the emancipators of women, conducted humiliating public unveilings during the last years of the armed struggle. The predictable effect was reinforcement of the cultural meaning of the veil as both Algerian and Islamic, and with the success of the nationalist movement women returned to wearing the veil on a mass scale. Also, it might be added somewhat cynically, men took power and were reluctant to share it with the women alongside whom they had struggled for national independence.

The mobilization of women initially around the issue of nationalism, with the addition of a feminist agenda, was a scenario that was replayed in a number of less known but courageous examples. These include the cases of the Sudan and Tunisia (Fluehr-Lobban 1980; Libidi 1987), the Yemen and Iraq, Syria and Lebanon. While in no instance did women come to power after independence, their agenda for social change was broadly accepted and implemented. Women have the right to vote in virtually every Arab-Muslim country, with the exception of the feudal kingdoms, such as Saudi Arabia and Kuwait, which experienced neither direct colonialism nor concomitant struggles for independence. In the Gulf War, which the United States claimed it entered for the preservation of the West's oil interests and democracy in the Arabian peninsula, it turned out to be only the former that was accurate, as the most fundamental democratic right—the right to vote—remained the exclusive right of men.

Education for women has expanded from elementary to higher education. Some Islamist movements strongly endorse education for women, as their secular predecessors did, and a significant proportion of the Islamist activists are women students. However, extremist states like that under Taliban rule in Afghanistan forbade public schooling for girls or public professions for women such as teaching or medicine. In the historically secular states, the professions are generally open to women. In fact, women formed a greater proportion of physicians and engineers in the Middle East than they did in the West until very recent times. Even in conservative Muslim countries, women are encouraged to become physicians or lawyers as a culturally appropriate means of serving a female clientele. The conflicts between career and family are not as acute as they are in the West due to the continued strength of the extended family and its ability to care for children at home, as well as the general availability of affordable daycare in countries with a history of feminist activism, such as Tunisia, Egypt, Iraq, and Indonesia.

Women as Public Officials and Heads of State

Women in Egypt, the Sudan, Tunisia, Iraq, Jordan, Syria, Turkey, Pakistan, Lebanon, Bangladesh, Malaysia, and Indonesia—indeed, in most Muslim countries—have been appointed to important ministerial posts or have been elected to public office within their respective governments, while others have served as their nation's ambassadors abroad or at the United Nations. It is only in the ultraconservative countries of the Arabian peninsula and the Gulf that women have been excluded from holding public office of any kind or having other basic rights as full citizens. Human rights activists worldwide now view this as unacceptable.

The influential Egyptian television industry is dominated by female employees and has numerous female officials in top leadership positions of this massive enterprise. Television news correspondents are commonly seen unveiled in Lebanon and Syria and on the popular pan-Arab network Al-Jazeera. The so-called glass ceiling, much commented upon in the United States as blocking women's achievement of the highest levels of government or business hierarchies, has not been as much of a barrier in these nations.

Thus there is a diverse range of historical experience in the Arab-Islamic world that includes secularist anticolonialist progressive movements as well as religious fundamentalist groups seeking a stronger role for Islam through the control and protection of women. In Saudi Arabia social norms of female seclusion are enforced legally and politically. Not only are women not permitted to vote. They also cannot drive, and they must obtain written permission from their male guardian (*al-wali*, recalling the marriage guardian) before they may travel. Kuwait is less restrictive, but women still lack the right to vote.

One of the most extreme examples of Islamist activism affecting women has occurred in Afghanistan after the rise to power of the Taliban in 1996. Some of the severest measures restricting the movements and activities of women were imposed, including the withdrawal of women from all formal public employment and mandatory head-to-toe veiling of all women in public. These measures plus physical punishment for noncompliance, including flogging, led to an unprecedented international outcry. Although the United

States supported the Afghani mujahideen (religious freedom fighters) who evolved into the Taliban when they were fighting against Soviet rule, the United States refused to recognize this government and isolated the regime internationally. International human rights groups protested the Taliban treatment of women, but much of the world seemed not to care until the attacks on the United States on September 11, 2001.

Since 1989, an Islamist regime in Sudan has also imposed severe restrictions upon public employment and "proper" dress of women. This is often described as Shariʿ dress, implying that it is prescribed by Islamic law. In extremist interpretations it becomes lawful to dress in hijab, and these regimes have mandated veiling and the most modest forms of dress. In extremist states such as Iran immediately after the Islamic Revolution, Saudi Arabia, Sudan, and Afghanistan, it became common for the "morals police" to arrest women and punish them with flogging or imprisonment. In other social arenas, women were forbidden to hold "demeaning" public jobs such as waiting on tables or pumping gas. Some women, especially those suspected of opposing the regime, were arrested for noncompliance with the proper public code of conduct or dress and were summarily tried, imprisoned, tortured, or flogged for their "non-Islamic" behavior. I have personally been involved in a number of political asylum cases offering expert testimony in support of women who have been subjected to these extremist interpretations of Islam.

Iran, now decades past its Islamic Revolution, has mollified some of its restrictions upon public female employment and activities. Strict enforcement and observance of veiling has been curtailed, with some younger women donning simple headscarves with blue jeans under their chadors.

The appropriate status of women today is a much-debated issue in the context of Islamist versus secular models for the development of society, as the earlier secular models of society are increasingly being challenged by more "authentic" Muslim values. This and other debates and tensions within contemporary Islamic society, including Islamist and anti-Islamist tendencies with respect to women and other social issues, are taken up in chapter 7.

5

National, Religious, and Ethnic Identity

Relations with the West

Islam originated in the seventh century of the common era within Arab culture that subsequently spread throughout southwest Asia, North Africa, and the Iberian Peninsula within its first century after the Hegira in 622, the beginning of the Muslim calendar. It was absorbed in succeeding centuries by cultures from eastern Asia westward to the African continent and to North America. Obviously, there is no single ethnicity attached to Islam, although there is the powerful, overriding concept of the Umma—the world community of believers—that does convey an international identity that transcends ethnicity for the 1.2 billion people who profess Islam. In terms of cultural and linguistic identity, there is no question that Arab society and the Arabic language have played the most important roles in the shaping of the faith of Islam and the cultural-religious identity that it conveys.

In the previous chapter the focus was on the collective identity at the micro level—male/female relations and others drawn from one's relationship to extended families and local community. In this chapter I focus on communal identity at the macro level—ethnic, national, religious, and regional. I examine ways that one's identity is constructed in relation to others who may be defined as outsiders to one's immediate social group, but nonetheless are citizens of nation-states. I also analyze how identity is constructed in terms of others defined as foreigners, Muslim and non-Muslim, and how various distinctions are made along religious, ethnic, and national lines. Beyond these social constructions of identity, Islam in Africa, Asia, and North America is also surveyed as an aid to the reader for an expanded understanding of Islamic societies in practice.

Religious Identity

The most fundamental identity of Muslims is that they are part of the Umma. In regions where the Islamic faith predominates, religious identity is taken for granted and is rarely articulated in relation to other creeds. In places where Muslim identity has assumed a political dimension, the concept has been attached to political parties such as the Umma Party of Sudan. Some Muslim scholars have asserted that the Umma constitutes an ethnic identity opening a new Islamic ethnography and anthropology (Ahmed 1986).

Islam, as the last of the revealed prophetic traditions beginning with Abraham, formally recognizes the prophets of Judaism and Christianity who preceded Muhammad. Abraham, Moses, and Jesus are venerated as prophets. As a result, special relations are enjoined between Muslims and Christians and Jews. For example, marriage is permissible between Muslim men and Christian or Jewish women as Kitabiyeen (people of the Book), and they are promised special protection under the governance of a Muslim state in return for paying taxes.

Throughout the Middle East, minority Christian and Jewish communities, while residentially segregated, have coexisted in relatively peaceful conditions with Muslim communities well into the modern period. Despite the chronic hostilities engendered by the Crusades, Christian communities in the Middle East did not experience communal violence against them, and Sephardic Jewish communities in southwest Asia and North Africa did not experience the type of intercommunal violence associated with the anti-Semitism rooted in European Christianity and experienced in the ghettos of eastern Europe or the pogroms of czarist Russia. This is not to portray an unduly romantic picture of goodwill and social harmony among the three religious groups, but to stress that repression of Christians and Jews was not a feature of early, medieval, or modern Islam. Indeed, Jewish scholarship was supported by the caliphates at Baghdad and Cordoba, with the books of the Talmud completed in Baghdad under the sponsorship of the Caliph. This contrasts sharply to the religious oppression and expulsion of Muslims and Jews in the Middle Ages in Europe, of which the Spanish Inquisition is the prime example.

Muslim/Christian Relations

Islam as a new revealed faith came only six centuries after the introduction of Christianity. As it spread, it replaced Christianity in many of the communities where it had only recently secured a place. However, Christians remained, and they now constitute nearly half the Lebanese population, over 10 percent of Egypt, and 12 percent of Syria. They are the guardians of

Christianity's holiest shrines in Nazareth, Bethlehem, and Jerusalem. The Crusaders' attempt to reclaim Christianity and "lost" territories, especially the Holy Land, is a bitterly remembered chapter in Muslim/Christian history. The seizure and sacking of Jerusalem in 1099 by the Faranj (the Frank or French, as Crusaders) was an epic moment in Muslim consciousness. An Arab account, *The Crusades through Arab Eyes* (Maalouf 1984), is a classic account by the "other" in the chronicles of the Crusades that offers an alternative perspective of a period that helped to shape modern Muslim/Christian relations. The word *al-Faranj* is still used in colloquial Arabic to refer to a foreigner and Westerner. In some colloquial dialects of Arabic the distinction is made between the Suq al-'Arab, the market where one buys locally made items, and the Suq al-Faranji, Western-style stores where one buys appliances and other foreign-made items.

Add to this early and highly negative episode in Christian/Muslim history the era of European colonialism, which introduced a new element of the power of European Christianity often allied with local indigenous Christian groups. With Islamic institutions either isolated or co-opted by colonialism, local Christian communities were strategically placed to work with colonial officials and to benefit more than Muslim communities, relatively speaking, from the presence of colonialism. The proselytizing of Western culture and values through Christianity and the use of missionaries encouraged by colonial governments naturally was not opposed by the Christian communities, while their role was perceived as collaborationist by local Muslim communities.

As a result, a segment of the nationalist movements advocated the restoration of Islam and, by extrapolation, the diminished influence of Christianity. Because many nationalist leaders saw the divisive role that religion played in this context, they rejected a political role for religion in the new postindependence states. However, others pressed for an Islamic model of government. In the immediate postcolonial period, Arab nationalism and secularism won the day and popular nationalist leaders were both Christian and Muslim.

Decades later, with the failure of secular Arab governments seriously to challenge Israeli expansion into their territories, with few political or economic advances made by secularist politics, and with the success of the Islamists in Iran, Pakistan, Afghanistan, and a myriad other struggles—the model of Islamic government has gained ground. This is certainly perceived as a threat to Arab-Christian communities. For example, in the southern Sudan, where chronic civil war has ravaged the countryside and resulted in the deaths or dislocation of millions of people, rebel forces define themselves as Christian and animist, waging their struggle against northern Muslim domination and Islamic fundamentalism.

As mentioned, Christian minority groups exist in significant numbers in Egypt; in Syria and Iraq; in the Sudan, with a 30 percent Christian and animist minority; and in Lebanon, where Maronite and Eastern Rite Christians represent almost half of the nation's population. These communities, including the nonminority Lebanese case, exist in relatively encapsulated groups, sharing common residential areas and socializing and marrying within the local group. In most ways their patterns of extended family life and endogamous marriage mirror their Muslim counterparts in each nation. Some Christian families have specialized in an area of manufacturing or trade, such as gold working or Oriental carpet sales, and have developed prosperous livelihoods within predominantly Muslim markets. Others have remained quite poor, like their fellow Muslim citizens in Egypt and the Sudan.

In Egypt, Copts are among the most influential national families, such as the family of former United Nations secretary general Boutros Boutros Ghali, and they are among the poorest of city dwellers, as they are disproportionately represented among the garbage collectors. This is partly explained by the Muslim prohibition against eating pork; in response, Copts have developed pig production and butchering in Egypt and used the substantial Cairene garbage heaps to feed their pigs. This lowly occupation can be quite lucrative, but it does reinforce Muslim ideas about the uncleanliness of pigs and their association with Christians.

Depending on the government in power, the Coptic Church and its leaders and institutions have been subjected to religious control and repression. The Coptic patriarch, Pope Shenouda, has often been under house arrest for speaking out against the government and its lack of representation of Copts and their interests. The successive waves of Islamist activism in Egypt have negatively impacted the Coptic community, especially in central Egypt near Assyut, which is a center of both Coptic concentration and militant Islamist activity. Armed attacks against Copts have alarmed the Christian community even as these have been staunchly opposed by the Egyptian government. Nonetheless, in folk religious culture, accounts of apparitions of the Virgin Mary in a Coptic neighborhood in Cairo were popularly accepted by Muslims and Christians alike as a sign and a warning to adopt a more religious path in social governance. Fewer assaults on Copts have occurred in metropolitan Cairo; however, the popular Christmas displays in the stores downtown have been curtailed due to Islamist pressure.

The Egyptian government has been criticized for succumbing to Islamist pressure by issuing permits for the construction of new mosques but not for new Coptic churches. Responding to internal and international criticism on its treatment of Copts, the government approved the construction, com-

Fig. 17. Archangel Michael Coptic Christian cathedral in Aswan, Egypt.

pleted in 2001, of the largest Coptic church in Egypt in Aswan where its steeples rise above the highest minarets in town.

In the Sudan, Christian leaders and communicants are identified with the southern resistance to northern dominance, most recently being perpetrated by an Islamist regime. In this country, Christianity is on the rise primarily as a reaction to intensified political Islamization (see Fluehr-Lobban, 1990). The fundamental problems are those of national unity, uneven economic development, and fair representation of the nation's multiple regions and ethnic groups, but the battleground rhetoric is religious, with Christians pitted against Muslims. Even before the Islamists came to power in 1989, the presence of Christian missionaries in the southern region was viewed as an example of neocolonialism, with a continuation of undue influence and interference from the West. Various governments, from independence in 1956 to the present, have engaged in the political expulsion of missionaries as agents of foreign governments and Western culture. Similar Christian/Muslim tensions exist in Chad and in Nigeria. A rising tide of Islamism and the institution of Shariʿa as provincial law in its twelve Muslim provinces in northern Nigeria have exacerbated Christian/Muslim tension. Intercommunal religious violence has resulted, and the fragile balance between the dominantly Muslim north and Christian and animist south of Africa's most populous nation has been disturbed.

Since the 1990s, the issue of slavery in Sudan has come to the world's attention. This revival of slavery is a consequence of the chronic civil war and its consequent lawlessness as well as the government turning a blind eye toward the revival of old patterns of Arab militias along the Bahr al-Ghazal border areas capturing and enslaving non-Muslim southerners. Media reports of this renewed enslavement and trade shocked Western audiences and revived Christian-based abolitionism and antipathies toward Islam. That Muslims engaged in slavery and their Muslim government did little to stop it helped to launch a western Christian crusade to end the practice by buying back slaves and emancipating them.

Muslim/Jewish Relations

Generally harmonious and collaborative relationships between Jewish and Muslim people can be documented within the histories of each community. As "protected" people (*dhimmis*) under the various Muslim caliphates, such as the Umayyads in Spain, Christian and Jewish communities enjoyed mutual respect and tolerance. Required by the Islamic states to pay a tax for protection (*jizya*), dhimmis could not openly confront the Islamic faith (Hourani 1991, 117). However, Christians and Jews held important government jobs, and Jewish scholars compiled the books of the Talmud in Baghdad under Abbasid protection. Jewish and Muslim scholars of the Middle Ages were responsible for translating the great Arabic works of science and philosophy from antiquity and introducing them to Europe. Under Ottoman rule, Jewish communities were ruled autonomously under the millet system of government. This continued until the fall of the Ottoman Empire after World War I.

The status of Jewish communities within Arab and Muslim societies grew more complicated after the creation of the state of Israel in 1948. Prior to this, Sephardic (or Middle Eastern Jewish) communities were scattered throughout the Maghrib in North Africa and in the Arabian peninsula and southwest Asia. The term *Sephardic,* meaning originating in Spain, excludes the long established Jewish communities that had no historical relationship to Spain or to the expulsion of Jews after 1492 (Eickelman 2001). Diaspora communities in North Africa existed for a long time, such as the community at al-Ghriba on the Isle of Jerba in Tunisia, which dates at least from the time of the fall of Jerusalem in 70 C.E. This synagogue, which we visited in 1990, was attacked by a cell of al-Qaeda in the fall of 2001, killing a number of German tourists.

Jewish communities lived in relative peace within predominantly Muslim areas until 1948, when many Sephardic Jews joined European Ashkenazi Jews in the newly created state of Israel. The war fought over the future of Palestine was a bitter one between the Zionists and Palestinians, but the Arab-Muslim world had no effective political response, since most of the region was still under European colonial control. Many Middle Eastern Jews elected to remain within the countries of their birth and ancestors, and

Fig. 18. A Torah in a synagogue in Fez, Morocco

for the most part nonhostile relations between Muslims and Jews continued until the humiliating defeat of Arab-Muslim armies in the 1967 war with Israel. This blow to Arab-Muslim pride and, ultimately, to Arab nationalism produced an emotional and subjective reaction against local Jewish communities, and in the aftermath of 1967 most left for Israel or the West. However, there remain significant communities of Sephardic Jewish minorities today in Tunisia, Morocco, Turkey, and Iran.

Subsequent events have exacerbated feelings on all sides. The failure of the Oslo peace process in the 1990s was a failure for East and West, Arab and Jew. The bloodier second intifada, begun early in Prime Minister Ariel Sharon's term of office in 2000, has escalated to the level of war threatening to engulf the region.

The conflict is about land, equitable use of its resources, and relative political control, autonomy, and security in the region of Palestine/Israel. The conflict is not about religion, so it can be hoped that a negotiated peace will bring about a resumption of the relations between Muslims and Jews that prevailed before 1948 and 1967. Ensuring that Jerusalem is open and accessible to the faithful of the Abrahamic tradition is crucial to the restoration of peaceful relations among Muslims, Jews, and Christians.

Ethnic Identity

The ethnic diversity found in Middle Eastern and Islamic societies is obscured by simple stereotypes regarding Arabs along with a basic ignorance of the cultural and linguistic geography of the region. Iranians, Pakistanis, and Afghanis are not Arabs, although they employ Arabic writing in their languages—Farsi in Iran, Urdu in Pakistan, and the linguistic majority Pashtun in Afghanistan. These are all Indo-European languages. The Berber language, Tamazigh, is widely spoken in North Africa from Morocco, Algeria, and Tunisia as far east as Siwa oasis in Egypt, while the Nubian language Rotana is spoken in southern Egypt and northern Sudan. The Kurdish language is spoken throughout Kurdistan straddling Turkey, Iraq, and Iran. These are not Semitic languages like Arabic or Hebrew, nor is their culture that of the Arabs. Likewise, the Turks, leaders of the Ottoman Empire and imperial rule of the region for five centuries, are not Arabs, and Turkish belongs to the Finno-Ugric language family. Before the reforms of Mustafa Kemal Atatürk in the 1920s, they too wrote their central Asian language using Arabic calligraphy. The Islamic Republics of Pakistan and Afghanistan employ Arabic script emphasizing Islamic religious identity over ethno-linguistic roots.

Arab Identity

Arab is an elusive ethnic, cultural, and linguistic term that has been used as a racial designation. Ethnologically, an Arab is one who traces descent from the Arab tribes of the Arabian peninsula. This would be simple enough were it not for the dramatic spread of Islam by the Arabs during the seventh century. After that great historical expansion and migration of people through the first jihad(s) in southwest Asia (contemporary Iraq, Iran, and Syria/Palestine) and North Africa from Egypt to Morocco to southern Europe, Arabs settled and mingled with local populations and forged a new Arab-Muslim identity in these areas. The tracing of descent through Arab tribes, especially through the line of the Prophet, the Quraysh, has always been favored with the honorific "Sayyid" and, perhaps, amplified beyond actual genealogy and is therefore more fictive than real.

This blending of people and cultures through the spread of Islam fostered indigenous concepts, such as "Afro-Arab" identity, that arose in the context of the Sudanese nationalist movement, as well as in Muslim East Africa, in Kenya and Tanzania. This was intended to solve the problem of having to identify exclusively with either African or Arab nations and cultures at the time of independence, and it flourished more as a political than as a cultural concept.

While the precise definition of who is an Arab is elusive, the sociological definition is more easily derived by simply asking people if they identify themselves as Arabs. The question is simple, but the answer is not. People who speak Arabic as a first language may identify themselves as Arabs in a generic sense, but they are as likely to identify themselves as Egyptian, or Palestinian, or Lebanese. The term ʿArab in the Arabic language has multiple meanings and derivations, and depending upon one's social background and place in society, they may evoke different responses. In its purest sense, ʿArab refers to nomads or Bedouin, meaning people who move about and use animal husbandry as the major economic adaptation. The colloquial Arabic term for automobile is "ʿarabiyya," or literally a thing that moves about.

Being nomadic and living in deserts or at the peripheries of settled, domesticated townspeople or urban dwellers, Arab nomads are not thought of as civilized in the ways that the more dominant agrarian or urban people see themselves. To be an Arab in this sense is to be somewhat uncouth living in a state of nature. Indeed, there is a historical antipathy between nomads and settled agriculturalists, evidenced in their conflicts over scarce resources, such as water and grazing lands. So one may readily hear disparaging references made to Arabs when the reference is to Bedouin or desert dwellers.

The most significant twentieth-century context of the term Arab is with the political movement of Arab nationalism, articulated by many nationalist leaders in anticolonial movements throughout the Middle East and given international recognition and regional meaning by Gamal Abdel Nasser. Nasser became the symbolic leader of Arab nationalism in the mid-1950s when Egypt nationalized the Suez Canal and Nasser stood up to the imperial pressure of Britain and France, allied with Israel, and succeeded in achieving Egyptian control over the canal. Dean Acheson, then U.S. secretary of state, sided with Egypt at a critical moment and helped to avoid all-out war over the Suez "crisis." Motivated by Arab nationalism, Nasser forged a short-lived union with Syria, known as the United Arab Republic (UAR). Long after Syria withdrew from this union, Egypt continued to refer to itself as the UAR, and Nasser was revered throughout the Arabic-speaking world as a great leader and people proudly identified themselves as Arabs.

After Nasser's death in 1969, the leadership of the Arab nationalist movement was unclear, and various spokesmen of this political philosophy took their turn, including Muammar Qaddafi of Libya, Yasir Arafat of the Palestine Liberation Organization, and the Ba'thist leaders Hafez Asad in Syria and Saddam Hussein in Iraq. The political appeal to the so-called Arab Nation made by these and other leaders proved to be powerful rhetoric, if not powerful politics. The first great blow to Arab nationalism came in the 1967 Six Day War, in which Israel invaded and seized territory from Egypt, Jordan, and Syria without drawing a concerted military response from the Arab Nation. This was a humiliating defeat to the Arab nations and the beginning of a popular skepticism of their leaders. The fatal blow to Arab nationalism came during the Gulf War of 1991, when the Arab nations of Kuwait and Saudi Arabia were pitted against the Arab nation of Iraq and its allies. Saddam Hussein placed the Islamic religious slogan, "Allahu akbar" (God is great), on the Iraqi flag, symbolically acknowledging the ascendance of Islamic political alternatives over Arab nationalism. In the second war against Iraq in 2003, Arab nationalism was not a factor; however, the response of the Muslim world to this perceived act of U.S. aggression was one of anger coupled with the widespread belief that the United States was against Islam.

Appeals to the Arab Nation continue to come from Palestinian nationalists, whose lack of a territorial base makes Arab nationalism a matter of essential politics. Some of the more eloquent spokesmen of Arab nationalism have been the Christian Palestinian leaders Naif Hawatmeh and George Habash. The juxtaposition of Arab and Israel in the usually hyphenated Arab-Israeli conflict adds to the sense of the Arabs being constituted as a single nation, although this amounts to a political chimera.

Arab nationalism has had a distinctly secular cast to its political rhetoric and practice, with religion either irrelevant, from the standpoint of politics, or kept separated from politics. Together with the rhetoric of the Arab Nation was the promise of democracy or the presentation of military regimes or single-party regimes as democratic. Failures of Arab solidarity, from the 1967 Six Day War to the 1991 Gulf War and 2003 war against Iraq, have seriously undermined the political viability of Arab nationalism, as has the failure to achieve economic security long promised by these regimes. While people may still respond emotionally to the call for Arab unity, the political dynamic is shifting away from Arab nationalism to political alternatives framed by Islamic discourse, generally referred as Islamist or Islamism, meaning political Islam.

So, perhaps the best definition of an Arab is someone who thinks of himself or herself as an Arab. This person speaks Arabic as a first language, may be Christian or Muslim, and may or may not claim descent in the long genealogy of the Arabs and their historical relationship to Islam. This definition leaves out the vast majority of the world's Muslims, most of whom are not Arabs and do not live in the Middle East. There are also numerous Muslim but non-Arab ethnic groups in the Middle East as well as the 3 million non-Arab, non-Muslim Jewish people living in Israel.

Racial Identity

The designations Semite and Semitic have been used to describe the Arab and Jewish peoples. In Euro-American history and culture, Semite has been applied to the Jewish presence in Western society, so that the negative referent "anti-Semitic" has been used almost exclusively to mean bigotry or racism as applied to Jewish people. Anti-Arab prejudice has witnessed an alarming increase in the West and can justifiably be included as another unfortunate form of anti-Semitism.

The Semites are an ancient people tracing their common linguistic heritage to Mesopotamia about 2500 B.C.E. The "sons of Shem" diverged into distinctive language and cultural groups that included the Arabs and Hebrews—the legendary descendants of the sons of Abraham, Ismail and Isaac —and also people speaking related Semitic languages, such as Aramaic and Amharic. According to some linguists, Semites living in the Sinai took the Egyptian alphabet and converted it into the first true alphabet in which a sign or letter represented a single sound. Thus, only a few dozen characters had to be memorized, and in this way literacy became accessible to ordinary people instead of a monopoly controlled by priests and scribes. The Hebrews also perfected monotheism and originated the idea of the single, unchallenged deity through the prophet Abraham, who is revered as progenitor to all of the Abrahamic faiths: Judaism, Christianity, and Islam (Peters 1982).

The Hebrews were already a distinctive people at the time of Babylonian captivity and in the tenth century B.C.E. when the Hebrew territories of Judea and Samaria were united into the kingdom of Israel under King David. This kingdom was short-lived, and after only a century of existence, the Hebrews moved into parts of southwest Asia, North Africa, the Iberian Peninsula, and other parts of Europe.

The Arabs settled and flourished in "al-Jazira al-Arabiyya," literally the "island of the Arabs," the Arabian peninsula. The northern Arabs were nomadic camel herders or oasis dwellers, and the southern Arabs developed commercial centers and urban life. Situated strategically along the trade routes of the Red Sea, Arabian Sea, and Indian Ocean, the island of the

Arabs was a natural crossroads in the East/West trade between the Mediterranean and the Indian Ocean. Into this context of international trade and commerce Islam was introduced, grounded in Arab culture, but comprehended outside Arabia. With the introduction of Islam the Abrahamic tradition of prophecy was complete, as was the divergence of the original Semites into distinctive religious and cultural communities.

After the great expansion of Islam in the first centuries after its introduction, when the caliphates were established in Baghdad, Damascus, and Andalusia in Spain, Jewish and Christian residents of these areas were officially protected as dhimmis. Jewish scholarship flourished, and while the communities remained separate, there is no evidence of intercommunal violence or systematic discrimination that we might call racism today. Indeed, there is every indication that the reason for the flowering of Andalusia was its multilingual, multicultural, and multireligious character. Scholars carried out their research and writing in Arabic, Latin, and Hebrew, and ordinary people spoke an Andalusian dialect of Arabic and Romance that developed into Spanish (Hourani 1991, 194). In 1492, with the ascendance of a Christian monarchy in Spain, both the Muslims (Moors) and the Jews were expelled and victimized in the infamous Spanish Inquisition. The Sephardic Jews, those fleeing from Spain to North Africa and parts of the Middle East, resettled in Arab-Muslim communities with whom they were already familiar. Again, no pattern of intercommunal, interreligious conflict is recorded, although no significant blending of the communities through intermarriage took place.

The experience of Jewish people in Europe and Russia, the Ashkenazim, was quite different. The religious blame placed on the Jews for the killing of Christ and the isolation of Jewish communities in reaction made them an easy target for religious and racial harassment, documented in the case of urban Jews in the ghettos of major European cities and the systematic pogroms of rural and urban Jews in czarist Russia. This historical context gave rise in Europe to the nineteenth-century Jewish nationalist movement, called Zionism, not in any Arab or Muslim capital where Jewish people historically resided. The fulfillment of Zionist aspirations after the end of World War II, with the creation of the state of Israel and the displacement of Palestinian Arab people, altered the preexisting relationship between Arab-Muslim and Jewish peoples.

An enmity engendered by politics has replaced the traditional tolerance between the religious-cultural groups. But I do not agree that this is racial at its core. Over the years I have heard many angry comments about Israeli politics from Muslim and Arab friends, but I have not heard the kind of anti-Semitic remarks and stereotypes that are common in the United States. This gives me a sense of optimism that a negotiated peace between Israel and its Arab neighbors will bring about a restoration of Arab-Muslim and Jewish relations as they once were, the essentials of this being tolerance, mutual respect, and peaceful coexistence. Is there a Semitic race? Race has been defined by anthropologists as a biologically distinct population sharing certain common physical features. This is a term that does not readily apply to either Arab or Jewish people, whose antiquity and influence over a great expanse of time and geography has been the antithesis of isolation. Semites, both Arabs and Jews, share a common ancient linguistic heritage, common religious roots as followers of Abrahamic faiths, and a period of shared history after the advent of Islam.

Anthropologists have abandoned the concept of race as misleading and lacking in scientific rigor. Race has been used to foster notions of purity, and it has been used to divide peoples purportedly not of the same racial stock. Human biologists and anthropologists have experimented with racial classifications and have generally found these to be hopelessly inadequate.

While scientific racial classification has all but disappeared, sociological categories based on group identity are nevertheless vital cultural and political constructs. The racial concept "black" means very little biologically or even physically, but it conveys a great deal of political and cultural meaning in the United States. The American Bureau of Census and a host of business, professional, and educational institutions keep statistics on American racial groups, including categories such as "Black/African American," "White/Caucasian," "Hispanic," "Native American," "Asian American," and "Other." Many Arabs and Muslims from the Middle East and North Africa have been confounded by these racial categories, and when asked to fill out these American forms, they have not known with which race they should identify. Some would say they are African but not black; others report that they are frequently taken for being Hispanic and have been addressed in Spanish in American cities with large Latino populations; others, in frustration, might check "Other," since nothing else seems to fit. Some affirmative action guidelines have sought to clarify the question of race for North Africans and Middle Eastern people including these groups as "White/Caucasian."

After September 11, 2001, there has been a great deal of racial profiling of Arabs, Middle Eastern, Central Asian, and South Asian men throughout the United States. There were cases of mistaken identity where Indian or Sikh men were taken into custody or racially harassed as Arabs because they were brown-skinned men with beards and turbans. As such incidents were reported I reflected that in all of the years of living in the Middle East and North Africa with my family—at one point during the buildup to the Gulf

War—there was not a single unpleasant incident that we experienced as Americans. We could have been racially or culturally profiled—and perhaps those days are coming—but hospitality and curiosity prevailed over hostility.

Islamic society, with its broad geographic and cultural scope, is a multiracial grouping. This is one of the Umma's most potent features. The fact that images of Allah, of the Prophet and his family, or any other form of idolatry are strictly forbidden in Islam means that as Islam spread it did not require the convert to accept a foreign image of God as "white" or any other picture of the deity in some human form. Allah, the supreme deity, as an abstraction, could be shaped in the mind of the convert.

There are numerous religious interpretations and historical studies that deal with the matter of race in Islam and Islamic society. The Qur'an is replete with passages that reveal an all-embracing, nonracialist view of humanity, where goodness is equated with righteous conduct. A hadith refers to humans being "like the teeth of a comb" with none superior to another save in the conduct of religion.

Notwithstanding religious preference for conversion to Islam and freedom from slave status, the practice of enslavement was present in Arab society at the time of the coming of Islam and has persisted into the twentieth century, including recent revivals in the context of the civil war in Sudan that have provoked an international outcry and protest of human rights abuses. Slavery was not legally abolished in Saudi Arabia until 1962. And the status of a "free" person or "slave" probably remains a significant category in such cases as the Rwala Bedouin society, where marriage between persons of slave and free origin is impossible or strongly stigmatized. Likewise in the Sudan, where slavery was officially abolished at the turn of the twentieth century, the slave status of persons remained a viable category for decades. I vividly recall my own shock when a local district commissioner in southern Kordofan in 1971 presented to my husband and me an individual who was described as a slave among the Baggara people. Sadly, this recollection took on new meaning when Sudanese social scientists reported that slavery was revived among the Baggara and neighboring Rizeigat and Messiriya Arabs, who conducted armed militia raids against southerners in the renewed civil war after 1983 (Mahmoud and Baldo 1987).

Although neither Christianity nor Islam made decisive theological statements against slavery in their histories, in modern times Islamic jurisprudence has opposed any legacy of slavery that would adversely affect the rights of persons of alleged slave origin. In a landmark case in the Sudan in 1973, the Shari'a High Court decided that a father's effort to block the marriage of his daughter to a man alleged to be the grandson of a slave was unfounded. The father had attempted to show that the proposed bride-groom and his family's background were not of equal status to his daughter and their family, an idea known as "equality of standard in marriage" (*al-kafa'a fi al-zowaj*) in Islamic jurisprudence. After a lengthy appeals process, the High Court judges concluded that Islam recognizes the equality of all people and that "there is no preference between an Arab and a non-Arab except by his God-fearing" (Fluehr-Lobban 1987, 127–29). This case and others like it ultimately resulted in changes in the personal status law in 1991 when pedigree or genealogy was removed as a condition restricting marriage.

On the other hand, slavery existed in the time of the Prophet, and it continued throughout the great Muslim empires and into the modern period. Middle Eastern slavery was carried out for military purposes to raise and expand armies, and for domestic use in wealthy households. The practice of slavery predated Islam, and the new religion did not oppose this but accepted this reality although it recognized certain legal rights of slaves in Muslim society. According to Islamic law, a free-born Muslim cannot be enslaved; slaves were captured from non-Muslim societies that were invaded or conquered. Slaves have the legal right to inherit property and conduct business, as such effects could result from a close master/slave relationship. Manumission or the freeing of a slave is recommended in the Qur'an as an act of contrition or expiation, and emancipated slaves can marry into the families of their former masters. Perhaps the best evidence for a unique Islamic approach to slavery, conversion to Islam, and manumission is the Mamluke dynasty which ruled Egypt and Syria from the mid-thirteenth to early sixteenth centuries. The Mamlukes were military slaves—recruited as slave-soldiers from conquered lands in Central Asia, eastern Europe, and North Africa—who converted to Islam, were freed, and then came to rule. One of the most popular and widespread of stories from the Arabian peninsula is that of Antar ibn Shaddad, the son of a slave woman, whose courage and adventures have been told and retold, probably since pre-Islamic times. Bilal, a former slave from Ethiopia, was the first *muezzin* (caller of the faithful to prayer) in Islam in Mecca and a favorite of the Prophet, of whom he remarked—"Verily as I journeyed into Paradise and was mounting the stairs of God, I heard your footsteps before me" (Atterbury 1899, 81). Equality of all people before God was a principle that the Prophet exemplified.

Although the institution of slavery was not formally rejected by Islam, it denied any color or caste status to slavery and revered many distinguished Muslims irrespective of race. Slaves could be elevated by deeds, religion, or knowledge, but they could also remain in servitude. Many slaves were taken from the Sudan, Ethiopia, and Somalia. While some were ultimately incorporated into Arab society, others retained the stigmas attached to a social underclass. To a great extent this correlates with race and phenotype. Dark-skinned Nubians, other Sudanese, and Africans may experience racial bigotry when they are traveling or working in countries where the legacy of slavery is still apparent, such as in the Arab Gulf countries. The term *'abd* (slave) has both a racial and class dimension. The term *zinji* is also used to refer to "blacks," and while it carries descriptive and sometimes pejorative meaning, it lacks the specific stigma of slavery.

The Legacy of Slavery

Slavery was practiced throughout the Ottoman Empire—in Europe and Asia as well as in Africa—primarily for military and domestic use. Plantation slavery, like that in the New World, was not a feature of this system until its limited development in the nineteenth century in response to world market demand for cotton. The Ottoman Turks enslaved southeast Europeans (Circassions), tribal peoples of central Asia, and Africans from *bilad as-Sudan* (Arabic for land of the blacks). Males were enslaved as recruits for the armies of the empire, and women and children were enslaved for domestic service. The mobility of status afforded by Islam, although it should not be overstated, did permit self-emancipation for years or merit of service, and military service made male opportunities greater. Female slaves in a master's house gave birth to free children and were freed upon the death of the master. Various studies of the status of enslaved persons in Ottoman and other Muslim societies offer a complex picture of their household and community status (Marmon 1999). For example, wealthy women with other women as their slaves or retainers were confined to their homes (or harems), while the slave woman was "free" to go about town on household errands (Tucker 1984, 191). Male slaves were often trusted to carry out the personal business of their masters. On the other hand, the childlike status of enslaved humans encouraged a paternalism familiar to American patterns of slavery. The stereotype of the Nubian slave is an eastern Ottoman one, reinforced by the Orientalist painters.

From a local perspective, slavery in nineteenth-century southern Sudan was a time when "the world was spoiled," according to Dinka writer Francis Deng (1978). The warfare, raiding, and capture of humans by soldiers in the Turco-Egyptian army was justified by the fact that the ethnic groups in the south of Sudan were not Muslims, and were, therefore, fair game. The British, who emerged from centuries of involvement in the Atlantic slave trade as champions of an antislavery campaign, encouraged the idea that Islam sanctioned the trade. They used this as part of a Christian crusade to rid the Sudan of Islamic rule under the Mahdi in the late nineteenth century. Indeed,

Fig. 19. Southern Sudanese scholar Dr. David Chand at a meeting of Sudan Studies Association.

efforts by the Mahdi to bring areas of the south under Islamic control are remembered by southerners as an encounter filled with bitterness and fear of Arabs and Muslims.

Phenotypically distinct, the southerners were ready targets for racist referents, most typically and painfully the term *'abd*. The south as a region was basically left out of the first postindependence government, and successive northern governments attempted to solve the "southern problem" through an imposed Islamization. Resistance to this solution has led to a chronic state of civil war between the Muslim north and the animist and Christian south (Fluehr-Lobban 1990).

Southern Sudanese anthropologist Jok Madut Jok (2001) has explored the legacy of racism from this historical relationship. He argues that the British colonizers allied with the northern slave trading merchant elites—who had previously carried out their raids for the Turks—and that neither had a serious interest in ending slavery. The formal end to slavery that the British introduced as part of their enlightened rule nonetheless preserved the relationships that were born in this trade. This leaves the country with a cruel legacy of slavery with a strong racist cast to it that must be confronted directly and resolved before Sudanese unity is achieved.

Ironically, the term for slave, *'abd,* used by northern "Arab" Sudanese in reference to southerners is frequently applied to them in the Arab heartland. This dual consciousness has been probed deeply by northern intellectuals (Mukhtar 2003), especially for the role that the legacy of race has played in the civil war. In a comparable vein, historian Eve Troutt Powell has examined the dual consciousness of Egyptians in the colonial service who were at once inferior and subordinate to the English and in the role of "master" to the northern Sudanese over whom they were given power and jurisdiction by the European authority. Such nuanced treatment of race is a new and promising field in regional studies that has produced dissertations and edited volumes that address race directly for the first time (Powell 2001; Smith 2004; Fluehr-Lobban and Rhodes 2003).

Major Non-Arab National and Ethnic Groups

There are many non-Arab nations in the Middle East and Central Asia and numerous non-Arab ethnic groups within majority Arab nations that are often confused with Arabs because they are part of a region or nation-state associated with the predominantly Arab world. The non-Arab nations of Turkey, Iran, Pakistan, and Afghanistan have already been mentioned. Few view the Jewish state of Israel as Arab, although the Arab minority constitutes 30–40 percent of the population.

Turkey and Iran

Turkic peoples embraced Islam by the eleventh and twelfth centuries, and the Turks of Central Asia came to be among the faith's great promoters and defenders. Under Islam's banner the Seljuk Turks carried Islam west to southwest Asia where their successors, the Ottomans, conquered Constantinople in 1453. In doing so they replaced Christian Byzantium with Muslim rule, and the powerful and long-lived Ottoman Empire was born. Turkic peoples speak Turkish, a language that belongs to the Ural-Altaic family with no relationship to Semitic languages, such as Arabic.

The Ottoman Empire deserves greater attention in Western and American schools, not only for its influential role in world affairs but also for its geographical and historical breadth. From the fifteenth to the twentieth centuries Ottoman rule dominated the core of the Middle East, including the holy lands of the Hijaz; most of North Africa—including a successful invasion of the Sudan in 1820, the Balkans, and significant regions of eastern Europe. The Ottoman Empire was only defeated in World War I by the Western Alliance as a result of its siding with the Axis powers and Germany. Significantly, Palestine—along with Trans-Jordan and other key parts of the Ottoman Empire—fell to British Mandate status after the breakup of the empire in 1918, and shortly thereafter Lord Balfour opened the door to Zionist emigration into Palestine. The Ottoman Empire spread the Hanafi school of law throughout its administration, and it was famous for its millet system, which offered cultural, linguistic, and religious autonomy to its territories. The Tanzimat reforms of the nineteenth century laid the basis for land and commercial reforms that paved the way to significant "modernization," while setting the stage for reforms in Islamic family law in the twentieth century whereby polygamy was outlawed and divorce law was reformed. In some locales, Ottoman rule is recalled as harsh, especially where it actively pursued the enslavement of Africans, Europeans, and some Asians for the empire's largely slave army and for domestic servitude in the empire.

In the wake of its defeat in the 1920s, Turkey underwent a program of secular reform and open westernization. Arabic script was banned in 1924 as was the wearing of the fez, the unique symbol of Turkish rule often mistaken by Westerners as Arab because it was worn throughout the empire. Kemal Atatürk was the architect of Turkey's decisive turn toward the West and away from its Muslim neighbors, an ambiguous relationship that remains to this day. Turkey's admission to NATO in 2001 was a significant step ensuring that it takes the "right" political stands in Euro-American relations with "the East."

In the last decades of the twentieth century and the early twenty-first century, Turkey's Islamist parties, the Rifah (Welfare) Party and the Justice and Development Party (AKP) have elected members to Parliament and to national office. The rise of Islamism was not supposed to have occurred in the state with the region's most secular history; however, Islamist leaders claim that they will show the way to moderate Islamism in political practice.

Iran

Islam reached Persia in its first century, although the branch of Shi'a Islam predominated after the decisive battles within the early Muslim community. However, empire was already a strong tradition with the Persian Empire dominating the region from the sixth through fourth centuries B.C.E. including territories in central Asia, the Middle East, and Egypt. It was Alexander the Great who overthrew the empire, but Parthian and Sassanid monarchies resumed control until Arab armies defeated the last Sassanid king in 637 C.E. However, Arabic did not displace the Farsi language, and as a result Islamic faith and culture became internationalized and more refined by Iranian heritage and is perhaps best remembered in the West for the works of astronomer-poet Omar Khayyam.

The majority Shi'a Muslims revere one of the twelve Shi'a imams, Reza, who lived in Iran and whose tomb in Meshed is the holiest shrine in Iran. The

Safavid dynasty claimed descent from the prophet Muhammad and ruled from the sixteenth century, making Shi'a Islam the official religion. As rivals of the Ottoman Empire that proclaimed itself the ruler and voice of all Muslims, the Persians conducted a war of words with Sunni Islam that never came to blows.

In terms of the growing influence of the United States in the Middle East, Iran provides a good example. The declining influence of the European powers after World War II saw the concomitant rise of the United States as a global power, especially in the bipolar world of the cold war. The critical oil reserves of the Persian Gulf countries of Iran and Iraq as well as the Arabian peninsula were, of course, well known and ever under the watchful eye of Europe and the United States. A nationalist and progressive regime under Mossadegh was overthrown in 1953 in a now openly admitted CIA-led coup d'état that reinstated the Pahlavi monarchy that began the rule of Mohammed Reza Pahlavi. His rule, self-styled as the "White Revolution," embarked upon a number of reforms aimed at Westernizing Iran. Like his father, who was crowned shah in 1925, he attempted to settle nomadic peoples, institute family law reforms by decree, and limit the influence of the mullahs, local preachers, teachers, and imams whose influence was likewise judged to be "backward." A close ally of America, the shah was a huge recipient of U.S. aid. He declared himself "king of kings" in a lavish celebration that was supposed to commemorate 2,500 years of Persian history in a display of conspicuous consumption that shocked his supporters and angered many Iranians.

On the eve of the modern era's first popular Islamic revolution, in Iran in 1979, the United States believed that the shah's position was secure and no one, especially the United States, was prepared for the sustained protests that catapulted Ayatollah Ruhollah Khomeini to political power. The success of the Iranian Revolution was a shock to the West, from which, it might be argued, it has still not recovered. The mobilization of masses of Muslims can still provoke dread, linked today with the fear of terrorism. But the Iranian revolution was primarily a revolt against the corruption, scandals, and shameless indulgence of the monarchy at the expense of poor Iranians. Islam and the mullahs provided the vehicle for this mass mobilization of women and men, and the possibility of this being replicated elsewhere was also born.

Non-Arab Minority Populations

Among the minority non-Arab populations are the Nubians of Egypt and Sudan; the Berbers of Morocco, Algeria, and Tunisia; and the Kurds who occupy parts of two non-Arab states, Iran and Turkey, and one Arab nation, Iraq. Many people who identify with these ethnic groups also speak Arabic as a second language, especially if they are living in less isolated towns and cities, but they do not identify themselves as Arabs.

Nubians

The Nubians of Egypt and the Sudan present a study in contrasts, for their status as an ethnic minority differs dramatically between the two states. Nubians occupy regions in Egypt south of the first cataract at the city of Aswan and in towns and villages along the Nile south to the Sudanese border and its major Nubian settlement from Wadi Halfa south to Dongola in northern Sudan. The unique civilization of Kush centered at Meroë ruled ancient Egypt for a time during the Twenty-fifth Dynasty and then developed its own culture, religion, and written language. Kushites ruled ancient Nubia from the fifth century B.C.E. to the fourth century C.E., when Nubia's kingdoms were Christianized. Nubia remained Christian for almost another millennium, until the penetration of Islamic influences in the thirteenth through fifteenth centuries (see Adams 1984; Lobban 2003 for a more comprehensive survey of this history).

Historically Nubia acted as the corridor to Africa (although Egypt is sometimes forgotten as part of Africa). And from ancient Pharaonic times through the days of the Ottoman Turks and the British, Nubia was a place for capturing slaves; "Nubian" was even a generalized referent for slaves. The trade in Nubian slaves was primarily for domestic labor and service in the armies of the ancient Egyptians and the Ottoman Empire. But Nubians were not enslaved upon as part of the Great Atlantic slave trade of the sixteenth through nineteenth centuries, which exploited West African slave markets. The legacy of slavery has lingered in the generally inferior status that Nubians experience in Egypt, but it has not acted as a barrier to social advancement and influence in the Sudan.

In the Sudan, Nubians and other northern, riverain peoples close to them, such as the Shayqiya and Ja'aliyin, were closely aligned with the English colonial administration and assumed many of the key government posts after independence. They have constituted, in effect, Sudan's ruling elite in marked contrast to the secondary status of Nubians to the north. Nubians in Egypt are called Saeedis, a neutral reference to their southern roots, generally south of Assiut. However, Saeedi also connotes rural, not urban, and a degree of cultural backwardness, darker skin color, and lower educational levels. This often translates into unskilled or semiskilled jobs when Nubians migrate to cities in the northern part of the country. By contrast, Nubians in Sudan move easily from their villages or towns in the north to professional positions in Khartoum in government, business, or the military without stig-matization. As part of Sudan's ruling elite, they have been responsible for the continued inferior status imposed on southern Sudanese.

Nubians are united through language and custom and speak a group of languages unrelated to Arabic known as Rotana, as well as various dialects such as Mahas and Kenuz-Dongolawi, which are spoken on either side of the Egyptian/Sudanese border (Fernea and Fernea 1991, 137). One of the distinctive features of Nubian history is the early conversion to Christianity of Nubian kingdoms, lasting until the fifteenth century. These kingdoms acted as a barrier to the penetration of Islam into Nubia and further south until after their collapse. Nubian social organization was matrilineal until the penetration of Islamic influence, but even today there are remnants of matrilineal social organization that clearly contrast with strongly patrilineal Arab traditions. One of these is the well-known Nubian pattern of post-marital residence with the bride's family until after the birth of the first child. Other remnant behaviors have been documented in a study of Nubian women (Jennings 1995) in which the role of women and matrilineal ties in the economics of marriage and the financial support of the couple has been demonstrated.

Nubia is also remembered for the great disruption and relocation of people that took place when the High Dam at Aswan was opened and Nubia was flooded. An international effort was mounted to save some of the antiq-uities in Nubia, and many sociological and anthropological studies were made of the process of removal and adjustment of Nubian peoples. Kom Ombo in Egypt and Khasm al-Girba in the Sudan became the major resettle-ment areas for the displaced Nubians. This massive relocation of Nubian people in the early 1960s, ironically, established a common sense of Nubian identity and in recent decades has sparked a cultural revival, including ef-forts to develop a system of writing and literary tradition. Nubians travel freely between Egypt and the Sudan visiting relatives, but to do so they must traverse the great Lake Nasser, which was created by the Aswan High Dam, a powerful reminder of how their communities were forever changed by the demands of the nation-states of which they are part. Nubians are an ancient Nile Valley people whose destiny is shaped by Egypt and Sudan, experienc-ing discrimination or elite status depending upon their location north or south of Aswan, Nubia's cultural capital.

Berbers

The Berbers are a non-Arab, pre-Islamic people of northwest Africa who occupy the interior and remote regions of what is today Tunisia, Algeria, and Morocco, as well as parts of Libya and western Egypt, notably at Siwa oasis. As a Saharan people with a distinctive linguistic and cultural history, they initially resisted Arab and Islamic penetration as they spread westward and south into the Maghrib. The Berber language, Amazigh or Tamazigh, is Afro-Asiatic and belongs to the great Semitic family that includes also Arabic and Hebrew. Both essentially nomadic, Arabs and Berbers shared a common lifestyle in adapting to a desert environment, but this is where the resemblance between Arab and Berber ends. The term *barbarian* is derived from the Greeks' encounter with the Berbers, whose language was non-Greek and therefore, in their perception, uncivilized. As the traditional inhabitants of the western Sahara from Morocco to Siwa oasis in Egypt near the Libyan border, they have controlled both desert and mountains, in the latter case seeking refuge as much as an economic habitat. In part due to the foreign pressure to which they have been subjected, but also as a result of their non-Arab ethnicity, the culture of hospitality with frequent visiting is generally not found among Berbers.

The Arab invasions began in the seventh century of the common era and the first century of Islam, and first affected the indigenous regions along the Mediterranean coast. As the invasions continued during the next several centuries, Arabic language, culture, and the religion of Islam penetrated the interior of North Africa and spread among the local Berber peoples. The Berbers resisted this intrusion, having previously fled into mountainous regions to escape Greek and Roman domination, thus the Berbers only accepted Islam very gradually. Their matrilineal traditions were also incompatible with Arab patrilineal-patriarchal ones. A famous case of resistance to the Arab invasions was led by the Berber warrior queen, known as "al-Kahina," who held back the invaders in the Maghrib from 693–98. When the Berbers did accept Islam, many did not follow the path of the religion of the ruling Arab dynasties, but accepted Kharijite ideas that permitted removal of an unpopular or unjust imam (Hourani 1991, 39), a practice more compatible with their egalitarian traditions. Some of the largest Berber confederations, such as the Sanhaja, were strong enough to resist altogether the Arab advance, and the westernmost part of Africa remained outside of Arab control (Abu-Lughod 1980, 44).

Extensive linkages of new Arab empires crisscrossed the Sahara east from Egypt and the East, known as the Mashriq, to the Maghrib in the west of North Africa, while north and south trade routes connected the Mediterranean to the interior. In their path, Berber culture gradually absorbed a generalized Arab-Islamic culture. Typically, this did not include fluency and literacy in Arabic or the great literary, scholastic traditions associated with this. The written Berber language, known as Tifnac, was a literate tradition carried mainly by women. It could not compete successfully with Arabic, however, and increasingly those Berbers who came within the sphere of urban life became Arabic speakers (Hourani 1991, 435). Outside of urban situations, Berber dialects continue to be widely spoken in Algeria and Morocco, in parts of Tunisia, south of the historically important Arab-Islamic city of Kairouan, and as far east as Libya and Siwa oasis in Egypt. However, the governments of Morocco and Algeria have not favored the continued use of the Berber language, seeing it as a threat to the dominance of the "Arab" state. Morocco banned any official use of Tamazigh, disallowing education in the Berber language or the registration of Berber names for children. In 2001, Berber protests in Algeria against their discrimination left sixty people dead and two thousand injured. In 2002, as May elections neared, Berber leaders threatened a boycott unless their demands were met for recognition of their rights. The Algerian government then announced that Tamazight would become an official language along with Arabic (*New York Times*, March 13, 2002).

A cultural and linguistic distinctiveness among Berbers has been maintained, with unique traditions maintained by large Berber groups in Morocco and Algeria, such as the Kabyle. Certain nomadic groups, such as the Tuareg of Morocco and Mauretania, have become famous in the ethnographic literature by the custom of male veiling. Berbers maintained their language, local organization, leadership, and sense of independence even during the era of French colonialism. Colonialism kept alive the divide between Arab and Berber, and in the case of colonial Morocco, Berber-speaking regions were formally removed from the jurisdiction of Islamic law, thus enforcing a policy of separation (Eickelman 1976, 256). The colonialists were surprised by the enthusiasm with which Berber peoples took up the nationalist struggle.

Much of their literature dealing with nationalist themes and Berber identity is written in French, since an educated Berber is likely to be more literate in French than in Arabic. The modern Arabic dialect spoken in the Maghrib is distinctive as well, and this is frequently attributed to the mixture of Berber and French words with Arabic vocabulary. Cultural encounters, like the one between Berbers and Arabs, and later with the French admixture, are rarely as clear as simple cultural domination by the invader. Today Berbers struggle for their distinctive cultural identity by opposing Arabizing tactics such as the Moroccan government's official nonrecognition of Berber names. Such resistance to assimilation is common, as the example of Berber culture shows.

Armenians

Armenians are the earliest Christians who once predominated in eastern Turkey, and whose autonomous Republic of Armenia, established under Soviet rule, now borders easternmost Turkey. In the last days of the Ottoman

Empire, as it was in defeat and decline from its alliance with Germany in World War I, Armenians were expelled from Turkey because the government suspected them of aiding the invading Russian armies. Hundreds of thousands fled and many more were executed in what many claim was the twentieth century's first genocide. Armenians fled to other parts of the Middle East, to Europe, and to the United States where they have kept alive this memory of persecution, death, and exile from their homelands.

Armenian minorities can be found in Lebanon (4 percent), where they have blended in with the nearly 50 percent eastern Christian groups, in Syria (4–5 percent), and in Egypt, where they have specialized as merchants and jewelers.

Kurds

Kurdistan, the homeland of the Kurdish people, is a region that stretches from the mountain ranges of the eastern Anatolian region in Turkey to northern Iraq and northwestern Iran. The Kurdish population of about 15 million people is another example of a substantial non-Arab group forming about 20 percent of Iraq, nearly 20 percent of Turkey, and about 7 percent of Iran. Although the largest number of Kurds live in Turkey, their status was, until recently, politically unrecognized in that country. In the early 1990s, the Turkish legislature abolished laws made at the time of the founding of the Turkish republic that made it illegal to speak Kurdish in public or to publish in the language. It is now legal for Kurds to speak their indigenous language, Kurmanci, for testifying in Turkish courts. However, their military struggle for greater autonomy has been met with greater repression in recent years.

The Kurds have not fared well in Iran or Iraq either. In northern Iraq, forced Arabization of Kurds has taken place since 1970 under Saddam Hussein as president, as Kurdish resistance increased to protect their cultural, linguistic, and political autonomy. Since the 1991 Gulf War, the U.S. and British planes have created a "safe haven" under which the Kurds have erected institutions of self-governance, such as a parliament and currency, and they have benefited from the Western-controlled "oil-for-food" program.

They have been historically repressed as a non-Arab minority in Iraq and as a non-Shi'a, non-Persian group in Iran. As members of the 'Alawi Islamic sect, they have been rejected by Sunni Muslims in Turkey and Iraq. Probably, like the Armenians and Palestinians, their status was better in the past when Kurdistan was administered autonomously under the Ottoman Empire. The call for an independent Kurdistan or autonomous Kurdish regions within the states where they are found is likely to increase in the coming years.

The 'Alawi sect, to which most Kurds belong, is a branch of Shi'a Islam marked by specialized religious practices. For example, fasting takes place during twelve days of the month of Muharram as commemoration of the twelve imams, and the fast is interpreted as a ritual of mourning for the martyrs at Karbala. Differences in prayer and in the performance of the faith associated with the major Islamic holidays, such as 'Eid al-Fitr and 'Eid al-Kabir, distinguish them as outsiders.

During the 1991 Gulf War there were many news reports about the repression of the Kurds and the use of biological warfare against them because of their opposition to Saddam Hussein. Their potential importance as a source of resistance to Baghdad resurfaced in the U.S. war in Iraq in 2003. There were also renewed fears, from Turkey and the other states with Kurdish minorities, that the Kurds might use the war as an opportunity to press for an independent state. As nomadic or semisedentary people at the periphery of the political center in Baghdad, they have been left out of the sweeping economic and social changes occurring in the nation. Kurdish nationalism has been a feature of "outsider" rule of the Kurds from the time of the Ottomans, through the period of the British Mandate, and since the time of Iraqi independence in 1958. During times of tension between the nations where the Kurds are found, they have been subject to manipulation, as during the period of the Iran-Iraq War and the Gulf War. A powerful theme in Kurdish folklore is that the Kurds have no reliable friends. At the moment there are few supranational calls for Kurdish independence. Perhaps as a part of the international response to end human rights abuses levied against the Kurds, the call for an independent Kurdistan will be heard.

Continental Perspectives

In an effort to broaden the scope of this volume, surveys of Islam and Muslims in Africa, Asia, and North America are provided. However, these are only brief surveys intended to introduce the reader to Islam as a global faith and the presence of Muslims on virtually every continent.

Islam in Africa

With the core of the Islamic world originating in the Middle East, it is often forgotten that the majority of the world's Muslims are in Asia, and that Islam predominates or is strongly represented in more than two-thirds of the African continent. Besides all of North Africa, in Saharan and West African nations Muslims are the majority of the population in Gambia, Guinea, Mali, Mauritania, Senegal, Chad, and Sudan, and they form 25–50 percent of the populations of Burkina Faso, Ivory Coast, Nigeria, and Sierra Leone. In East Africa Muslims form a significant percentage of Kenya and Tanzania (27 percent), and they are a 99 percent majority in Somalia. In South Africa, after the end of apartheid, the mostly ethnic Malays and other Asians who make up the 5 percent Muslim population have used Islam to assert their common racial and religious identity.

Nigeria

Nigeria as Africa's most populous nation, at 110 million, is about half Muslim, making it, after Egypt, the largest of Africa's many Islamic countries. The overwhelming majority of Nigerian Muslims live in the northern half of the country bordering the predominantly Muslim nations of Burkina Faso, Niger, and Chad. The major Muslim ethnic groups are the Hausa and Fulani with important cities at Sokoto, Kano, Zaria, and Maiduguri. The roots of Islam in the north can be traced to the spread of Islam across the Sahara where the first Muslim kingdoms of ancient Ghana and later Mali and Songhai can be traced to the tenth through fifteenth centuries C.E. Major Muslim historical states in Nigeria were found at Zaria, Kano, Kanem, and Bornu that gave birth to great jihadist movements that spread Islam in the region. Puritanical reformist jihads such as that led by Shehu Uthman Dan Fodio between 1804 and 1812 imposed Fulani rule over the Hausa, absorbing them into one people known today as the Hausa-Fulani. The Qadiriyya Sufi brotherhood is especially strong and played a key role in this nineteenth-century movement, which also sought to purify and revive Islamic society.

These kingdoms remained intact until the present and were the perfect tools of English colonialist use of indirect rule after 1903 whereby local leaders continued to exercise power in the name of the British Crown. Islamic law and Shari'a courts were retained, and a powerful class of religious scholars perfected a version of Islamic orthodoxy. Cults labeled "superstitious," like the Bori spirit possession cult popular with women, were officially suppressed but continued underground. However, Muslim women's status following independence in education and other measures of advance has suffered in comparison with women in the southern part of Nigeria, many of whom succeeded in commercial, political, and educational enterprises.

Until recently, Nigerian Islam has been tolerant, permissive, and responsive to local custom. While the strictest seclusion of women was practiced among the Hausa, Muslim women in Nigeria have been vocal in advocating their rights based upon Islamic principles and values (Calloway and Creevy 1994, 5, 15). It is often difficult to differentiate between Muslim and non-

Muslim women in Nigeria apart from regional identity and names, since women's clothing, including brightly colored long dresses and head wraps, is part of national culture. This is a positive feature of Nigerian culture and unlike Muslim majority/minority relations elsewhere.

Muslims in Nigeria are often pitted politically against the majority ethnic groups of the south, the Yorubas and Igbos. The capital city of Lagos in the predominantly Christian and animist south, Nigeria's largest city, contains a sizable Muslim minority population. Although a political balance has been established among Muslim, Christian, and animist elements and a number of Nigeria's military leaders have been Muslim, religious-ethnic tensions have spilled over into violent conflict over the past decade. Islam and Christianity have peacefully coexisted for over a century in Nigeria, blending with a common background mixing animism and ancestor worship with these great world religions. However, tensions have mounted with the rise of political Islam. Between 2000 and 2002, all twelve northern Nigerian states made Shari'a state law, imposing the harshest penalties of the amputation of limbs for theft and stoning for adultery. Several stoning cases have attracted the attention of international human rights groups. Some charge that the Shari'a was imposed to target the enemies of the state's ruling elite in Lagos, while others claim that Islamic law has improved life with the closing of bars, gambling houses, and brothels. The Christian minority fears the political as well as cultural dominance of the Muslims. Although the federalism of the Nigerian constitution allowed local autonomy and thus the institution of Shari'a, this did not become widespread until President Obasanjo was elected in 1999, ending fifteen years of military dictatorship.

A federal republic since independence in 1960, its major regions have traditionally been well balanced in terms of political power and religion, which has been viewed as a private matter. Nigeria's wave of Islamism rising over the past two decades has resulted in Muslim activists having Shari'a made provincial law in northern regional governments. Beginning in Zamfara in the far north and spreading south to the midland regions with mixed Christian and Muslim communities, such as in Katsina and Jos, intercommunal violence has resulted in attacks on churches and mosques and in some cases great loss of life. Muslim/Christian fighting erupted in Kano in the north in the wake of the U.S. war in Afghanistan in 2001 which Nigerian Islamists were protesting.

A political crisis over stoning sentences that were handed down against northern Muslims—especially the case of Amina Lawal, whose sentence was to be carried out after she had weaned her baby—led to an international boycott of the 2002 Miss World Pageant, which was to be held in Lagos but was moved to London in response to the outcry.

Swahili Culture of East Africa: Lamu Island, Kenya

Swahili culture and language dominates coastal East Africa, where an Islamic society developed that is a blend of Bantu African culture and Omani and south Arabian peoples. Swahili culture took shape between the thirteenth and fifteenth centuries, plying a trade in slaves and ivory as well as in the exotic spices of cinnamon and cloves in their dhows along the trade winds of the Indian Ocean. It may be best known to the world through the island of Zanzibar, a center of the trade. The Swahili language is heavily influenced by Arabic and is the national language of Kenya and Tanzania; it is widely spoken throughout coastal east Africa and Uganda. Though strongly associated with the spread of Islam, it is not exclusively spoken by Muslims.

The Swahili language became popular in the United States during the rise of the Black Power movement of the 1960s and 1970s as a symbol of Africa. Maulana Karenga used Swahili east African and Islamic values and principles to develop the Afrocentric rites of Kwanzaa now widely celebrated by African Americans and others as an alternative or an addition to Christmas. The principles of Kwanzaa are taken directly from the Swahili language and Islamic culture of east Africa. These include Umoja (unity), Kujichagulia (self-determination), Ujima (collective work and responsibility), Ujamaa (cooperative economic unity), Nia (purpose), Kuumba (creativity), and Imani (faith).

Mombasa, a major port city in Kenya, still has a thriving dhow trade along the ancient Indian Ocean routes. Extant Swahili communities such as that on the island of Lamu, which I visited in 1996, maintain a lifestyle similar to that established in the sixteenth century. The narrow streets, able to accommodate only two persons walking side by side or a single donkey, prohibit vehicular traffic. Close-knit families with centuries of shared economic and human relations living in closely constructed homes and communities weave the social fabric of the island together in a web of family, religious, and economic ties. The only strangers on the island are the European tourists who arrive in increasing numbers for the beaches and magnificent snorkeling offshore in the rich marine diversity of the Indian Ocean. They have little or no contact with the Lamu locals.

Lamu is exclusively Muslim and almost evenly divided between Sunni and Shi'a Islam with separate mosques and Qur'anic schools (*madrasas*), which are mainly attended by boys. Sufi orders are prevalent in both communities, and when I visited I witnessed a *dhikr* for a local holy man, Sheikh Habib Swela, who had died about twenty years earlier and whose veneration was in its early stages of development. The seclusion of women is widely practiced, and the women of Lamu appear in public fully veiled. As with other conservative Muslim societies, women in the confines of homes are strong figures and active preservers of Lamu's unique culture. Others migrate to Kenya's major cities or to the United States to seek higher education, as with the happy occasion when I had a student from Lamu in my class the year of her graduation.

Islam in Asia

The majority of the world's 1.2 billion Muslims live in Asia. Islam emerged in Asia, in the Hijaz in its southwestern corner, the Arabian peninsula, and spread to east and central Asia as well as to the Maghrib in the west in the first century after its introduction. The three nations with the largest number of Muslims are in Asia: Indonesia (population of over 215 million), Pakistan (141 million), and India (over 1 billion), with 270 million Muslims. Distinctive in culture as well as architecture, Islam in Asia represents both the face of universal Islam and a myriad different historical, linguistic, and national experiences with Islamic history and practice. With clear links to the Middle East, Islam in Asia took on distinctive cultural expression through language and subsequent political developments.

Central Asia

Islam spread to central Asia with the first Muslim dynasty, the Umayyads, and later the Abbasids as rulers of the early Muslim caliphates who brought the regions of Uzbekistan, Kazakhstan, Tajikistan, Kyrgyzstan, and Azerbaijan into the realm of Islam (Dar al-Islam). The growth of Islam was reinforced by the pilgrimage routes that flourished along trade routes and brought growing numbers of Muslims into continuous contact with non-Muslims (Eickelman and Piscatori 1990). The Muslim population of Central Asia and the Caucasus is estimated at 55 million (Eickelman 2001, 13). That dramatic first century of Islam brought the growing Muslim nation into conflict with the Chinese superpower competing for the control of central Asia, and Afghanistan came under Muslim rule. The Arabs stayed in Asia for two centuries and left a lasting imprint not only of the faith of Islam but of Arabic language and its writing system. Samarkand became a cultural and scientific center as well as a famed religious city. Its most famous mosque, Bibi Khanum, named for ruler Timur's favorite wife, is of legendary beauty and was restored after the end of Soviet rule in Uzbekistan. Soviet rule in these regions for most of the twentieth century had a dramatic impact—from forced unveilings of Muslim women in central Asia by politically correct communists bent upon "liberating" women in the East to the closing of all but the most historically significant mosques, such as in Samarkand, and destruction of others to forbid open worship or observance of the five pillars by Muslims. Russification, practiced in all of the Soviet Republics, meant the substitution of the Cyrillic alphabet for Arabic writing. Revival of Islam and Muslim practice in the post-Soviet era and conversion back to Arabic or Latin was only one of many symbolic changes from Soviet rule (Eickelman 2001, 4).

Afghanistan

Like Iran and Turkey, Afghanistan is not an Arab country. America learned this after September 11, 2001. However, it is a Muslim nation. Afghanis are distinguished by ethnicity, language, and religion as well as by sociopolitical structure. Pashtuns make up 40–50 percent; Tajiks, Hazaras, and Uzbeks are ethnic minorities among the nation's 20 million people. Afghanistan's mountainous terrain and lack of infrastructure have kept long-standing tribal and social institutions unchanged. Among Pashtuns, Turkmens, and Uzbeks, essentially tribal political structures still play an important role, emphasizing descent from a common ancestor. Were it not for the rise of the Taliban and its close association with Osama bin Laden, Afghanistan would have remained obscure in the West, known better as a source of drugs than for its politics.

The rise of Pashtuns to political control of Afghanistan coincided with the "modernizer" kings of the Musahiban dynasty such as Nadir Khan (1929–33) and his successors, Zahir Shah (1933–73) and Daud Khan (1973–78), who attempted to centralize basic institutions in an effort to build a nation. The majority of non-Pashtun Afghans rejected the idea that Afghani identity would be equated with being Pashtun. Various Muslim factions, later known as the mujahideen (those who struggle in the name of religion), emphasized the unity of the Muslim Umma, including Sunni and Shi'a Afghanis. In April 1992, the Taliban overthrew the Soviet-backed regime. It is important to recall that the United States materially and politically backed these mujahideen, Osama bin Laden among them, while they were fighting the communists in Kabul.

Despite efforts by the first post-Soviet government to ensure that the Islamic state would be equitable and rejecting any privilege or discrimination based on race, ethnic, tribal, or linguistic differences, civil war ensued. It was this civil war among the mujahideen factions that brought about the dominance of the Pashtuns over the Uzbeks and Hazaras and brought them to power, as Pashtuns dominated the Taliban movement. *Taliban* is the Arabic word for "students," as many of the Pashtun Islamists had been students together in the Islamic religious madrasas in Pakistan while the resistance to Soviet rule was being waged. Under the Taliban, Afghanistan experienced one of the most severe cases of Islamic extremism. Taliban rule was harsh against all whom it judged to be contrary to its ideal of Muslim behavior, interpreted by the Taliban scholars in the most conservative manner, unlike the majority of the world's Islamic nations. The Taliban punished women for appearing in public without their burqas or for working outside the home as teachers or doctors, persecuted alleged homosexuals and fornicators, carried out stoning penalties for adultery, prevented any creative musical or artistic activity that was not Islamic calligraphy or art, and abolished television and cinema as irreligious images. International attention was drawn to this extreme view that any statues or "idols" were forbidden when the Taliban in 1991 dynamited two 1,500-year-old colossal statues of the Buddha in the Bamiyan Valley.

After the attacks on September 11, 2001, with the links to al-Qaeda that held a base through the alliance of Osama bin Laden and Mullah Omar, leader of the Taliban, the United States invaded Afghanistan, secured control over Kabul, and installed Ahmad Karzai as president. But civil war and the old reign of the warlords resumed. The Northern Alliance backed by the United States was made up primarily of non-Pashtuns, thus the ethnic rivalry between Pashtun and non-Pashtun in Afghanistan was reinforced.

Some ethnic markers of Pashtun dominance remain. Horsemanship and horse culture remains a strong marker of Pashtun masculinity, defined as courage, competition, and host generosity in the national sport of "buzkashi" (Azoy 2003, 11). The game is played with a goat or calf carcass with which riders vie for control, serving as a metaphor for political competition. However, to Westerners, buzkashi reveals the wild, fierce, and primitive nature of the Afghanis. The Soviet occupation of Afghanistan and resistance to it have been described as "the real buzkashi." Indeed, the game was banned by the Soviets as "backward," and after the Taliban took power it was banned again with the argument that horses should be preserved for "God's work," that is jihad, but eventually the Taliban acknowledged the national rather than irreligious essence of this sport.

South and East Asia

Pakistan, India, and Bangladesh

Nearly half of the world's Muslims live in south and southeast Asia. The multiple faces of Asian Islam help to decentralize the stereotypical view that Islam is concentrated in the Middle East. The approximate 250 million Middle Eastern Muslims constitute less than a quarter of world Islam. India and Pakistan are nuclear powers, while Indonesia and Malaysia are key economic and political powers in east Asia.

Pakistan was created in 1947 in the breakup of British colonial India in order to solve the problem of interreligious conflicts between Hindus and Muslims. Colonial "West Pakistan" became independent Pakistan, and East Pakistan became Bangladesh later, in 1971. With a population of 141 million that is 97 percent Muslim, it is among the largest of the Islamic nations. The majority are Sunni Muslims; however, Shi'a Muslims form 20 percent of the population.

The Turks initially spread Islam through the Khyber Pass across the Indus and Ganges plains, making Islam the dominant religion of Pakistan and northern India. Together Pakistan and India contain more Muslims than in the core of the Middle East, with nearly 20 percent of India's 1 billion people being Muslim. Later Pathan invasions from Afghanistan from the eighth to the thirteenth centuries continued the infusion of Muslims, and Islam came to prevail in Pakistan. From Kabul through the Khyber Pass to Peshawar and Islamabad, Islam established itself among the highest geographical locales close to the Himalayas. The Pathans in 1313 brought Islam to Kashmir in the Himalayas, and Indian Sultan Sikander made it a Muslim state in the fourteenth century.

The Moghul dynasty, founded by Babur, a descendant of the great central Asian leaders Timur and Genghis Khan, became the symbol of Indian Islamic empire from the fifteenth to the nineteenth centuries. Under the sultans of Delhi, Muslims and Hindus deeply influenced each other, synthesizing the fabled Moghul civilization. Its best known architectural achievement, the Taj Mahal, was built for Queen Mumtaz Mahal, wife of Shah Jahan. It remains a symbol and reminder of the grandeur of this Indian Muslim civilization.

By the fourteenth century Islam reached as far south in India as Bombay, Hyderabad, and Goa, also spread by the Moghuls. The British ousted the Moghuls in 1858 at the beginning of their vast colonial enterprise, adopting a policy of indirect rule that left intact certain nonpolitical Muslim institutions and Islamic family law. Also, a strong Sufi influence survived and prevailed under indirect rule. At the end of British rule, Muslim/Hindu tensions about the future of a postindependence Indian state led to partition being the only viable solution. The Islamic Republic of Pakistan was created in 1947 and that of Bangladesh (East Pakistan) was formed in 1971.

Bangladesh has a population of 129 million who are mainly Bengali. There is a 10 percent Hindu minority. It is notable that Bangladesh has had several women as heads of state, the last two being Khalida Zia and Sheikha Hassina.

Indonesia and Malaysia

It surprises many new to the study of Islam that the majority of world Muslims live in Asia. The state with the largest Muslim population is Indonesia, at more than 215 million citizens, with Malaysia and the Philippines having significant Muslim populations. Together the populations of Indonesia and Malaysia equal the number of Muslims in the Middle East, yet this core of southeast Asian Islam has been viewed as outside the heartland of the Middle Eastern centers of Islam and Muslims. The Malay peninsula, Sumatra, and Java as well as other regions of the archipelago constitute the core of this center of Asian Islam.

Islam entered coastal Sumatra and other parts of Indonesia by way of the straits of Malacca beginning around the thirteenth century. From Sumatra Islam spread to Java and then to other areas of the Indonesian archipelago. Javanese are the largest ethnic group at 70 percent.

Malaysia has been described as the crossroads of Asia where goods and ideas from the Middle East, India, and China were widely exchanged during a period of vibrant trade stretching from the fifteenth to eighteenth centuries (which in turn were built upon trade patterns dating back some two thousand years). It is an ethnic mosaic comprised of Malays—just over half the population who are Muslim—ethnic Chinese who constitute about a quarter of the population, Indians (some of whom are Muslim), Eurasians, and others who make up the remainder of the population who are generally non-Muslim (Peletz 2002, 6).

Malaysia and other south Asian Muslim societies are unique in global Islam in that they have retained patterns of matrilineal descent and inheritance despite the notable patriarchal traditions associated with Islam and its institutions. Women, in many respects, are the economic centers, while male roles within matrilineal families have been characterized by Michael Peletz as relatively weak, being "neither reasonable nor responsible" (1995).

Malays are Sunni Muslims who formally follow the Shafi'i school of Islamic jurisprudence, but they also have preserved significant areas of *adat,* or custom, much of which predates Islamic influence in the area. As with many of the Muslim societies under review here, Malaysia was colonized by Great Britain, in stages, beginning in the late eighteenth century, although the period of high colonialism began in the 1870s. The British helped formalize and in some cases actually introduced Islamic courts in areas under its jurisdiction retaining essential elements of Islamic law administered by local Muslim judges but relegating Islamic law to family and personal status matters, while administering English law in more serious matters of criminal and civil law. "Kadi-justice," or "Mohammedan law," came to be regarded widely by the English and Europeans as capricious, without precedent, and untrustworthy (Peletz 2002, 49).

Much of the same historical pattern described for Malaysia applies to Singapore and Indonesia as well.

Fig. 20. Malaysian children at Friday prayers in Kelantan, Malaysia. Courtesy of Michael Peletz and Susan Henry.

China and the Silk Road

Islam reached into China in Xinjiang at Kahsgar and Urumqi and as far east as Xian through the Silk Road that linked Europe with the lands far to its east and the riches of China. This longest of the world's trade routes stretched over seven thousand miles between the two most important cities of Asia, Baghdad and Ch'ang-an (now Xian). Indeed, Baghdad with a population of 1.5 million and Ch'ang-an at 1–2 million were the two largest cities of the world in the eighth through tenth centuries, and their leaders, the Abbasid caliph and the T'ang emperor, were the two most powerful on earth. Both

Fig. 21. A mosque in Ho Chi Minh City, Vietnam.

ruled ethnically heterogeneous populations—Arabs, Jews, Persians, and Turks in Baghdad, and Uighurs, Turks, Arabs, Persians, and Kindus in Ch'ang-an. This is an important historical reminder, as the United States stands as the sole superpower, when 1,200 years ago the western powers were weak and not global contenders, and the United States was not to become a state for a millennium.

The spread of Islam to the east depended upon sea trade routes, much as the spread of Islam in Africa followed trans-Saharan trade routes. Besides the Silk Trade routes, Islam also entered China by way of its trading ports on the South China Sea.

The majority of China's 16 million Muslims are of Turkic extraction living in Xinjiang province. Their numbers in an overall Chinese population of over 1 billion makes them a distinct minority community. The other Chinese Muslims are Hui, ethnic Chinese who have intermarried with Muslim immigrants. They live in oases in central and western China along the old Silk Road routes. These communities date from the tenth century.

In the twentieth century, Muslim Chinese were forced to practice their faith discreetly, especially after the advent of the communist era and the Maoist Cultural Revolution. Between 1966 and 1971, most mosques were destroyed or closed. After the death of Mao, Chinese Muslims were once again able to travel to make the hajj, and mosques and religious schools were reopened.

Social Class in Ideology and Practice

While Islamic and Arab society are egalitarian in fundamental ideology of religion and family and community life, hierarchical differences have been evident since the earliest days of state and empire. Travel to any major metropolis in the Middle East reveals great discrepancies between rich and poor, even observed at the most superficial level. Egyptian Nobel laureate Naguib Mahfouz brought international attention to the conditions of urban life in Cairo, especially in his classic *Midaq Alley*. The maintenance of the egalitarian ethos, like the myth of democracy in America, is a powerful ideology that can be drawn upon to mobilize masses of people and to shape everyday interactions. But the historical record is filled with evidence that class differences have been pronounced in every aspect of urban and rural life.

Large urban-based families engaged in local and international commerce comprised the nascent bourgeoisie of the medieval Muslim state. Feudal lords governed every aspect of the economy and society of the peasants they controlled. They became rich and powerful and used the traditional ideology of *nasab* to suggest a genealogical connection to their rule and influence. The European powers were only too happy to use these indigenous notables to assist in their own economic and political control of their colonies. With independence, these powerful families were only partly diminished by land reforms and government regulations that followed popular control of national resources. In Egypt and other countries that underwent significant land reform, the reformer, Gamal Abdel Nasser, became a hero to the peasants. However, in other cases, such as the Sudan, the notables themselves came to power and nationalized the apparatus of government without altering the traditional centers of power and wealth.

The oil industry in countries of the Arabian peninsula and the Persian Gulf has expanded the economic gap with the non-oil-producing countries, which have become labor-exporting countries. The last decades of the twentieth century witnessed the opening up of Middle Eastern economies to largely unregulated Western investment, what the Egyptians called *infitah*. The gap between rich and poor within nations has become as dramatic as the gap between rich and poor states in the Middle East. The factor of class difference has become more evident as the focus has shifted from outside economic control to domestic class differentiation.

The major modern economic contradiction in the Arab Middle East has been the extraordinary wealth generated by the oil-producing countries and the inability of dominantly agrarian economies elsewhere to compete. In response, these capital-poor countries have devised economic strategies that were supposed to open up local economies to compensate for being left out of the oil boom. Egypt, Sudan, Jordan, Syria, former North Yemen, and Tunisia have all followed economic policies that can be considered infitah. These policies have included measures that relax controls over the economy to facilitate the entrance of foreign, Western capital, the productive investment of domestic capital, and the export of domestic labor to the oil-producing or former colonial countries. The results have been less than dramatic,

Fig. 22. Kentucky Fried Chicken restaurant in Cairo.

for the loosely regulated foreign investments tend to stifle rather than stimulate indigenous capital. Thus the economic growth is largely foreign and extractive rather than of the type which develops an infrastructure and lays the base for long-term, sustainable development.

Domestic labor is not mobilized for long-term projects and is valuable primarily because it is cheap. However, with the rising costs of commodities due to the artificial injection of wealth into the local economy and emphasis on consumer items, poorly paid local workers can no longer afford the high cost of living in their own countries. Domestic skilled laborers must migrate elsewhere for employment, usually to the Arabian peninsula or to oil-rich countries of the Persian Gulf, less often to Europe and the United States. In turn, the domestic economy has become increasingly dependent on the remittances of workers abroad. During the economic boom of the 1980s in oil production, the economies of poorer countries were buoyed by these workers' remittances, in Egypt, accounting for about one-fifth of its GNP. But with the economic downturn of the late twentieth century, local economies have suffered both the return of workers who are not easily absorbed into the domestic economy and the loss of their remittances.

Globalization and the Effects of Large-Scale Labor Migration

The ripple effect of this regional imbalance between capital-producing and labor-exporting nations is felt in virtually every city, town, and village in the region. The oil-rich countries, with acute labor shortages for their expanding economies, are able to employ schoolteachers and university professors, as well as domestics, car drivers, and other service personnel from all over the Arab and Islamic world. Saudi Arabia's working class is mostly foreign, including large numbers of Yemenis, Egyptians, Sudanese, and Muslim workers from non-Arab countries such as Malaysia and Pakistan. Emigration to Saudi Arabia, Kuwait, or other oil-rich countries, in the sense of long-term residence and eventual citizenship, is out of the question due to tight regulation of foreign workers. The overflow may choose Europe and America as destinations for economic relief where they usually enter these countries illegally and become super-exploited, undocumented workers. Since September 11, 2001, illegal immigrants to the United States from the Middle East have become more vulnerable for expulsion.

The outflow of semiskilled and skilled labor from the poorer Muslim and Arab countries usually means the loss of that nation's youngest and most productive workers. The initial drain came from the cities of the poorer countries, but eventually a continuous process of rural to urban labor migration within the country was carried forward to its logical extension. Towns and villages have been drained of agricultural workers, and many villages have been all but abandoned to women, the very old and the very young. There is even a slight increase in the number of women workers migrating from the rural areas to the city and then to the labor-importing countries, even though culturally this is risky and unacceptable.

Some young men intend to work abroad only long enough to earn enough money to marry and settle down at home. However, the ever-weakening local economies cannot reabsorb workers accustomed to higher wages and certain levels of food and commodity consumption. Married men working outside of their countries are nevertheless still responsible for the support of their families, according to Islamic law, and those who fail to do so may find a court case against them by their wives. There has been a sharp increase in nonsupport cases during this period of massive expatriate labor migration. The Shari'a courts, with a high responsibility to the Umma, cooperate internationally to litigate such cases. A summons can be issued in Cairo or Khartoum and be received in Jidda, where it is delivered to the accused party, in this case a husband and father who is not supporting his family.

Relations with Westerners

There are a number of indigenous categories in Islam and Arab society that reflect conceptions about "the other," in this case especially the Western outsider. There are, of course, numerous examples of how Arabs and Muslims describe their own "others"—Sudanese concepts of Egyptians and vice versa; how Saudis view Malaysian Muslims, and so forth; but since the intended audience for this work is Western and American, the focus is on Muslim and Arab views of Westerners.

The main word for foreigner, meaning Westerner, is *al-gharib*, coming from the root meaning "from the West" but also connoting that which is strange or foreign. The term could be compared favorably to our use of "the East," the Orient, to mean the strange and exotic. "Orientals" for the West are both Near Eastern and Far Eastern peoples, reflecting a Eurocentric point of view where the "East" is defined in relation to being "near" or "far" from the West. Orientalism is the study of the East by the West.

Al-ajnabi is the term used for foreigner in modern standard Arabic. Referents that stem directly from colonial contact include *khawaja* for a European or white person, probably begun in Ottoman Turkish times to indicate a foreign ruler or person of wealth and power, and carried forward into European colonial times with similar meaning. The term *faranj* was applied to the French foreign colonial and commercial presence in the Levant.

All of these terms are in active use in the Arab world today, and each has its own distinctive secular historical context. From the point of view of Islam, the world is historically divided into Muslim and non-Muslim, the *Dar al-Islam* (the abode of peace) and *Dar al-Harb* (the place of war). Originally concepts in the early decades of the faith that divided regions that had embraced Islam by will or force from those that could be subject to jihad for the spread of the religion, this division has been invoked by Islamists to justify holy war against the West and has been criticized by liberal Muslim thinkers such as Muhammad Sa'id al-'Ashmawy, who sees the revival of this old division as dangerous for the tense and misunderstood relations between Westerners and Muslims today (1998). Appropriate to the early centuries of Islam as it was spreading more through conquest than by trade, this was an accurate division of the world into Muslim and non-Muslim. Decades of Western colonial rule placed most Islamic societies in a defensive position, where the struggle was one of maintaining the essentials of Islam in the face of foreign rule and economic control. The contemporary jihadist call to establish or regain Islamic ascendancy recalls this division of the world into the place of Islam and peace and the place of war.

Vigorous nationalist movements were witnessed in every British and French colony, but soon after independence the local politicians and merchants almost invariably welcomed foreigners' return as guests in the new nations. Americans, lacking the particular history of a colonial relationship, nevertheless have been treated more or less in the same category as former colonialists and therefore as powerful foreigners. As the United States assumed the leadership of the West after World War II, the power or motive of some individual Americans may have been misinterpreted. When my husband, Richard, and I first went to the Sudan, some acquaintances joked that the CIA was becoming even more sophisticated, sending nice young Americans to learn colloquial Arabic in order to be better spies on the people.

While Americans and Europeans historically were not distinguished except by the more cosmopolitan sectors of society, African Americans have had a different experience than Euro-Americans. Often taken for North African or Arab, they may be approached as a fellow countryperson, until the first impression is corrected. Many Arabs and Africans are interested in the historical experience and contemporary status of African Americans in the United States and may include black Americans with other third world peoples, but in nearly every case blacks are distinguished from other Americans.

Westerners may be thought of in stereotypical ways, as the West stereotypes Muslims and Arabs. Western life is generalized as being of high standard, and the idea of poor people in these wealthy countries may be challenging to communicate. Whiskey drinking is thought to be common for

Western men (perhaps a holdover from colonial times), while Western women may be considered to be of looser morals, like the women portrayed in Hollywood films. Both sexes are seen as living the good life, preferring nightclubs to more serious activities. The "Wild West" image of the cowboy has taken root whereby American society is thought to be violent and dangerous; this was reinforced by the presidencies of Texans George Bush and George W. Bush. With sexuality less regulated and sexual relations easily accessible, Western society is generally viewed as decadent. Women's relatively greater freedom in this respect is not necessarily envied. Within an Islamic framework, Western women are seen as unprotected and therefore easy prey for sexual exploitation. The Western family is a particular target for Islamist propaganda that exhorts Muslim activists not to mimic Western values. The high rate of divorce in the West and the growing number of single-parent families, usually headed by women, are viewed as examples of women's vulnerable condition. The drug problem and the prevalence of AIDS and other sexually transmitted diseases are well publicized with the conclusion often reached that Western society is out of control. It is with fear and trepidation that sons are sent to the West to study, and daughters are rarely permitted to study abroad. To a great extent, only dire circumstances, such as enforced exile due to repressive regimes, bring significant numbers of women as migrants to the West. Women are not usually economic migrants.

Western education, however, is admired. Young people leave their countries to study in the technical areas because the technological advancement of the West is much admired. Students are encouraged to study the physical and biological sciences, engineering, medicine, and computer technology in Europe and the United States. It is hoped that they will return home to utilize these skills in the development and welfare of their countries. This is not always the case, for the temptations of the West are powerful, in terms of a comfortable material life free from the traditional responsibilities to the extended family. Some young men stay for an extended period of time to complete their studies; they enjoy the relatively greater freedom possible in the West, but then return home to marry. Others remain in the West, marry, and adapt to cultural and religious differences.

Apart from the unusual contact with visitors, like anthropologists or other academics who have come to stay for extended visits, most foreigners conducting business in the Muslim areas of the Middle East fall into the category of either tourists or governmental and nongovernmental professionals, such as diplomats or aid workers. The tourists are readily identifiable by their national costume and travel gear. In most places and situations they are welcomed with traditional Arab hospitality. There are a few exceptions to this general rule. Visits to the interior of mosques are generally not permitted in the Maghrib and have been curtailed in places where Islamist activism has been a feature of local politics. But such visits are welcomed in Egypt, Syria, and Turkey, for example, where some of the most beautiful examples of Islamic architecture are found. The normal hospitality found throughout the region is compromised by the European custom of nude sunbathing and nude swimming, which is found throughout the northern rim of the Mediterranean but is not acceptable in the Muslim southern Mediterranean. Some Europeans, apparently oblivious to the fact that they are visiting a Muslim country, will visit the southern Mediterranean public beaches and dress (or undress) as though they were visiting the Côte d'Azure. In Tunisia and in parts of Muslim East Africa, such as Zanzibar and Lamu, where some of the most beautiful beaches can be found and where tourism is officially encouraged, many Muslims who are offended by open nudity blame their government rather than the visitors for permitting the practice. Lacking this custom at home, Americans are not guilty of this cultural offense, but they are also less likely to travel to these areas simply for the beaches because they prefer the Caribbean, which is closer.

Of the Western professionals resident or visiting the region, there is likely to be more contact with the businessman than the diplomat, whose range of public activities may be somewhat circumscribed. It is the unusual diplomat or spouse who involves himself or herself with the social life of the host country, but those who do so are much admired. American diplomats trained for work in Arab-Muslim countries in recent years are generally well prepared in language and cultural areas, such that public events as might be sponsored by the American Cultural Center can be conducted by them in the Arabic language.

The Western journalists or businessmen, most often lacking sufficient language training, use English to conduct their business. To be effective, they need to become culturally sensitive to develop their relationships. Men interact best with other men and should expect evening engagements not to include the wife of the colleague, unless the invitation is to the man's home. Even at home, in more conservative contexts, the wife may make only a perfunctory appearance, or none at all. Western women, as business representatives or journalists, will do their best work interviewing or conducting business with other women. However, it is likely that their local contacts are men. Avoiding appointments at night or in isolated places reduces the ambiguity and possible misinterpretation of Western/Middle Eastern male/female relations.

Recalling Arab and Islamic values of hospitality and generosity, it is imperative that the host pay the bill, for example, after a meeting at a restaurant. Despite insistence of intent to pay or share the bill as is the Western style, it is shameful to permit the guest to pay even part of a bill. The Westerner must permit the Arab-Muslim host to display his generosity when he is the guest; Dutch treat arrangements are inappropriate and are a Western solution to this awkward problem. Multiple meetings may also be necessary in order to accomplish the task at hand, so the Westerner should gauge the length of stay accordingly. Also, typically, the work day often ends earlier than in the West, so morning meetings are better than afternoons. Arab and Muslim etiquette prevents a person from saying no directly, so picking up on nuance of meaning is important, even when the language of communication is English. Unsophisticated Westerners may interpret the indirect no as slyness or the possibility of a deferred decision, but in this case persistence usually will not pay off.

Western notions of time and of being on time may have to be adjusted in order to allay frustration. Arab and Middle Eastern society moves at a slower, more socially inclusive pace. One is never in such a hurry that there is no time to stop and chat with a neighbor or associate. Also, telephones, public transportation, and other means of communication and getting about may not be as efficient as the Westerner expects, so patience is also an asset. Allowing a half-hour or more to the appointed time may still be within a local definition of being on time, so the experienced Westerner may add this amount of time to an appointment and arrive just as his or her guest arrives. As a more relaxed relationship develops, different concepts of time can be discussed and joked about, such as "Is that 10 o'clock Western or Eastern time?" The Sudanese refer to Western time as appearing on the hour, *'ala shoka,* meaning, "as on the prong of the fork."

Relations with the United States after September 11, 2001

The shock that the United States felt on September 11, 2001, was felt around the world. Our daughter Nichola was studying at the American University in Cairo at the time of the attacks on the World Trade Center and the Pentagon. She remained in Egypt for four months thereafter, and my husband and I led two tours in Egypt within months. It is a grave error to think that the Arab and Muslim world rejoiced at the success of the terrorist acts against America. It is another kind of denial of their humanity to believe so strongly that the deaths of Americans were met with overt demonstrations of happiness throughout the Muslim world. While the U.S. media focused on these kinds of reactions in the region, far more common were reactions of sadness and empathy, of anxiety and fear of U.S. retaliation. Our daughter reported many expressions of sympathy made to her by Egyptians accompanied by frank discussions of U.S. policies in the Israeli/Palestinian conflict and in the

Gulf, including the lengthy U.S. boycott of Iraq. Her own thinking on these matters deepened as her perspective became more complex through an extended dialogue with friends. Our own discussions with Egyptians from many walks of life, in Arabic and in English, only four months after the attacks, revealed this same sympathy for the U.S. losses that inevitably led to questions about U.S. policies. Chief among their concerns was the imbalanced support of Israel to the long-term detriment of the Palestinian people, to whom they believe America is indifferent. This visit took place during some of the bloodiest days of the second intifada, and many people asked me how Americans could not be moved by seeing the daily suffering of the Palestinians on television. I remarked that television coverage of the conflict differs in our respective parts of the world—their coverage of the Palestinians may be greater, while U.S. coverage of Israel may be greater. There has been little or no U.S. media interest in the effects of the boycott of Iraq, which has harmed civilians far more than the Iraqi military or Saddam Hussein.

There is widespread belief that America is hostile to Islam and to Muslims. An American, like myself, with a good command of spoken Arabic and an understanding of Islam is often met with disbelief, and my abilities are praised beyond real achievement. Anticipating a surprised reaction, I took a supply of the new 'Eid Mubarak (Blessed Holiday) stamps that the U.S. Post Office issued for the 2001–2002 Muslim holiday season celebrating the 'Eid al-Fitr that fell around the time of Christmas and Chanukah. To its credit, the Post Office had decided to issue this stamp before September 11; however, its reception was not especially popular. Showing this stamp and offering it as a gift to Egyptians invariably resulted in their immense surprise and immediate pleasure at this official acknowledgment of Islam and Muslim holidays in the United States.

In the wake of September 11, American specialists on the Middle East and Islam received many invitations to speak for the media and at public gatherings. These included local and national radio, television, journal, and newspaper interviews, as well as guest lectures at universities, public libraries, community groups, and churches. Almost invariably the inspiration for the invitation came from a desire to know more, to fill in some of the missing pieces that many Americans believe have been left out of their education and exposure to the Middle East and Islamic worlds. While the discussion was often emotional and passionate with a wide range of points of view expressed from diverse voices, the exchange often ended with a frank recognition of American ignorance of the region. It was also often agreed that this is no longer tenable for future informed decision making as citizens and as a government.

I also continued visiting local mosques with my students. Other community groups, such as the local Committee for the Humanities, followed national initiatives to promote programs for greater cultural awareness of Islam and the Muslims around us. They, too, conducted visits to local mosques whose imams opened the doors to this interest in greater public understanding of Islam and Muslims. About twenty-five of my students were delighted by one visit for Friday prayers that the imam devoted his sermon to their having paid a visit, emphasizing the need for the Muslim and non-Muslim communities to reach out to one another. Citing a familiar passage from the Qur'an that God has made mankind into different nations and tribes so that "ye can come to know one another" (sura 49:13), he announced that the sermons for the coming weeks would be directed toward and open to the public for a better understanding of the five pillars and the basic beliefs and practices of Muslims. Having made similar visits to local mosques for years prior to 9/11, this expressed desire for mutual understanding is an undoubted effect of the tragic events of September 11, 2001.

6

Islamic Law: The Foundation of Muslim Practice and a Measure of Social and Political Change

Islamic law is based on the immutable holy sources of the Qur'an and Sunna and is therefore a religious law in theory—al-fiqh, or jurisprudence—and Shari'a, the law in practice. The Qur'an, as the revealed word of God, and the teachings and the practice of the Messenger of God, Muhammad, are fundamental sources that have been interpreted over the ages but cannot be altered. However, the various schools of jurisprudence that have developed since the introduction of Islam, primarily in the first century after the Hegira (seventh to eighth centuries C.E.), reveal that the law is not static or immutable. These schools include the Maliki, Hanafi, Hanbali, and Shafi', as well as others that are a bit more obscure, which had their origins and influence in various parts of the original core of the early Islamic world. For example, the Maliki school grew out of the customs in practice in Medina and Mecca and spread throughout North and West Africa, while the Hanafi school spread with the Ottoman Empire. The differences in interpretation between the different schools are, relatively speaking, rather minor and do not represent doctrinal or factional differences in Islamic law.

Shari'a, as a religious law, is comprehensive and theoretically applies to all legal matters that we would differentiate in the West as civil, criminal, and family law. There is even a system of economics, banking, and finance that has grown out of Islamic prescriptions. In practice, in the modern period, Islamic Shari'a was circumscribed by Ottoman rule, which secularized the law in commerce and trade and relegated the Shari'a more to a law governing personal status matters of Muslims. The colonial powers reinforced and amplified this model, introduced their own Western laws in civil and criminal areas, and left Islamic law to govern family matters almost exclusively. Thus the current movement by the Islamists to restore the comprehensive role of the Shari'a in Islamic society does have historical legitimacy. However, Western and Muslim critics have questioned the compatibility of Islamic law with the standards and demands of the modern state in terms of protecting the rights of non-Muslims and women. This issue is addressed in chapter 7.

Each of the countries of the Arab-Muslim Middle East share Islamic culture, and they share, to varying degrees, Arabic language and culture. Most are nations with a background of European colonialism, French rule in the case of the Maghrib and the Levant, Italian rule in Libya, and British rule in the cases of the Nile Valley countries of the Sudan and Egypt, Jordan, Palestine, Iraq, and the oil nations of the Persian Gulf and Arabian Peninsula. Each country has been governed, since independence or the formation of a new nation, essentially by a monarchy or single party or military monopoly that has effectively excluded democratic elections or referenda on the subjects of family and social change or on any other matter.

Shari'a in Arabic means the "correct path," and in a religious sense it is quite clear that this means adhering to a correctly guided life that is upright and conforming to the teachings and practice of Islam. Living in a Shar'i way can be used to describe a proper home for a husband and wife, or living with one's family and assisting them rather than living alone in a flat, or to describe the revived form of Islamic dress that many young Muslim women are adopting. All are examples of proper conduct guided by the religion of Islam. From an Islamic point of view, there is little distinction between sacred and secular, and the different contextual use of terms like Shar'i and Shari'a is more noticeable to the Western non-Muslim than to the Muslim, for whom religion and society more comfortably commingle. The past development and future role of Islamic law in Muslim societies is a critical part of the contemporary debate regarding the "correct path" for Islamic nations to pursue into the twenty-first century.

For thirteen centuries, Islamic law has developed within Muslim communities and states comprehending civil, criminal, and family legal matters. Interpretations of the holy sources have developed through discussion and commentary relying upon the judgment of the jurists and scholars of the golden ages of Muslim caliphates—from Baghdad to Cordoba, from the Maghrib to central and south Asia. Great scholars such as al-Ghazali wrote detailed opinions upon multiple subjects relating to Muslim life, Islamic civil society, family relations, and relations with non-Muslims. These opinions are remarkable and worthy of greater weight than the Orientalist view of Max Weber that "Kadi justice" was no more than capricious decision making by Islamic judges who decided cases whimsically and not based on the more "logical" Western use of precedent.

For example, as early as the tenth century, Muslim jurists determined that since the Qur'an was silent on contraception birth control was permissible in Islamic society (Musallam 1986, 16). The method discussed was coitus interruptus, or male withdrawal. Medieval Arab medical texts also noted female techniques, such as vaginal suppositories or other barriers to the womb. "Spilling the seed," or male withdrawal, was forbidden in Jewish and Christian law, so this Islamic interpretation was novel and presaged developments in the twentieth century debates over theological and secular legal interpretations of birth control and the right to life. Al-Ghazali (1058–1111), one of the most influential of early jurists, argued that contraception for reasons of economy or to protect a wife from dangerous childbirth was lawful, but contraception to prevent the birth of daughters was not (Musallam 1986, 22). The right of a wife to sexual fulfillment in Muslim marriage intrigues and surprises Westerners accustomed to views of Eastern women as disempowered.

Islamic legal opinions regarding slavery and manumission are summarized in chapter 5 in the discussion of race and enslavement of non-Muslims. Slavery was acknowledged as part of existing social conditions when Islam began in the Hijaz and although it was not banned, legal opinion held that its practice was mollified by recommending kind treatment of slaves, including marriage, property, and inheritance rights, as well as heavenly reward for manumission, or freeing of slaves.

Interpretations regarding the treatment of non-Muslims living within Muslim states favored Kitabiyeen (Jews and Christians) over pagans, who were not endowed with the same rights as either Muslim or Kitabiyeen. The idea of a multireligious Islamic state may be viewed either as a contradiction in terms or as an idea to be developed further by Muslim reformers.

Islamic Law during Colonialism

More than twelve centuries of Islamic societies in local and state practice in Africa and Asia preceded the colonization of most of the Muslim world by European powers. Colonizing pressures from Europe threatened the Ottoman Empire and forced it into decline before its demise after World War I. Ottoman Hanafi law spread as official law throughout its empire, while local traditions favored Maliki traditions—especially in Africa—and Shafi'i traditions were favored in parts of Asia, while the Hanbali school was adopted by the Wahhabis in Arabia.

In 1798, with the Napoleonic invasion of Egypt, the era of European colonialism of "the Orient" began in earnest. Britain and France particularly vied for control of the trade routes and the natural resources. Lord Nelson's defeat of Napoleon secured Egypt for Britain, and for much of the nineteenth century Britain made strategic alliances with the Ottomans in their pursuit of empire. From Egypt they sought to control the Nile Valley, but met with resistance from the Sudanese Mahdi, Muhammad Ahmed, whose jihad against the foreign invader prevented British rule, beginning with the battle at Khartoum (1884–85). The Mahdi ruled much of the country until 1898, when the British returned in force under H. H. Kitchener with gunboats and gatling guns. They overcame Sudanese resistance, slaughtering over ten thousand one morning at the battle of Omdurman.

In 1885 the major European powers met in Berlin to divide up the African continent into spheres of influence. In Islamic Africa, British colonial rule was extended with and without resistance not only in Egypt and the Sudan but also in Uganda, Kenya, Tanganyika, South Africa, Rhodesia, Zambia, Nigeria, Ghana, and Sierre Leone. France, the political rival, colonized Algeria in 1830 and the rest of the Maghrib before the end of the century. The French secured Senegal, Ivory Coast, and the Sahelian countries of Mali, Niger, and Chad with their armies.

In Asia, the British secured India, Pakistan, Ceylon, Burma, and Thailand along with the major Muslim countries of Malaysia and Indonesia.

Colonial attitudes toward Shari'a were generalized and filtered through the indirect rule of the British, who used an English governor general and local rulers and officials as intermediaries, and the direct rule of the French, who placed themselves in official positions from the top down through the colonial hierarchy. Islamic law was treated as a form of "customary" law and relegated to personal status or family law matters. European-based law was imposed in the more politically important areas of property, civil, and criminal law. Certain Islamic institutions were retained or created—such as mosques, Islamic schools for training local imams, and "Mohammedan" courts with Muslim judges administering to family law needs. Emphasis was placed on controlling Islamic institutions and keeping them within the bounds of the colonial government without suppressing them altogether. However, monitoring the activities of the Muslim 'ulama under colonial rule was routine.

Lord Cromer, the architect of English colonialism in Egypt and the Sudan, wrote to the governor general of Sudan about how to handle the 'ulama at the Kadi School. Cromer wrote that he did not like the "tone" of the Grand Kadi's report, which desired the teaching of "pure Mohammedan law without alteration or amendment." "This is sheer nonsense," Cromer exclaimed. "Mohammedan law more than anything else is what is keeping the Mohammedans back. I am inclined to think that a Kadi who holds these views is not the man you want for the job, although I recognize that it is probably difficult to get anybody better. They are pretty well all of them alike, so I would advise keeping a careful watch over him, and not trusting him too far" (Cromer to Wingate, 11 February 1907, Sudan Archives, University of Durham).

The Indian Penal Code was created by the English to introduce Western criminal law into the East and was adapted to multiple colonial holdings in the Islamic and other colonies. French Napoleonic law was applied in their colonies consistent with direct rule. In Egypt, Tunisia, Lebanon, and other former French colonies, the tradition was established of using three sitting judges in civil cases. (Although French occupation of Egypt only lasted from 1798 until 1803, this tradition continues to this day.) Local qadis administered personal status family law from Malaysia and Indonesia, to India, to British-controlled Middle East and North Africa, but they suffered less pay, lower status, poorer facilities, and political isolation from the central government and from their colleagues in the civil and criminal division of the judiciary. This imposed inferior status during colonialism was keenly felt such that when opportunities for enhanced status for Islamic governance and Muslim institutions appeared—such as with various Islamist political movements—qadis and members of the ʿulama class of religious scholars embraced these opportunities, even if they were not committed Islamists. This broader colonial historical background to understanding calls for the restoration or full implementation of Shariʿa as state law is often ignored in Western discourse on the rise of Islamism. The Shariʿa judges and members of the High Court with whom I worked told me of this inherited sense of inferiority as well as of their nearly universal celebration when Shariʿa was made state law.

Fig. 23. Sudanese ʿulama, religious scholars, and judges of the High Court in Khartoum.

Punishment in Islam

Hadd (*hudud*, pl.) penalties—including flogging, amputation, and stoning for crimes of immorality, theft, fornication and adultery—are much discussed in the West as inhumane, uncivilized, or barbaric. Such penalties are Qur'anic, meaning they are mentioned specifically in the Holy Book, and as such are of such clear intent by God that their application is accepted. But over the centuries they have been the subject of much debate about their application because they are so severe.

> As for the thief, both male and female, cut off their hands.
> It is the reward of their own deeds, an exemplary punishment from
> Allah. (sura 5:38)

> But who so repents after his wrongdoing and amends,
> lo! Allah will relent toward him. Lo! Allah is Forgiving, Merciful.
> (sura 5:39, Pickthall translation)

The standard of proof of the crimes punishable by hudud penalties requires the admission of the guilty person or the testimony of four full witnesses (meaning four men or double the number of women). This requirement is so difficult to fulfill that the intent appears to be that hudud penalties should be used rarely, as examples. In Sudan since Shariᶜa became state law under Numeiri after 1983, and in the period of the rule of the National Islamic Front after 1989 when extremist interpretations prevailed, hundreds of amputations have been carried out by the Islamist Courts of Prompt Justice. Some of these amputees were not Muslims but were southerners displaced by the chronic civil war; it is not permissible to apply hadd punishments to non-Muslims. And many were poor men of the street, homeless vagrants accused or caught stealing, presumably from economic need. International human rights groups have criticized this application of hudud not only as cruel but as un-Islamic, since they were applied against non-Muslims and failed the stringent Islamic test of proof. The amputees in Sudan have organized themselves into mutual aid societies and are being assisted by Muslims who disapprove of the wrongful carrying out of these harsh penalties.

For example, in the case of adultery, both the man and the woman are to receive hadd punishments.

> The adulterer and the adulteress, scourge ye each one of them [with]
> a hundred stripes. And let not pity for the two withhold you from
> obedience to Allah, if ye believe in Allah and the Last Day. And let
> a party of believers witness their punishment. (sura 24:2)

And those who accuse honorable women but bring not four witnesses, scourge them with eighty stripes, and never (afterward)
accept their testimony—they indeed are evil doers. (sura 24:4)

Save those who afterward repent and make amends. (For such) lo!
Allah is Forgiving, Merciful. (sura 24:5, Pickthall translation)

In each case where the hadd punishment is mentioned, the Qur'an adds that
repentance and amendment yield God's forgiveness and mercy. However,
the contemporary sentencing and application of the hudud penalties seem to
have held neither to the standard of proof nor to the invocation of God's
mercy.

Studies of the application of hudud penalties in the past cannot as yet
answer the question of the frequency of their application within the caliphates or Muslim empires, such as the Moghuls or Ottomans. However, in
the context of politicized Islamist states, such as Sudan, Afghanistan under
the Taliban, Saudi Arabia, or Nigeria, the application of hudud punishments
has raised many religious, political, and human rights questions. Most common has been the application of flogging for "immoral" behavior and amputation for theft. Sentences of stoning for adultery have been handed down
in Sudan and Nigeria, but have not been carried out.

Islamic criminal law and hudud penalties are legal in countries where a
comprehensive Shari'a is applied: Iran, Pakistan, Saudi Arabia, Afghanistan
under the Taliban, Sudan, and northern Nigeria. The hadd punishment of
stoning for adultery has been applied not only in Sudan but also in northern
Nigeria, where Islamism has been on the rise. In Sudan there was an international outcry because the penalty was levied against a Christian woman
from the south who was a refugee in Khartoum from the civil war waged
there. International human rights groups protested the application of Islamic law against a non-Muslim as well as the cruelty of the punishment.
The Islamist government of Sudan backed down, as did the Nigerian government in the ruling by its Supreme Court in the case of Salfiya Hussaini, a
Muslim woman from the northern city of Sokoto who had been convicted of
having sex outside of wedlock and sentenced to death by stoning. She was
the first of two women convicted since a dozen northern Nigerian states had
instituted Shari'a as state law; the second was sentenced in Katsina state
after President Olusegun Obasanjo declared beheadings, amputations, and
stonings unconstitutional (*Providence Journal,* March 26, 2002). International pressure included the withdrawal of the Miss World Pageant from
Nigeria, moving it to London in 2002 in protest of the government's failure
to deal decisively with the stoning cases. Nigeria's delicate constitutional
balance among its multiple ethnicities and between its Muslim north and

Christian and animist south suggests that a major constitutional and political crisis would develop if a stoning sentence were carried out. Nigerian Muslim critics fear the intercommunal violence between Christians and Muslims that will spread if the sentence is applied, and they point out correctly that the Qur'an is clear about punishing both the man and the woman, not just the woman whose pregnancy clearly marks her.

The hudud punishments have been applied and executed in countries where Islamism (political Islam) or Wahhabism (conservative and puritanical interpretations) are in force using the apparatus of the state, such as in Sudan, northern Nigeria, or Saudi Arabia. Application of these severe punishments may be used to exhibit the unlimited power and Islamic character of the state, or they may be used to terrify their potential opponents. It is significant that they are not applied in Muslim countries that are officially secular states, such as in Indonesia or Egypt.

Contemporary Banking and Finance

The religious inspiration for an Islamic system of economics stems from the Qur'anic prohibition on usury, *riba,* which in itself derives from the fundamental principle of *tawheed,* the unity and oneness of God, and the relationship of cooperation and equity that is commanded between Muslims. *Riba* literally means "an increase" and was the subject of the last revelation of the Prophet; riba is usually interpreted as any form of direct interest charges upon money loaned or borrowed. Financial dealings that unite and provide support for the Umma have been favored. Waqf (awqaf, pl.) is a religiously inspired bequest of land or funding for the construction or maintenance of beneficial projects, such as the building of mosques, schools, and medical facilities that benefit the Muslim community. A waqf is a special testamentary bequest made in God's name that is permanent and cannot be sold or transferred without the intervention of local religious leaders. This explains why mosques built under waqf regulation centuries before the present are still standing and are maintained. A special family waqf could also be nominated to increase the share of inheritance to a needy Qur'anic heir, but could not be used to disinherit a proscribed relative in Muslim inheritance. Likewise, zakat—religious almsgiving and one of the five pillars—is a compulsory obligation to financially or materially assist the needy in the Muslim community. The Islamic states have imposed a zakat tax to enforce this religious obligation.

By analogy, that which divides the Muslim community, such as unjust economic practices involved in usury, is forbidden in Islam. The Qur'an specifically condemns the taking of interest on loans as a form of expropriation, since it claims more from a person's capital than its fair value. Likewise, it is commonly said that it is wrong to profit from another person's hardship, the assumption being that only a needy person would seek a loan.

Islam encourages commerce, trade, and economic growth. However, any financial dealings that involve charging interest are banned, as are trade and commerce in commodities that are forbidden, such as pork, alcohol, or drugs. The selling of products that are known to cause harm to humans, such as guns and tobacco, is considered by some religious scholars as *haram* (forbidden) or *makruh* (reprehensible). The sale of stolen property is also forbidden, although it is permitted in much of Western civil law.

The fundamental ban on interest charges led in the 1970s to the creation of new Islamic banks and institutions of investment. An interesting, but less well known, aspect to the current revival of Islam has been the creation of Islamic alternatives in the economic sphere. The Islamic banking and finance movement was synthesized by a combination of religious philosophy and practical need to meet the economic demands of Muslims engaging in local and international commerce. The Islamic banks were started with capital from Saudi Arabia, Dubai, and Bahrain, which have continued to play a dominant role in the ownership of these alternative financial institutions. Ironically, while the finance capital originates in the Gulf among some of its richest families (e.g., in the Faisal Islamic banks), most of the Islamic banks have been established in the poorer Arab states, chiefly Egypt, Sudan, and Jordan, where they have come to dominate smaller local banking needs. It is virtually impossible to separate the movement to promote Islamic economics from the movement to restore Islamic principles in government and society, thus Islamic banking is very much tied to Islamic revival. After 9/11, some Islamic banks were alleged to be funnels for funding al-Qaeda operatives; however, Western banks could just as well have been involved.

The rules regarding Islamic banking and investment, while common in theory, may vary in practice. The Islamic alternatives that have been devised to avoid charging interest emphasize partnership and profit-sharing in investment. A common type of loan from an Islamic bank is known as *mudarabah*, whereby the bank loans money to a client to finance a business venture in return for which the bank receives a specified percentage of the net profits of the business for a designated period. Share of the profits provides for repayment of the principal plus a profit for the bank to pass on to its depositors. Should a mudarabah enterprise lose money or fail to thrive, the bank, the borrower, and the bank's depositors all jointly absorb the loss. This puts into practice the basic Islamic principle that lenders and borrowers of capital should share risks and rewards.

Another commonly used technique is *murabahah,* whereby the bank purchases goods in its own name and takes title to these goods, and then sells them at an agreed-upon markup. The profit that the bank derives is justified in terms of the service rendered. This technique is frequently used for the financing of trade.

Trade and commerce must conform to Islamic teachings; commercial dealings with alcohol, drugs, pork products, pornography, and sexually exploitative material are forbidden. Some interpretations also forbid the sale of guns, ammunition, and any other deadly weapons. The Taliban in Afghanistan curtailed the drug trade during their years of rule; however, other Afghani governments observed no contradiction in the international trade in drugs, especially after 9/11 and the U.S. invasion that toppled the Taliban. Shortly after the end of the Taliban regime, the international drug trade resumed as a lucrative means of fueling various movements. Some scholars make a sharp distinction over the application of the rules of investment and trade between Muslims, where rules are essential, and with non-Muslims, where they are not.

To be clear, Islam does not condemn profit taking from legitimate businesses so long as the accumulation of wealth is not based on interest earned by loaning money. For example, loans made by the Islamic Development Bank to poorer Islamic countries using capital from the richer Arab-Muslim nations are interest-free. This stands in marked contrast to the interest-bearing loans made by the Western capitalist nations whose banking systems and economies are founded on loaning money at prescribed interest rates. Often poorer nations use their entire GNP to pay off the interest on loans from Western financial institutions like the World Bank or International Monetary Fund. While loans from the Islamic Development Bank may have other strings attached that make them less desirable, the element of long-term indebtedness is absent.

The Islamic banking movement reflects popular Islamist sentiment and propagandizes for it. In the Sudan, the Islamic banking movement is closely tied to the growth of the National Islamic Front and is largely responsible for funding it. Islamic banks have come to dominate all banking transactions under the current Islamist regime, having been favored by the government as being exempt from state regulation. The banks have offered opportunities to small and medium-sized business ventures that have aided in their mass appeal, and have served to break the monopoly of some of the old merchant families that have dominated trade and commerce since colonial times. With 60 percent of the capital being foreign based, typically Saudi or other Gulf money, the stability of the banks depends on the maintenance of good ties with these nations. During the 1991 Gulf War, the Sudan sided with Iraq and thus incurred the wrath of Saudi Arabia, which in turn limited its flow of capital into the country. Sudan turned to Iran for economic and military assistance, which has also Islamized its banking system.

The Islamic banking and financial institutions have not always lived up to the high standards expected of them. In Egypt, for example, Islamic investment corporations established envious reputations for very high rates of return on money invested, sometimes as high as 20–25 percent. These high returns brought more capital to the Islamic alternative, not necessarily for religious motives. Standing outside of government regulation, some improprieties were inevitable. During the late 1980s, there was a scandal in Egypt involving corruption and misrepresentation of monies invested in several of the largest Islamic investment corporations, with the result that the government stepped in and imposed strict guidelines over what had been a laissez-faire economic situation.

The challenge presented by the very existence and dramatic growth of the Islamic banks is one that is faced by secular regimes, fearful of their ties to the Islamic revival movements but reluctant to restrain them for fear of popular resistance. The Islamic banks present an indigenous challenge to the Western financial institutions, like the English-based Barclay's Bank, the French Credit Lyonaise, or Citibank, which have been accustomed to controlling the movement of foreign capital in many Arab-Muslim nations; they may find that regional Islamic financial institutions will replace the international flow of capital among Muslim nations.

Likewise, an economic system that operates on totally different premises, such as the Islamic ban on charging interest, has a broad appeal among the debt-ridden nations of the world and poor people in general. In my own teaching about Islamic concepts, I find that many of my students, who are themselves struggling to make ends meet, are attracted to the ideas of Islamic economics. Even the more cynical among them, who see banking fees and service charges as a form of "interest" taken by the Islamic banks, yield the point that the system is more open to the poorer echelons of society and would have popular appeal. Some of my Muslim students point with pride to the economic alternatives that have sprung up within Muslim communities whereby mortgages on houses and car loans are made using Islamic principles that bypass the usurious loans made by American banks. These loans involve the joint purchase of the house, for example, by a group of Muslim investors who receive "rent" or "use" payments from the occupant of the home, who is also an investor; when the home is eventually sold and a profit presumably made, all of the investors share in the profit made from the sale of the home. Islamic investment corporations have been established in a number of U.S. and Canadian cities to handle these alternative economic transactions for Muslims seeking a banking method that conforms to their religious principles.

In a related vein, American Muslims are advised not to use VISA or MasterCard because they charge interest rates for the unpaid balance. It is, or has been, preferable to choose the American Express card, which charges an annual service fee instead of charging interest.

To many non-Muslim Americans, including the students I have taught over the years, many of these ideas make sense as a collective approach to solving what are otherwise individual financial problems. However, the social collectivity, based on religion or some other common bond, is difficult to create in Western society, which has been erected so fundamentally upon individualism.

Development Programs

A number of solutions to the dramatic regional economic imbalances between rich and poor Arab and Muslim states have been proposed, involving Western technology, Arab or Muslim capital, and indigenous labor. The potential partnership for purposes of economic development of Western technology purchased by Arab capital and managed by local labor has been more attractive in theory than in practice. Western technological ventures have been more interested in contract work than in a long-term commitment to development projects, while Arab capital has been less willing to risk long-term ventures.

Various Arab development funds have been organized for several decades on the principle that surplus Arab capital, generated in the oil-producing countries with their relatively small populations and limited agricultural resources, should be invested in the capital-poor nations with large labor pools and greater agricultural potential. In fact, the flow of Arab capital into poorer nations has been timid, due to politically generated risks of failure and elevated expectations of the recipient nations. Nationalistic considerations came into play when foreign investors, Arab and non-Arab, sought to buy into safer ventures, such as real estate.

The common bond of Islam between capital-rich and capital-poor nations in the region has engendered a religiously based system of financing and investment, with the creation of various alternate Islamic financial and investment institutions in the 1970s, including the Islamic Development Bank and private Islamic banks, such as the Faisal Islamic Bank, relying heavily on Saudi capital, the Baraka Group of Bahrain, and others. These financial groups and development banks employ the investment alternative of shared ventures, where the capital is provided by one partner and the labor and management of the project are provided by the other partner.

Together they share the risks and profits in proportions agreed upon in advance of the undertaking.

As a religiously based alternative for economic investment, there is much to be admired in theory in Islamic investment. With their philosophy of sharing capital and labor, risk and profit, they have helped to mobilize indigenous small businesses that had been alienated and rejected by the power of traditional wealth concentrated in the hands of a few families. However, the Islamic banks have also acted as a funnel for controlled investment, such as financing Islamic Jihad, the al-Qaeda organization of Osama bin Laden, or the National Islamic Front in the Sudan, which have pursued a political agenda of Islamization and militant and violent actions against the rational economic interests of the nation and region as a whole. It is ironic that the religiously correct Islamic banks and financial groups operate primarily outside the Arabian Peninsula, while the major Western banks are favored within these oil-producing countries.

Family Law

Although different in the particulars of the historical development of family law matters, the laws of each country all derive from a common Islamic base of interpretation of the fundamental sources of Shari'a, the Qur'an and Sunna. Many predominantly Islamic states have religious and cultural minorities who have been historically exempted from Muslim family laws. Moreover, each country has been affected by recent revisions of Muslim family law, especially concerning marriage and divorce. Child betrothal has virtually disappeared, and the right of the woman, not her father, to choose her husband has been supported in the law. The previous unilateral right of the husband to divorce has been seriously undermined, with a corresponding rise in the legal interpretation and actual practice of the wife's right to judicial divorce. This began in North Africa as early as 1915 when the Ottoman Empire introduced judicial divorce for women; Sudan and Egypt later followed this example. This legal development was consistent with the Maliki religious interpretation that a woman should not be harmed in her marriage. Thus, the initial grounds that were recognized for women seeking divorce in court were injury or harm, at first interpreted as physical harm, such as beating, abandonment, or failure to support, but later incorporating notions of psychological abuse, such as insult. Change in the reform of the divorce laws is uneven and still ongoing, as women in Kuwait and Saudi Arabia lack this right and Jordan granted women the right to judicial divorce in 2002 after a government human rights commission recommended the change.

The right of a wife and the duty of a husband to support the family have been reinforced strongly in the recent decades of economic growth in some Arab-Muslim countries and relative stagnation in others. With massive labor migration from poorer to richer Arab countries, the stress placed on the family has been observed most acutely in the sharp rise in cases of nonsupport raised by wives against husbands who are labor migrants. One of the advantages of the Umma is the idea that national boundaries can be irrelevant in Islamic family law cases, such that Muslim courts of differing nations recognize the actions and decisions from other national Islamic courts.

Even though there are great commonalities in the religious law and practice of Muslim communities, each nation has its own unique political developments in relation to the larger issue of secularism versus Islamic revival. The focus of this section compares three nations in North Africa with regard to the development of family law and the degree to which this body of law has been affected by secular or Islamist trends over the past several decades. These countries are Tunisia, with a history of secular rule and a liberal (by Western standards) family law policy; Egypt, with a secular history of family law development but a growing Islamist movement; and Sudan, with a secular history that was fundamentally altered when Islamic law (Shari'a) was declared state law in 1983. Developments in North Africa are compared with Malaysia in an effort to compare the practice of Muslim family law in African and Asian Islamic communities. Examination of these cases aids in the understanding of the complexities underlying Islamic society and family issues and reveals that there is no single, monolithic system of law governing all Islamic contexts.

Tunisia's first postindependence president, Habib Bourguiba (1957–87), was among the pioneers, after Kemal Atatürk in Turkey, to revolutionize Islamic family law under an enlightened and liberal philosophy that promised to emancipate women through legal change. Today this secular approach to law and government is under question by Islamist forces who seek legal reform and restoration of the more traditional Shari'a as part of their larger political agenda. Egypt has a unified court system whereby Islamic family law is applied under the same general jurisdiction as its more Western-derived civil and criminal codes. However, Islamism has had a powerful impact upon Egyptian society, with a majority of young, educated women turning to an Islamic style of dress, and with increasing demand that Islamic law play a greater role in a reconstructed, more religiously based government. And in the Sudan, the military regime, guided by the Islamist National Islamic Front, that seized power in 1989 has reinforced the 1983 decision that Islamic law is state law. The family law was codified in 1991, and only Islamic law is applied in civil and criminal matters, a fact which has fanned the flames of the chronic civil war between the north and the south.

These countries represent points on a continuum of secular to Islamist approaches to law and government. The Sudan is an Islamic state with Shari'a as national law which alienates a significant portion of its population. Egypt is a secular state that retained intact most of the substance of Muslim family law, but has a large Islamist movement pressing for a greater role for Islamic law in the state. Tunisia is a secular state that has significantly revised Islamic law in theory and in practice, but it has a growing Islamist trend that would return Shari'a family law to its original status.

Tunisia

Tunisia most radically altered the traditional content of Islamic family law, and Tunisian law would undergo the most dramatic change were the Islamist trend to become dominant. The introduction of Islam to the Maghrib occurred in Tunisia Kairouan, established as the center of Maghrib Islam after 670 C.E. The Zaytouna Mosque in Tunis became the center of higher Islamic studies, and more than twenty thousand Islamic schools, or *kuttabs*, were established throughout the country. Ottoman rule, overseen by the infamous corsairs, led the country into a crippling foreign debt that opened the way to French colonialism.

During French colonial rule, between 1888 and 1956, the historic Zaytouna Mosque and University was eclipsed by the secular, westernized Sidiqi College which produced a new breed of Francophone intellectuals. In 1932 a new law allowed Tunisians to acquire French nationality; this assimilation was backed by the highest religious authority, the Sheikh al-Islam and Mufti, who issued a fatwa permitting "French" Tunisians to remain Muslim as long as they performed their religious duties and were buried in Muslim cemeteries.

The nationalist leader Habib Bourguiba led the country to independence through the secular Dastour (Constitution) Party. The party's attitude toward Islam was revolutionary, and reforms were issued by decree without even pro forma approval of the Tunisian religious scholars, the 'ulama. This contrasts markedly with developments in Egypt, where the powerful 'ulama, associated with the great international Al-Azhar University, has had an important role in both the colonial and postindependence states. This resulted in the overall weakening of the Zaytouna Islamic University during colonialism and its lack of renewal after independence. In fact, Zaytouna Mosque and University was neutralized by government appointment of faculty and selection of imams, with passive and ineffectual 'ulama and was finally closed during Bourguiba's rule (Handal 1989). Instead of using traditional interpretation by Tunisia's 'ulama, Bourguiba used his personal interpretation of Islam, and tried to espouse its true spirit by moving away from orthodoxy of law.

Besides changing family law, Bourguiba tried to do away with traditional Maghribi folk worship of saints, the *marabout,* and the wearing of the veil, both of which he viewed as symbols of the past. Family planning was seen as consistent with an Islamic view, and some of the most liberal programs favoring the limitation of family size were sponsored by the Tunisian government. More controversial was Bourguiba's recommendation to end Ramadan fasting as part of a "jihad against underdevelopment" because he regarded fasting/feasting as expensive and inefficient. The Shari'a courts were integrated into a "modern" legal system, and Zaytouna University became a department of the newly created University of Tunis in 1961.

The new Code of Personal Status, ratified in 1956, became the most significant reform of newly independent Tunisia. Its most salient features included the abolition of polygamy, which was made punishable by prison and a fine of 24,000 dinars. This legal reform necessitated some explanation and a period of legal tolerance by the government. In 1964 the government issued a new decree concerning invalid marriages (i.e., polygamous marriages), whereby the court enforced the dower payment and established that the children of such marriages were the legitimate heirs to both their parents' lineages.

Divorce reforms were also controversial, with the recognition of the right of both wife and husband to initiate divorce. This radically altered the traditional unilateral right of the husband to divorce using the triple pronouncement without the intervention of the courts, and it required a court appearance for both parties in divorce cases. In 1968 this trend toward equalizing the legal roles of men and women was carried further. The right of the wife to seek employment or choose a profession demanding work outside of the home was established without the necessity of prior permission from her husband.

Amended again in 1981, the law granted the divorced woman priority in the custody of the children and all legal maintenance (*nafaqa*) to which she was accustomed in married life, which continues as a debt upon the husband's resources even until his death, with payment to stop only if the condition of the woman improves. This unleashed something of a backlash against the reform movement as having gone too far, and the topic still provoked animated discussion when I raised the subject in 1990. Critics at the time contended that it unfairly discriminated against men and placed them on the defensive. A part of the backlash that the reformed divorce law unleashed came from female judges, lawyers, and educators, as well as from male legal professionals. Divorce cases initiated by women increased, as did cases initiated by men (Sherif-Stanford 1984, 93), so it might be inferred that the divorce reform had an initial destabilizing effect resulting in more divorce, rather than what was perhaps the intention of the law—to inhibit divorce by men.

Arranged marriage also was abolished, and a legal age of twenty-one for the groom and eighteen for the bride was established. Dower was greatly reduced in legal status and explicitly made the legal property of the wife, while the wife's right to refuse cohabitation if the dower was not paid according to negotiated amounts and time of payments was reaffirmed.

Added to these revolutionary changes, Bourguiba and his reformers attacked the veil as a symbol of female subordination. Moreover, the French language was made the official language of instruction, and Bourguiba promoted a Franco-Tunisian synthesis and a Mediterranean Islam. Emphasis was placed on modern education, and literacy rates dramatically increased, while the percentage of girls attending school rose to 40 percent.

Regarding property and inheritance, support was given to the Islamic principle that the husband has no right to control his wife's property, estates, or earnings. However, the wife may contribute to the family budget if she desires. This was amended in 1968 to state that "the wife is her husband's responsibility no matter what her economic condition," and if the husband is away, she can legally demand that support from her husband. This has marked bearing upon the large number of men who migrate abroad for work, especially to France and other European countries, and whose families may suffer economic hardship as a result.

The inheritance code follows traditional Islamic law regarding female inheritance, which is half that of male heirs, but does make the children, the wife, and the grandparents the primary heirs. Only if these heirs are not available does the estate revert to traditional Muslim inheritance, where other members of the extended family are included. This had the effect of strengthening nuclear family ties and lineal ties between parents and children, over the broader Islamic concept of the extended family.

Optional legal wills are possible, written and registered with the Ministry of Justice for leaving property to people, charities, and religious shrines provided that such assets do not exceed the Islamic bequeathable third. In one study (Sherif-Stanford 1984, 90), two-thirds of Tunisians interviewed said they have left the optional one-third to wives, daughters, mothers, and sisters who would otherwise inherit half or less than their male relatives, depending on the relationship, suggesting a societal response to changes in family life.

The Tunisian Code of Personal Status was issued at the time of national independence when the desire for change and modernization was at its height. However, it was not achieved by political mobilization and activism of women, although many women were significant leaders in the struggle for

Tunisian independence (Libidi 1987). Instead, these radical changes in the law were introduced by fiat, by decree from above at the presidential level. Bourguiba himself created the National Union of Tunisian Women (UNFT), and he referred to the members as soldiers in a holy war against ignorance and illiteracy (Sherif-Stanford 1984, 83). For its work in modernizing women's status, the UNFT received the United Nations award for outstanding achievement in human rights, and Kurt Waldheim cited Tunisia as an example to other Arab societies. Bourguiba and legal reform are inextricably linked, as shown by the fact that the commemoration of the institution of the Tunisian Code of Personal Status is celebrated on Bourguiba's birthday.

Islamist activism has become a feature of contemporary Tunisian politics, with its inevitable social policy recommendations. The first organized Islamist activity was Ittijah al-Islami, which evolved to become the an-Nahda (Renaissance) Party. Its main thesis is that economic and social development must take into account religious values. Unlike the Bourguibist reform movement, it has mobilized young women in significant numbers. An-Nahda relies on the Qur'an and Sunna as fundamental sources but rejects "doctrinal sectarianism" and tolerates differences of opinion. Followers reject the idea of class conflict, seeing the overriding power of the Umma as a great unifier. However, the movement allies itself with the poor and has its greatest mass following there.

With respect to law, an-Nahda sees a great disparity between Islamic Shari'a and the law as applied in Tunisia today. To bring about change, the Islamist task is to resocialize the masses and then establish the Islamic order, based on democracy and *shura*, or consultation (Shahin 1990). An-Nahda calls upon the Tunisian people to fight against the Jahiliya (period of ignorance before Islam) created by Bourguiba and his successor, Ben-Ali. They see the Tunisian Code of Personal Status as a revision and not a reform of Islamic Shari'a. An-Nahda has called for the return of polygamy as a permissible form of marriage. Some have called on women to stop working outside of the home and return to domestic life; others have denounced *ikhtilat*, open socializing between men and women. Female members of an-Nahda have supported women working outside the home, saying that women are needed as doctors, nurses, and teachers to work with girls. As for Islamic dress or other outward signs of personal religious conviction, these should be a matter of choice for women.

An-Nahda is a movement led by educated, disaffected young Tunisians, with a relatively high participation of women, thus challenging the secular idea that Islam is against women's participation in public life. Reviving the practice of the Shari'a is the goal of the movement, but this is to be achieved primarily through education.

Tunisia is an example of legal reform in the family law area from the top down, one of the most radical and revolutionary changes in the Shari'a family law. To the degree that one-party, one-man rule has become unpopular in Tunisia and the Islamist path represents an apparently democratic alternative, the issue of increasing Islamization and restoring Shari'a remains alive.

Egypt

After independence in 1952, Egypt retained traditional Shari'a in the law of personal status, while it combined the Shari'a family law with French- and English-derived codes of civil and criminal law into a single system. The personal status courts have separate facilities but are administered as part of a comprehensive system of Egyptian law.

Historically, the Shari'a was the law in effect from the early times of the introduction of Islam into Egypt during its first great century of expansion. From the Ottoman period, after the fifteenth century of the common era, Shari'a remained in effect until the nineteenth century, when colonialist legal reform introduced Western-inspired codes in all areas except the law of personal status. During English colonialism, Egyptian family law was left unchanged until family law reforms of 1920 and 1929.

Reforms in 1920 and 1929 drew upon various schools of Islamic jurisprudence, and introduced judicial divorce initiated by women on the grounds of desertion, incarceration, terminal illness of the husband, or lack of maintenance. In addition, restrictions were placed on a husband's right of repudiation of the marriage by pronouncement of *talaq* (divorce), making sure that it must be a clear, sober, and deliberate decision. These reforms left out draft proposals on the restriction of polygamy, with King Fuad refusing to support the controversial recommendation to limit plural marriages, resulting in families that husbands could not maintain adequately (Esposito 1982, 60).

The constitution in 1956 established equal public rights for women and men, extended suffrage to women, and gave women the right to hold state offices at all levels. Recommendations to amend the family law were proposed by the Ministry of Social Affairs in 1943, 1945, and 1969, and each time they failed (ibid.). Proposals to reform polygamy and certain aspects of the divorce laws were advanced in 1960, when the governments of Egypt and Syria formed the United Arab Republic and merged elements of Syrian and Egyptian laws. The abolition of *bayt al-ta'a*, the right of a husband to retrieve by police force a wife who has fled the conjugal home, was proposed, but it was adamantly opposed by the Egyptian 'ulama, and in any event the issue was made moot by the end of union of the two countries.

In 1966 the reformers again proposed abolishing bayt al-ta'a as well as making eleven amendments to 1929 law. These reforms included obligating the husband to pay the wife's medical expenses; allowing a wife to stipulate in the marriage contract that she can be employed; forbidding a husband to take a second wife without the permission of his first wife; requiring attempted reconciliation by family councils prior to litigation in divorce cases; requiring temporary maintenance for a wife before legal proceedings; allowing divorce only after reconciliation attempts fail; requiring an additional year of support for a divorced woman; preventing repudiation by an irate husband; viewing polygamy as an injury to the first wife and a potential ground for divorce; ruling that remarriage does not nullify a woman's right to custody of her children; and ending the practice of requiring children to be taken to a police station for visitation with noncustodial parents.

Bayt al-ta'a was finally abolished in 1967 by a decree of the minister of justice, with specific mention being made of a ban on the issuance of an order of obedience by force. The decree was immediately challenged by the National Assembly as an inappropriate method of changing the law, and there was controversy and resistance among the judges, many of whom refused to comply with the new order (Fluehr-Lobban and Bardsley-Sirois 1990, 41). There was lively debate in the Assembly; however, few members were willing to go on record as supporting the rule of obedience by police action, and so the matter ended there.

In 1970, after the death of Gamal Abdel Nasser, Anwar al-Sadat assumed power and felt the growing strength of the Muslim conservatives. After the subject of the future status of the Shari'a was openly debated in 1975 within the Arab Socialist Union, the conservatives were successful in advancing the view that the Shari'a alone would constitute the basis of any reform of Egyptian law. The most innovative legal reform of the family law since independence was put forward by Sadat in 1979 in Law 44, widely referred to as "Jehan's law" because of the influence of Mrs. Jehan Sadat on the development of the various proposals. Although challenged on constitutional grounds in 1985, Law 44 was reintroduced as Law 100, and it survived almost completely intact and represented the most significant set of reforms in family law since 1929.

Major provisions of Law 44 included the following:

a. A notary public must obtain information from both parties when registering a divorce so that a husband could no longer divorce without the wife's knowledge.
b. A second marriage constituted an injury (*darar*) to the first wife and was a ground for divorce, even if not stipulated in the marriage contract.

c. The mother was favored as custodial parent and had the right to inhabit the conjugal dwelling during the period of custody.

d. The wife was entitled to legal separation if continued married life caused her unbearable harm.

e. Conditions under which the wife was entitled to maintenance were liberalized, and she had the right to divorce if maintenance ceased.

f. The wife was entitled to an indemnity (*mut'a*) over and above the legal support to which she was entitled in the event she had been repudiated without her consent or without apparent cause on her part.

Law 100, revising Law 44, declared that the second marriage did not necessarily constitute harm to the first wife. They argued that, according to Maliki law, injury can be caused by desertion, beating, and insulting, but not by marriage to another woman. The wife seeking divorce can always resort to *khul'* (mutual, negotiated divorce), which is preferable to *tafriq* (separation by court order).

Under Law 100, the burden of proof is on the wife to demonstrate the harm, physical or psychological. If not proven, she can be divorced, but she is not entitled to mut'a, a benefit or compensation that can only be awarded by a judge in cases of proven harm or abuse (*talaq al-darar*).

The law was hailed by feminists and liberals as a significant landmark toward the liberation of women. However, anticipating opposition from Muslim conservatives in 1979, Sadat secured the endorsement of the law by a number of 'ulama from the minister of awqaf, the mufti of Egypt, and the sheikh of Al-Azhar University. All concurred that the law was in conformity with Shari'a principles and Islamic jurisprudence, in addition to being conducive to social justice and family harmony. Nonetheless, the Muslim Brotherhood strenuously objected, disputing the authenticity of the state-controlled 'ulama's endorsement. Their attack on the entire law focused on the denial of the husband's right to unconditional polygamy. They claimed that to do so would be to repudiate Islam, and the interpretation that polygamy would be a harm to the first wife insinuates that the Prophet and his companions, the Saheban, permitted injury. However, the innovative mut'a—an amount of money due to the divorced wife and justified as a divorce transition benefit that extends beyond the few months of support due to the wife during the normal three-month *'idda* period—was seen as a benevolence that would find favor in the eyes of God. Qur'anic texts and jurists have supported mut'a compensation but left the matter "to the wealthy according to his means and the poor according to his means" (sura 2:236). The law now recognizes that times have changed and that a woman's welfare can no longer be left to a man's sense of honor and obligation. The courts determine the amount of the mut'a depending on the husband's condition and the circumstances of the divorce.

As part of the compromise legislation responding to masculine backlash, the husband was still obliged to provide adequate rental housing to his divorced wife and their minor children, but he has the exclusive right to his dwelling, which he owns as his private property and which he provided at the time of the marriage. Further, upon her loss of the right to custody, the wife also loses the right to the residence, so the primacy of the welfare of the children is favored over the financial condition of the divorced wife. Without children, the divorced wife must depend on her parents or relatives, and failing them, there is no government safety net or welfare program. With the government officially promoting family planning and the reduction of family size, the message of the revised law to married women is that larger families and minor children may provide legal and financial security.

In January 2000 President Hosni Mubarak signed into law amendments to the Personal Status Law that amounted to a quiet revolution. Discussed for a number of years and approved by the sheikhs at Al-Azhar University, the changes amended features of the law of marriage and divorce. Negotiated divorce was revived, allowing a couple to agree to the terms of divorce while keeping the case from being heard in court. Mandatory mediation for sixty days, a requirement in all divorce cases, was retained.

Most interesting was the official recognition of 'urfi, or customary marriage, which was acknowledged in Islamic law but was not legal in Egypt. Customary marriage requires only the agreement of the couple to the contract of marriage with their two witnesses. 'Urfi marriage need not include the consent of parents or the payment of the usual substantial dower. Interestingly, some religious conservatives as well as liberal feminists have found fault with the legalization of customary marriage. They argue that it might be used as a form of temporary marriage where couples marry as a matter of pleasure or convenience—like mut'a marriage in Shi'a Islam, which has a questionable reputation. The potentially less binding nature of the customary marriage raises concerns about deteriorating morals and women ending up with fewer rights, minus the dower, as the price for greater freedom in marriage and divorce.

Most significant is that the changes were innovated using the principles and methods with an Islamic framework employing Islamic institutions and interpretations with appeal to a broad audience. This effective embrace of Islam for reform of the personal status law by activists that have been historically secular reveals the potential for Islam to be a source of positive social change (Singerman 2003).

Egypt is clearly a nation and a society torn between its secular political

Fig. 24. Women judges and lawyers in Khartoum.

history since independence under Nasser, Sadat, and Mubarak, and its intensifying Islamist movement, which has both popular roots and a powerful legitimizing authority coming from the center of Muslim learning at Al-Azhar University. The Egyptian legislature and courts have attempted to steer a middle course between the conservative Islamists and the secular reformers. In the new family law Egypt has combined conservative and liberal tendencies adopting a political path that appeases secular concerns while using an Islamic framework to carry out its reforms. The decade of discussion that it took to do so is laudable, but it also speaks to the powerful contravening tendencies at work in the society (Fluehr-Lobban and Moore 2000).

Sudan

The Sudanese converted to Islam later than Egypt or Tunisia, with Muslim kingdoms and a significant spread of the religion taking place only after the fifteenth century of the common era. The Funj Kingdom at Sinnar was the first to install Islamic courts and have religious teachers and interpreters of the Shari'a. Cultural and religious influence of Islam penetrated Bilad as-Sudan (Muslim Africa across the Sahara) more from the west than from either the Nile Valley or Red Sea routes. Christian kingdoms in Nubia halted the spread of Islam south from Egypt until their fall in the fifteenth century. However, the African pilgrimage route to the holy places passed through the Sudan. The pilgrims from West Africa provided a continuous infusion of Islamic religion and customs since the first Islamic states.

The West African influence of Islamic tradition brought with it Maliki customs and law, an interpretation grounded in everyday practice in Mecca after the introduction of Islam. Ottoman conquest and administration of the Sudan after 1821 brought Hanafi law, where it blended with local interpretation and practice not only in Sudan but also in Egypt and other parts of the Ottoman Empire in Africa. The success of the Mahdist uprising in the late nineteenth century, an uprising as much against the abusive administration and corrupt practice of Islam by the Ottoman Turks as it was against European intrusion, brought the first independent Islamic republic, which lasted from 1885 until 1898. Following British reconquest, colonial rule lasted from 1898 to 1956, during which time "Mohammedan law" was relegated to the arena of personal status law alone, but administered throughout the Muslim regions of the country through a separate system of courts. I have written extensively about the development of Shari'a law in the twentieth century in the Sudan (see Fluehr-Lobban 1983, 1987), and I offer the following summary of the major points that characterized its application until Islamic law was made state law in 1983. Making Shari'a the state law precipitated renewed civil war and deepened the political crisis in the Sudan up to the present time.

The Sudan was one of the first dominantly Muslim nations in the twentieth century to modify the traditional unilateral right of the husband to divorce and to introduce the woman's right to a judicial divorce. A clear continuation of this legal trend is evident in the Tunisian abolition of this right of the husband to divorce by repudiation in the early 1960s. The Sudanese Judicial Circular 17 (ca. 1915) opened "the door of interpretation" in family matters regarding the potential for harm or abuse of the wife in a marriage, consistent with Maliki interpretation that such harm is contrary to Islam and social harmony. Divorce initiated by women is permitted on the grounds of physical cruelty (*talaq al-darar*) and desertion by the husband (*talaq khawf al-fitnah*). Beyond this, the law, as presented in Circular 17, provides a procedure and means for the wife to obtain maintenance payments from the husband who is absent for any reason or from the husband who has failed to maintain his wife adequately. This lack of support is viewed as a source of harm to the wife.

Many of these reforms anticipated developments that were not to occur in Egypt until the Family Law Reform of 1929; indeed most of the Grand Qadis of the Sudan, appointed by the English during colonial times, were Egyptian, and they may have tested these reforms first in the Sudan before their introduction in Egypt. The major mechanism for modification and interpretation of the law has been the judicial circulars that have been issued by the Grand Qadis until the courts were merged in 1980 and the position of Grand Qadi was eliminated. The judicial circulars had the effect of law.

The broad principle of protecting the wife against harm in the marriage is a rich one and was built upon again in 1973, after independence, in Circular 59, which recognized mental cruelty as another form of harm and thus a ground for divorce (Fluehr-Lobban 1983, 88). The right of a Muslim husband to divorce his wife by triple pronouncement, ideally on three occasions separated by three-month intervals, was long recognized as subject to abuse, especially by *talaq talata,* the triple pronouncement of divorce made on a single occasion, often in a fit of rage or under the influence of alcohol. The Sudan followed Egypt in 1935 by making the triple pronouncement illegal and by making a formal legal requirement of three separate and deliberate declarations of divorce.

The wife's right to marital support, particularly if the husband is absent, was safeguarded in law, and the issue of consent in marriage was addressed. In 1935 the strict Hanafi rule that an underage or adult woman could be betrothed with only the consent of the male marriage guardian, usually the father, was reaffirmed. Using Maliki instead of Hanafi interpretations, a divorced mother was allowed to retain custody of her son, beyond the usual seven years, to the time of puberty, while the custody of the daughter may be extended from nine years to the time of the consummation of her marriage. By 1960, under feminist pressure, this was reformed to make full and express consent to marriage the right of the woman.

As in Egypt, a similar retraction of bayt al-taʿa occurred in Sudan in 1970 under pressure from organized agitation by women's groups, especially the Sudanese Women's Union. Shariʿa law in the Sudan had a separate and unique means of development through the use of judicial circulars throughout most of the twentieth century, and it represented an enlightened approach to family law issues.

During the sixteen years of al-Numeiri's military rule (1969–85), dramatic developments affected the future of Shariʿa law in the country. The civil and Shariʿa courts were combined in 1980, and in 1983 al-Numeiri made Islamic law the state law, despite the negative impact this was certain to have on the large non-Muslim population of the south. Civil war broke out again in the south in 1983 over this issue and has continued, with a central point being the withdrawal of the state-imposed Islamic law. Since 1989 an Islamist government has been in power and has reasserted the supremacy of Shariʿa in the country, while secessionist sentiments in the southern movement have been revived and the future of the nation appears in jeopardy.

The current Islamist military government, with a civil war raging and an unpopular international record on human rights, quickly turned its attention to the area of family law after seizing power in June 1989. The Conference on the Role of Women in National Salvation recommended in January 1990 that a code of personal status law be drafted. A legislative committee drew up the 1991 Act on Personal Law for Muslims, which was passed by the ruling military and the Council of Ministers and put into effect on July 24, 1991. The new code brings together in five volumes the collective wisdom of Islamic family law in the Sudan dealing with marriage, divorce, guardianship and property, trusts, gifts and entertainment, inheritance, loans, and relations with relatives.

This first codification of the personal status law is not innovative, but it does put into a single set of books the background and interpretations of legal development in the Sudan. It consistently favors Maliki interpretations over Hanafi law, and it makes explicit points in the law that had previously only been decided in high court cases. For example, it recognizes the woman's increased authority in marriage and expressly rejects the six conditions to be met in Hanafi law for a valid marriage to be effected; religion, freedom, job or craft, financial situation, place of residence, and reasonable pedigree. These conditions when applied in Sudan created many ethnic and racial problems, especially over the issues of pedigree and parentage, with several famous cases of objections by marriage guardians to a future son-in-law with alleged slavery in his background (see Fluehr-Lobban 1987, 127–29). The new law requires only mutual respect between the two families; the financial situation of the families is also removed, such that competence in marriage can only be measured by "the practice of religion and good morals" (El-Rasoul 1991, 29).

The new law widens the concept of maintenance payments to include education and medical treatment for the wife, which were excluded under the previous Hanafi interpretation. A new ruling was instituted regarding engagement gifts; previously, if the engagement was broken, the gifts had to be returned, according to the Hanafi school. Under the new code, if the fiancé breaks off the engagement without reasonable cause, the gifts do not have to be returned, consistent with Maliki law. Matters regarding domestic possessions and furniture are also treated flexibly in the new code, taking into consideration the development of Sudanese society. Previously, if the husband and wife argued over the marital possessions, women were typically granted only their clothes and jewelry. Because it is not clear any longer what is "suitable possession to man or woman," the new code provides for the division of possessions equally between them (El-Rasoul 1991, 29).

The major drafter of the code, Sheikh Siddiq Abdel Hai, believes that the code will have a positive effect on the unification of the sources of the law and will bring about an end to the conflict and contradictions that occurred in the past in balancing the Hanafi and Maliki schools. Clearly set out in easily comprehensible language, the new personal status code can save the time of judges and lawyers, who now have a ready reference to many questions.

Tunisia, Egypt, and the Sudan Compared

In each country we have examined, Islamic law is a political issue, whether it is to be limited to family matters or it will command a greater role in state law and government. Shariʿa law and its future place in each of these predominantly Muslim nations has become a major part of the dialogue and, increasingly, of the political confrontation between Islamists and their secular opponents. Under Islamist pressure, Egypt has formally taken the position that the Shariʿa constitutes its source of legislation. The Sudan had taken a similar step even before Islamic law was made state law, bowing to growing Islamist pressures. Tunisia, with its dramatically secularized Islamic family law, is faced with a potentially powerful Islamist movement that seeks to restore the Shariʿa to its rightful place in a Muslim society.

While issues of family law may seem less important than the place of Shariʿa in state politics, in fact many of the battles between Islamist and secular reformers have been waged within the boundaries of Islamic family law. The British colonial authorities favored a policy that gave autonomy to the development of Islamic law in Egypt and the Sudan, in contrast to the direct method of colonial rule adopted by the French. With the ʿulama retained in positions of religious and legal power, the development of Islamic family law in Egypt and the Sudan was slow and deliberate, proceeding along a basically Islamic path. However, the ʿulama in Tunisia were already weakened and neutralized by the colonial state before Bourguiba introduced his sweeping reforms, so he had little to fear from their opposition and little tradition of reform to build upon. It has been left to a new generation of activists, inspired by Islamic revival but not led by any of the traditional ʿulama, to challenge the Bourguiba legacy.

In all three countries certain areas of the law were more accommodating to legal reform and change than others. The relative ease and ready acceptance of the elimination of the triple pronouncement of divorce in each country suggests a broad consensus on the need to limit the potential and real abuse that had resulted from unilateral and hasty divorce of wives in this fashion. Likewise, the recognition of the woman's right to initiate divorce and to be divorced on the grounds of economic neglect, desertion, and harm demonstrates wide agreement. The strengthening of the wife's right to maintenance and its enforcement has not been challenged, nor has the extension of the period of the mother's custody of her children after divorce. However, the caution with which the subject of polygamy has been approached in Egypt and the controversy over its limited restriction reveal the sensitive nature of this issue. The abolition of polygamy in Tunisia was, perhaps, the most notable and internationally recognized feature of the package of reforms undertaken there. The abolition of polygamy has not been a serious part of the agenda for legal reform in the Sudan and has historically appeared only in feminist tracts. However, rates of polygamy are extremely low in all three countries and have been declining. The confrontations over the abolition, restriction, or retention of polygamy have been more symbolic than real. Fruitful arguments have ensued over the question of whether a practice specifically mentioned in the Qur'an as permissible can be seen as wrong or can be amended.

Matters of family law affect all citizens of a nation, and when the fundamentals of the law derive from a religious base, as in Muslim societies, the sensibilities aroused can be of a deeply personal and spiritual nature. The dynamics of family law reform in the three countries examined reflect a complex blend of social, religious, and political change in the twentieth century. The role of Islam and its basic institutions, the status of women and the family, and the relationship of the family to the modern Muslim state are among the most pressing issues of the day.

Malaysia

Islam was introduced into Malaysia in the fifteenth century by traders from Indonesia. The early Aceh state administered Islamic law, including the hadd penalty for theft, throughout the seventeenth century, as did Brunei from the sixteenth century (Peletz 2002, 28). Islamic judges probably acted to sanction and legitimize the local rulers' wishes rather than acting as 'ulama interpreting and applying Islamic jurisprudence. In Malaysia, as elsewhere, state Islamic law must be distinguished from local practice—*adat,* or custom. Adat norms are so powerful in the region that kadis incorporated adat into Islamic law that historically has reserved a secure place for local custom elsewhere. Thus, for example, theft could be sanctioned by kadis using adat fines and ridicule, rather than the harsher Islamic hadd sanction of amputation.

In the late nineteenth century, by which time British colonialism was in full force, the colonial focus shifted to the contrast between local Malay judicial practice and its conflict with British judicial ideals. The colonial officials discredited existing local legal practice as "clumsy and inefficient" but also, significantly, as brutal and backward (Peletz 2002, 38–42) in order to provide the needed rationale for the substitution of enlightened, civilized law from England. This was accomplished between 1840 and 1890, and the Malaysian courts were reorganized along lines similar to colonial practice in India and Islamic Africa. The Indian Penal Code, applied equally in Africa and Asia, was introduced along with a parallel and inferior "Mohamedan" court system. Since kadi or *kathi* were generalized terms for judge, the colonizers were uncomfortable with the use of the term for judges both in their civil and criminal courts and in the Islamic courts. A solution in Malaysia, as elsewhere, was the invention of "Mixed Courts" that administered both Shari'a and civil (i.e., Western) law and permitted oversight, including revision of judgments made by insufficiently indoctrinated kadis. The strength of adat regarding women's rights in traditional matrilineal inheritance precipitated more than one controversy between old and new leadership in Malaysia, and indigenous and Western interpretations and applications of law (Peletz 2002, 58).

The Islamic courts were established as a separate and unequal system in Malaysia, comparable to other colonial settings. Moreover, cases heard in the religious courts could be appealed in the secular courts, but not the reverse.

Michael Peletz's anthropological study of contemporary cases in the Islamic courts reveals the normative character of Muslim family courts as the formal step in dispute resolution after informal, extralegal efforts have failed. As elsewhere, the majority of litigants—two-thirds or more—are women, seeing relief from the courts as a last resort. According to Peletz, men fare better in court than women. Requests for divorce are aired and mediated; desertions by husbands are formally noted, leading to the most commonly heard case, demands by wives for support (*nafaqa, nafkah*).

As with other anthropological studies of Islamic courts, the greatest number of cases deal with maintenance, resulting from negligence, desertion, and divorce. Divorce cases account for 41 percent and 18 percent of cases raised by women, respectively, in 1987–88 and 1990–91. Seventy percent of cases initiated by men in Kempas court in 1990–91, whether in monogamous or multiple unions, revealed the widespread exercise of the male prerogative of divorce pronouncement, or another form of divorce recognized in Malaysia—*fasakh* (annulment) or *tebus* (compensation paid to husband). Peletz documents that divorce has decreased (1988) in Malaysia, perhaps as a benefit of rising incomes witnessed in the Asian economic boom in the late twentieth century.

There are a nearly equal number of cases by women requesting maintenance (28 percent) and by men charging negligence (29 percent), and this is a striking demonstration of the two sides of this marital coin. The inclusion of assault and child abuse categories within official Muslim religious courts is unusual, as is the specific charge of illicit affairs. In other Islamic courts these issues are more likely to be embedded in divorce or maintenance cases. The number of males in polygynous unions seeking divorce suggests economic distress or stress in such marriages from the relative power of women in matrilineal Muslim societies.

Notably absent is the common ground for divorce sought by women in North Africa, complaining of harm or abuse. However, the high number of desertion cases—male and female—speaks to the overall economic stresses in the region forcing males to migrate out of their local communities for better employment opportunities. This compares accurately with desertion and maintenance cases in other poorer Muslim societies where male out-migration has added stress to the usual family patterns. It is often difficult to determine whether divorce rates have increased or decreased under contemporary global economic pressures. This is because comparative studies of Islamic law in space are rare enough, and those employing temporal comparisons of the application of Islamic law during Ottoman and colonial times, for example, are utterly lacking. This is made more problematical by the absence of statistical recordkeeping in precolonial times. However, comparison of colonial and postcolonial patterns of case law would be both possible and useful.

Changing Family Patterns and Implications for Muslim Family Law

From a social scientific perspective, the changes in family law are reflective of changes that have been taking place in Muslim societies for generations. These are especially dramatic with respect to the status of women, for whom major social change took place in the twentieth century, especially in the decades since the advent of independence.

Most impressive has been the entry of women into the workforce. Women represent significant numbers where the economic need is the greatest, but educated middle-class women have entered into the professions in ever-increasing numbers as well. Egypt and Tunisia have the greatest number (25 percent) of women undertaking salaried employment outside the home. Even in a country as traditionally conservative as the Sudan, the participation of women in the workforce has more than doubled in the past few decades, from 7 percent to 15 percent of all women. The percentage of women in the workforce in Iran increased in the 1980s. This may seem low by Western standards, where typically well over 50 percent of women work for wages. But similar economic and social forces are at work in the Arab-Muslim world and are occurring at a more rapid pace than in the West. Since such work by women may be considered shameful according to Arab and

Islamic values, it is usually undertaken only under the worst of economic and social conditions. Historically, women driven to work by personal circumstances were looked upon as the most pitiable of humans. The idea that women might work in factories, in government or business offices, or in gender-mixed situations was unthinkable only a generation or two ago. But the shame is beginning to be replaced with a sense of dignity in work, and many women have entered professions seen as "male," such as engineering, medicine, or law.

Of course, women work, as do men, whether they reside in the urban centers or in the countryside. Apart from the domestic work, growing numbers of women are working in the informal economic sector as street vendors, maids and domestics, or in craft production (such as carpet weaving). This work, although described as self-employment, places women in highly dependent positions whereby their livelihood or supplement to family income depends upon their relations with economic middlemen or those who hire them unofficially. Needless to say, the transience, vulnerability, and lack of benefits that a person working in the informal sector receives represent hardships for these working women. Despite often difficult working conditions, the entry of women into the informal sector is an offshoot of the larger social transformation that has brought women into the formal working sector (see Lobban 1998).

This economic participation of women amounts to a social transformation in the postindependence period, and to be sure, it correlates highly with the era of secular politics and the state support for the emancipation of women. With Islamist agitation, the propriety of women in the workforce is under intense scrutiny. This trend is discussed more fully in chapter 7.

An interesting survey of five hundred Sudanese women with an average age of twenty-six and ten years of marriage was conducted under the auspices of the Ahfad University College for women (Grotberg and Washi 1991), a pioneer in women's education in the Sudan and in the Muslim world generally. Sixty percent of these women married traditionally, that is, they married their first cousins, usually father's brother's son. Thirteen percent were salaried employees. Those who indicated that they exercised personal choice in the selection of their husbands had significantly lower fertility rates. These women had, on average, 3.5 children, while the general fertility rate for Muslim Sudanese women is 6.0 children. In contrast, the ideal "modern" family is described by these women as having two children. The average educational level of women in the sample was middle school, and their husbands were generally better educated, with some secondary school training.

Family Planning Movement

An untutored Western response to fundamentalism in the Muslim world projects onto that social reality the forces at work in one's own society. Thus, "fundamentalism" in the Islamic world might suggest a ban or hostility toward birth control and family planning, as that issue has divided liberal and conservative religion in the West. In fact, there has been no comparable right-to-life movement in the Muslim world, and family planning information has entered Islamic society without much rancorous theological or political struggle. The accepted religious interpretation of the beginning of life is at the time of "quickening," or the time when the mother feels life in her body. Thus abortion in the early stages of the development of the fetus is not a moral problem. However, if that abortion is linked to immoral and illicit sexual conduct, then the consequences are grave. Indeed, because sexual activity is so controlled and constrained in the Muslim world, the emphasis in birth control has been placed on preventing pregnancy within the context of a married woman's life. The idea that birth control information and devices should be made available to unmarried women is anathema to every basic value of Islamic society and sexuality.

The family planning movement has entered Arab-Muslim society, generally speaking, as a by-product of the movement for female emancipation, which in turn was linked to the nationalist movements. Family planning clinics initially were introduced with the idea that the full incorporation of women's labor and participation in the newly independent nation required smaller families.

In the case of the nations we have been examining, family planning movements were enthusiastically endorsed and promoted by the official women's organizations, such as the National Union of Tunisian Women, the Sudanese Women's Union, and the Egyptian Women's Union. To assist the working woman, accessible and inexpensive daycare centers were also established by these women's organizations. For urban, relatively better educated working women, family size did decrease. However, in Egypt, where family planning was embraced as government policy and the emphasis shifted to rural women reducing the number of pregnancies, the results were far less successful. Egypt became recognized as an exception to the rule that urbanization curtails family size; large numbers of Egyptian peasants were streaming into Egypt's cities and still fellahin women were bearing an average of seven children. Government propaganda and international financial aid for family planning programs instilled questions in the minds of many Egyptians as to motives, and the government got the message that the limited success and unenthusiastic response from people was a form of passive resistance. The programs then shifted to a more decentralized approach, involving local women cooperating with family planning clinics, without the apparent heavy hand of the government, and a greater success rate has been achieved.

Numerous studies have shown that the most effective way to reduce population is to promote education for women. There is a powerful and persuasive correlation between the number of years of a woman's education and the number of her children. The correlation is an inverse one: the greater the educational level, the fewer the children. In Grotberg and Washi's study of young married Sudanese women, lower fertility rates correlate not only with education but also with the following set of attitudes: (1) a man and a woman can be friends, (2) strict segregation of the sexes can be relaxed, (3) a woman can choose to work outside of the home, (4) women can be involved in politics, and (5) women and men are equally competent and should enjoy equal rights.

These attitudes are just beginning to emerge in many Middle Eastern Muslim states, and the rates of change are uneven in the various countries. However, on the matter of family planning, there has not been the resistance and social turbulence that has been witnessed in many Western nations, driven by a theological interpretation that life begins at conception and that reproduction is a legitimate matter for the state.

Economic Pressures on the Family

Despite rapid and massive urbanization in the Arab and Muslim worlds, much of traditional family structure remains intact. However, some cracks in the foundation of social life are becoming visible. Although the majority of people in the Middle Eastern nations now live in cities, the integrity of the extended family has generally been upheld. Elsewhere urbanization has had a devastating effect on the extended family, and it is likely to have profound effects on the Muslim extended family in the Middle East in the future. In other regions the nuclear family has come to replace the extended family, and in other places the nuclear family has broken down into matrifocal (single mother–headed household) units. Despite massive rural to urban migration and male out-migration from poorer nations to richer ones, the essential qualities of the extended family have held together. That is, family members speak of the larger extended family as a unit experiencing either good or bad times economically, and poor economies at home have brought about a necessary alliance between family members.

However, this is in the short term; in the long term the extended family may not fare so well in the absence of physical or residential unity to reinforce the ideology of family solidarity. In each of the three countries where I have conducted studies of Islamic family law, one of the major areas of concern is the failure of husbands/fathers who have migrated abroad for work to provide adequate economic support to those whom they are bound legally to support. Primarily, this affects the immediate nuclear family, and the majority of court cases have been suits brought by wives against husbands. But with most people still residing in some form of a communal-extended household, the impact is greater than on the nuclear family alone. These changes in the stability of family life may lead to even greater problems if present trends continue, especially if the economic imbalances in the region continue to foster massive rural to urban migration and expatriate migration.

7

Liberalism, Moderation, or Extremism

The Future of the State in Muslim Societies

There is no more pressing or compelling question in contemporary Islamic societies than what constitutes the future of the state in majority Muslim states. Parallel trends exist between developments in the Muslim world and in the West. Moreover, after September 11, 2001, there is little doubt that the future of Islamic societies and their political systems is more entwined than ever with the United States as the single most powerful western and world power. The United States now takes the "Islamic threat" seriously, as the debate over which country or region constitutes the chief enemy of the West is now apparently resolved. Islamic extremism has replaced the former Soviet Union as the new "evil empire" as represented in organizations such as Islamic Jihad and the al-Qaeda group of Osama bin Laden.

Extremism Flourishes in the Absence of Democracy

The West has seen clearly the face of Islamic extremism in Afghanistan— with the oppression of women and girls and bans on all images, from televisions and cinema to ancient Buddhist statues. But the West has not been shown the face of democracy in the region or the struggles that have been waged for democracy in the Muslim world and the Middle East. The desire for democratic societies is not the sole province of the West; nor is the love of freedom of thought, expression, and movement, as well as the cherished freedom of the press.

The political philosophy of secular democracy dominated the Arab nationalist movements that led to independence in the 1950s and 1960s in

North Africa and the Middle East, while movements calling for Islamic government were generally marginalized in the period of the independence struggles and after the end of colonialism. Well-known secular democratic movements, such as the Arab socialism of Gamal Abdel Nasser, influenced Syrian and Iraqi Baʿathism, as well as the foundation of the Palestine Liberation Organization. One by one, military regimes seized power and ruled autocratically for decades, intolerant of popular democratic organizations, such as trade unions, women's unions, and youth groups.

With the humiliating Arab defeat in the Six Day War of June 1967 when Israel occupied Egypt, Syria, and Jordan without adequate Arab retaliation, the Islamist "fundamentalist" trend—which had been part of the independence movement but lacked mass appeal—became a real alternative to secular democracy. With the success of the 1979 Islamic Revolution in Iran, Islamists were encouraged by the first popular movement to institute an Islamic Republic replacing the U.S.–backed corrupt monarchy of the Shah Reza Pahlavi.

Following this came an international call for Muslim brother-soldiers to join the Afghani mujahideen to drive out the Soviet army, which had occupied the country in 1979 and threatened the popular base of Islam. This group of mujahideen fighters was armed and backed by the United States as it fought communism based in Kabul. The lack of critical human intelligence deflected interest and attention in U.S. intelligence circles away from this international cadre of mujahideen, who had been emboldened by their success in Afghanistan. Instead, U.S. policy in the region focused on isolating Iran; defeating Iraq and imposing on it after its defeat in the Gulf War a crippling international boycott; protecting the West's oil in the Gulf; and supporting our critical allies—Israel and Egypt—in the Palestinian-Israeli struggle. Insufficient attention was paid to the growth of the Islamist movements, such as Hamas among the Palestinians. Hamas (al-harakah al-muqawamah al-Islamiyah—Islamic resistance movement) has effectively displaced the secular Palestine Liberation Organization for its superior resistance to the Israeli occupation of Palestine in two intifadas, from 1987 to 1992 and from 2000 to the present moment in the absence of a post-Oslo peace process. Unaware of this dramatic growth of an international Islamist movement, the United States unwittingly admitted Sheikh Omar Abdel Rahman, later tried and convicted of planning the first attack on the World Trade Center, and, again lacking critical human intelligence, could not screen the second band of attackers whose deadly, catastrophic attacks changed the world in a day. As this is being written, yet another humiliating defeat has been inflicted by the United States on the Iraqi people and, by extension, on the Arab and Muslim peoples. It may be that it is not so much

Table 7.1. Types of States (Selected, as of 2004)

Military Regimes	Monarchies	Parliamentary Democracies
Egypt	Kingdom of Saudi Arabia	Lebanon
Pakistan	Kuwait	Turkey
Syria	Jordan Hashemite Kingdom	Israel*
Libya	Morocco	Iranian Islamic Republic
Tunisia	United Arab Emirates	Indonesia
Sudan	Qatar	
Malaysia	Dubai	
Iraq		
Algeria		

*Excluding the occupied territories.

that Arab nationalism has died but that it has morphed into something much greater: Muslim solidarity in the face of external, neo-imperial threats.

There is no substitute—satellite or other remote listening devices—for socially based intelligence and face-to-face interaction. Human intelligence also means using America's own experts on Muslim and Arab cultures, as well as its own diverse Muslim population.

Most Arab states are military regimes or monarchies. Although military heads of state often appear in suits, their power is maintained by armies and may be dictatorial and relatively stable, or unstable and prone to successive coups. Monarchies are more stable with the tradition and legitimacy of royal families, perhaps claiming descent from the Prophet Muhammad. Many of these undemocratic governments are closely allied with the United States. A number of parliamentary democracies exist in the region, although Israel is often described as the region's only democracy. Table 7.1 contains a partial list of these regimes.

What Are the Islamist Movements?

Islamists make political use of religion to seek the installation of an Islamic state in their respective countries. Islamic states are ideally conceived in the minds of many Muslims, perhaps harkening back to the days of the righteous caliphates in early Islam to serve as models for replacing the military regimes or feudal monarchies that have oppressed Muslims since the end of colonialism. An Islamic state is a theocracy where the ruler is a pious Muslim who applies Shari'a or Islamic law as the sole law in force and where Islamic institutions prevail in civic and social life. In Islamic states with non-Muslim minorities, Islamists argue that "people of the Book"—Christians and Jews

—are protected by paying a tax for their protected status as *dhimmis* to the state. Scholars have finally settled on the term *Islamist* to describe those who advocate the Islamic state as a viable model.

After the Iranian Revolution, Western academics struggled with terminology. What should one call this seemingly new Islamic activism? The terms *Islamic resurgence* or *revival* were used by those who have been called the "Accomodationists," meaning those scholars who saw the rise of political Islam as primarily in reaction to local dictatorial regimes and not as a direct political threat to the West. Constructive engagement with Muslim activists could support a new kind of indigenous democracy. Scholars who disagreed viewed such activism, which they called "fundamentalist" or "militant" Islamic movements, as directing their political anger at the West. These "Confrontationists" see political Islam as a threat to the West in need of containment at least, with elimination as a better option (Gerges 1999).

If American experts can be divided into two camps, Muslim public opinion is at least as divided. While the American public has immersed itself in a national crash course about world Islam, the Muslim world has also engaged in much reflection about its relationship with the West and the rest of the world.

Countless Muslim democrats have resisted dictatorial regimes and repression in their countries. Many human rights groups and activists have struggled to survive in order to advocate agendas that support the rights of political dissenters, feminist activists, human rights activists, and other democrats. Muslim reformers have been executed for apostasy by Islamist regimes, for example, Mahmoud Mohamed Taha in Sudan in 1985 on the eve of the restoration of democracy. Anti-extremist writers, such as Muhammad Sa'id al-'Ashmawy in Egypt, have lived for decades under armed protection in their homes for fear of attack by militant Islamists (al-'Ashmawy 1998). In the largest and longest hunger strike in modern history, forty women starved themselves to death in 2002 to protest against the military government of Turkey and for the rights of political prisoners. They use henna marriage rites to induct new hunger strikers into the struggle (Anderson 2001). And there are American Muslims who seek to construct an agenda of engagement both internally within Islam and externally with global equity and justice movements.

Recent developments in Iran reveal that major debates are vigorous about gender equity, parliamentary democracy, and the criticism that too much power in the hands of a single Muslim leader is undemocratic. Rather than developing a model that would represent a retreat from Islamic governance, Islamic democracy would include a parliamentary system with public referenda that would operate within the framework of Islamic law and religious institutions. In Turkey in 2002, the Islamic Justice and Development Party (AKP) supplanted the two previous Islamist parties—the Virtue and Welfare Parties, which had been banned for undermining the secular state in place since the 1920s—in popular elections and announced that its rule would be one expressing to the world the face of a moderate Islam, a Muslim democracy.

In every Muslim and Arab country there are democratic activists and human rights advocates seeking an end to totalitarian regimes and more open societies. Many of the governments they oppose are supported by the United States, making flight to the United States for political asylum problematical. However, for the undemocratic regimes on the U.S. list of terrorist countries—Iran, Iraq, Sudan—political refugees have fled to the United States for haven in great numbers. Exiles from repressive regimes, exemplified by Dr. Mahgoub el-Tigani Mahmoud, founder of the Sudanese Human Rights Organization in Cairo, have come to the United States and Europe for refuge yet face stereotyping by people who are ignorant of their struggles. In short, there is a broad spectrum of political and religious views that the United States barely comprehends.

Several cases highlight the nature of the democratic, reformist, and anti-extremist movements that exist in Arab and Muslim countries today.

Movements for Democracy

Mahmoud Mohamed Taha and the Sudanese Republican Brothers Movement

As Sudan Islamized its law in 1983—imposing Shari'a as state law in the country moving toward an Islamic state despite its one-third non-Muslim population in the south—Mahmoud Mohamed Taha, leader of the Republican Brothers movement, campaigned against this imposition as a distortion of Islam and Shari'a. He opposed the *hadd* penalty of amputation; he opposed the application of a *jizya* tax imposed upon Christians and Jews for their protection as a violation of their equal civil rights; and he opposed the imposition of Shari'a as dividing north and south and fueling the civil war. "Religious fanaticism and backward religious ideology can achieve for the people only upheaval and civil war"; symbolically this declaration against the Islamist trend was issued on December 25, 1984 (Taha 1987). Within two weeks Ustadh Mahmoud and four others were arrested and found guilty of sedition, apostasy, and disturbing public tranquility. All were sentenced to death. The four others charged were given the opportunity to recant and save their lives. Taha was not given that opportunity, and he was hanged on January 18, 1985. Within three months the military dictator who signed the decree was ousted. The transitional government ruled that the trial was completely illegal and that the proceedings and execution were null and void. This act of state terror against the leader of the Republican movement—seventy-six years old at the time of his hanging—resulted not only in recantations by the four charged with Taha but the release of four hundred men and women detained upon their agreement to dismantle their organization and cease to propagate the liberal Islamic views of Mahmoud Mohamed Taha. The Arab Human Rights Organization declared a day in his honor and memory, January 18, the day of his execution.

On the matter of apostasy, the Qur'an says that it is a religious sin: "Then whosoever will, let him believe, and whosoever will, let him disbelieve" (sura 29:18). The Prophet never used this punishment, according to Sunna and Hadith.

Taha's reformist "second message of Islam" is based upon the difference between the earlier Meccan texts of the Qur'an and the later Medinan texts as a basis for novel interpretations of historical Shari'a/Islamic law whereby full rights and equality irrespective of sex or religion can be upheld. Disciples of Taha, notably Abdullahi An-Na'im, have developed his ideas, calling for nothing less than an Islamic Reformation primarily as historical Shari'a is reformed. Taha's ideas have appeal for educated liberal Muslims, women, and non-Muslims living in predominantly Islamic countries. Many potential supporters are intimidated by established state religious institutions and orthodoxy, but examples of Islamist rule, such as Afghanistan, Iran, and Sudan, will eventually produce many converts to reformist Islam (An-Na'im 1990) or a return to secularism within emerging democracies, if they are encouraged.

Muhammad Sa'id al-'Ashmawy

Dr. Muhammad Sa'id al-'Ashmawy is an Egyptian jurist and former chief justice of the High Court of Cairo who began writing against the growing politicization of Islam in 1979. Two years later, Anwar al-Sadat was assassinated by the militant Islamist group Takfir wa Hijra in the first public appearance of violent extremism in Islam. Since 1979, 'Ashmawy's writings have stressed that the political trend in Islam is not the real Islam but rather a political ideology similar to fascism, Nazism, or other totalitarian doctrines. The French translation of his work, *L'Islamism contre Islam*, captures this idea. A *Reader's Digest* essay written by 'Ashmawy was titled "Hijacking Islam," and the book that I edited of his writings, *Against Islamic Extremism*, speaks to this basic message. His books in Arabic—*Roots of Islamic Law; Essence of Islam; Political Islam*, published in Cairo—were subjected to Islamist criticism and threats. One of their leaders wrote in an

Fig. 25. Dr. Muhammad Saʿid al-ʿAshmawy (center) with Sheikh Ahmad Shalaby and author, al-Azhar University. Gift to the author from the American University in Cairo.

Islamist newspaper, "Judge ʿAshmawy must be silenced," a coded signal for his elimination. In 1980, ʿAshmawy opposed the Islamist position that non-Muslims are heathens and that Islam respects all faiths, especially the Christians and Jews, whom they prefer to call "crusaders and Zionists." The Egyptian minister of waqfs then instructed imams at the local mosques during their sermons at Friday prayers to expose ʿAshmawy as an apostate whose blood could be shed by the Faithful. In 1996, his continued rejection of the idea that Christians and Jews are infidels—at that time espoused in a fatwa by the late sheikh of al-Azhar—was rebutted by ʿAshmawy. He then became the target of a witch hunt in the Saudi London-based al-Muslimoun (the Muslim Faithful) and was denied the opportunity to refute his critics in the timid Egyptian press. ʿAshmawy cites the Qurʾanic verse "the faithful, Jews and Christians and whoever believes in God, and does what is right, shall have nothing to fear or regret" (ʿAshmawy, personal communication, 2001).

Since the early 1980s ʿAshmawy has been forced to live under the protection of the Egyptian government, which has battled extremism and terrorism. Two armed guards survey his apartment, one at the entry to his apartment building in Zamalek and the other outside his apartment door. I became quite familiar with the routine of being cleared by these guards before my meetings with Judge ʿAshmawy.

'Ashmawy was one of the first to oppose political Islam in Egypt. He has made the following points:

1) Shari'a—Islamic law—is treated by the Islamists as divinely inspired and immutable; however, it is a man-made jurisprudence and therefore not immune to criticism or amendment.

2) Interpretation of Qur'anic texts should be based on study of the historical context in which they were revealed.

3) Any pronouncement or action made by a ruler or an activist in the name of Islam is devoid of any sacredness or immunity and is subject to the same human critique and accountability as any other words or deeds.

'Ashmawy is sensitive to the points of conflict and debate between the West and the Islamic world. Jihad, he argues, is the most sensitive of these in both regions. To non-Muslims, jihad is a holy war against them; to many Muslims, jihad is a religious duty to guide non-Muslims to the true faith. Militants believe that jihad is a divine injunction to impose Islam upon non-Muslims. According to 'Ashmawy, only a minority of Muslims live jihad's true moral and spiritual meaning. "Fight in this way of God against those who fight against you, but begin not hostilities. Lo, Allah loveth not aggressors" (sura 2:190). After the first successful battle at Badr (624 C.E.), Muhammad announced: "We have turned from the minor jihad to the major one," with the battle being the minor jihad, and spiritual struggle being the major one. Jihad is always major, as the Prophet said, when one fights the negative elements in oneself in order to grow in serenity and strength. Jihad as defensive warfare is the minor jihad, not to be confused with the major jihad; the major jihad implies self-improvement and legitimate self-defense. The belief that jihad is war against all of the infidels until Islam is the sole faith on earth is a grave departure from the original meaning of jihad.

After the attacks of September 11, 2001, 'Ashmawy wrote a message to Americans. For the paperback edition of *Against Islamic Extremism,* it arrived too late to be published.

My long confrontation with Islamism was never confined to print media but also extended to lectures, conferences, and meetings with influential people all over the globe from San Francisco to Jakarta. I forewarned in my work about the unconventional warfare Islamism will wage against all humanity in the name of religion. Though many were convinced of the validity of my ideas, no action was taken to prevent the rising terrorist phenomenon. Almost all of the governments were courting the militants out of fear from their growing influ-

ence. Had they heeded my advice the attacks of the 11 September trag-
edy and the subsequent war would have been nipped in the bud. Ideologies are not fought off by military or police measures but with right,
just, and persuasive ideas. How can warfare by the police prevent sui-
cide bombers when the perpetrators have the inner conviction that
they are performing a religious act of martyrdom for which God will
reward them generously in paradise. *Against Islamic Extremism* con-
tributes to saving humanity from religious ideology and its twin, international religious terrorism. (October 2001)

Sisters in Islam

A core group of feminist scholars has been active in Malaysia endeavoring
to provide alternative interpretations of Qur'an and Sunna from the overwhelmingly male-dominated 'ulama in both historical and contemporary
Islamic societies. Publishing many of their pamphlets in English, they have
exerted an influence far beyond Malaysia. I learned of their work in 1996 in
Madras, India, while on the Semester at Sea visiting one of hundreds of
India's Women's Police Stations devoted to the problem of domestic violence. Female police officers are called to intervene in cases of violence
against women, and one of them showed me the Sisters in Islam pamphlet
Are Muslim Men Allowed to Beat Their Wives? Sisters in Islam is a small
organization largely appointed by the government that engages in critical
feminist discourse on the rights of women in Islam and in Muslim societies,
as well as other issues relating to Islam in the contemporary world. For
example, they are among the first to take up the issue of the *hudud* penalties
in Islamic criminal law, such as stoning for adultery or amputation of limbs
for theft.

Anthropologist Michael Peletz interviewed several members. Their mul-
tilateral world is immediately apparent: "We were against the World Trade
Center bombings, but we are also against the U.S. bombing in Afghanistan."
The Sisters in Islam, they say, "want a consistent, principled, liberal, progressive Islam." They disagreed with the national Pan-Malaysian Islamic
Party, which believed that the Taliban "protected" women. They criticized
Taliban—their position on women, culture, dance, hudud, which they say
represents the intolerant, extremist side of Islam. They don't believe in
ijtihad [legal innovation] and have medieval, unthinking, ahistorical minds
and no ability to deal with differences of opinion within Islam. Zainah
Anwar, a leader of Sisters in Islam, has been accused of insulting the Prophet
and disgracing Islam (Peletz 2002, 22–24).

In their earliest pamphlets, they explain their agenda and method:

Sisters in Islam is a group of Muslim women studying and researching the status of women in Islam. We have come together because we want to achieve the rights granted to us by Islam. Islamic resurgence in the past two decades has affected the lives of Muslims all over the world. It has prompted among many of the Faithful a renewed endeavor to understand the meaning of Islam as a comprehensive way of life. We believe that women and men who constitute the ummah must participate as equal partners in this noble effort.

We are concerned over certain attitudes towards women prevalent in the Muslim world today. From its very outset, Islam was a liberating religion that uplifted the status of women and gave them rights that were considered revolutionary 1,400 years ago. In spite of this founding spirit, Muslim practices today oppress women and deny them the equality and human dignity granted in the Qur'an.

Our research has shown that oppressive interpretations of the Qur'an are influenced mostly by cultural practices and values which regard women as inferior and subordinate to men. It is not Islam that oppresses women, but human beings with all their weaknesses who have failed to understand Allah's intentions.

It has been a liberating experience for us to return to the Qur'an and study Allah's actual words in an effort to understand their true meaning. The Qur'an teaches "love and mercy" (30:21) between men and women, that men and women are each other's garment (2:187), that "be you male or female, you are members of one another" (3:195), and that "men and women are protectors, one of another" (9:71)

In this spirit of equality and justice so insistently enjoined by the Qur'an that guides our efforts, we now wish to share our findings with our sisters and brothers in the hope that together we can create a world where equality and justice may now prevail. (*Are Women and Men Equal before Allah?* 1991)

Pamphlets and working papers tackle some of the thorniest issues affecting women's status in Islam: *Are Muslim Men Allowed to Beat Their Wives?* (1990), *Islam, Reproductive Health, and Women's Rights* (2000), *Islam and Family Planning* (2001), and *Women as Judges* (2002). Forthcoming works in English include *Islam and Polygamy, Islamic Family Law and Justice for Muslim Women,* and *Biographies of Muslim Women Role Models.*

Progressive Muslims

Numerous works have appeared since the events of September 11, 2001, that underscore liberal and progressive thought and tolerance within Islam. Many of these, like my own work featuring one who opposed Islamic extremism, were published before 9/11, but such works became urgent after 9/11. The association in the public mind of violence and extremism with the world of Islam and Muslims required at least an academic response. Likewise, Muslim scholars were mobilized to defend the faith and expose its extremist advocates and practitioners as wrongful. *Liberal Islam* (Kurzman 1998), *The Place of Tolerance in Islam* (Abou El Fadl 2002), and *Progressive Muslims* (Safi 2003) are just a few examples. One of the most positive developments is that Muslim voices are being heard in a credible way, albeit in a time of crisis for the West.

The essential thesis of Khaled Abou El Fadl is that extremist groups have long been ejected from mainstream Islam. An American example of this is the nonacceptance of the theology of the Nation of Islam, whose historical racial chauvinism has no place in Islamic history or practice. Today, dialogue and accommodation by Nation of Islam ministers and imams has moved some groups closer to the mainstream, but it is they, not Islam, who have changed. Further, he argues that first colonial and later weak Muslim states have not had a vigorous class of ʿulama but most were co-opted by the needs and ambitions of the state and have become discredited. This vacuum has provided opportunities for amateurs like Osama bin Laden to wreak havoc with Qurʾanic scripture, making hatred, vengeance, and murder a sacred duty. His writings and those of his contributors seek to deny legitimacy to those who would raise the banner of Islam as moral or religious justification for their acts.

Omid Safi's introductory essay in *Progressive Muslims,* entitled "The Times They Are a-Changin': A Muslim Quest for Justice, Gender Equality, and Pluralism," places contemporary Muslim discourse squarely within democratic and pluralistic dialogues of the West and the rest of the world. In other words, Muslims are no different from other humans or humanistic traditions. This obvious fact should hardly need mentioning, much less require academic tracts to demonstrate its validity. Safi challenges Muslim progressives to think not only more deeply about the Qurʾan and the life of the Prophet but also about the life we all share as human beings, indeed all life, on this planet. At the same time Safi acknowledges that Muslim "modernizers" of the past have lacked a certain authenticity for Muslims as their writings may have been intended for a Western audience, or they may have been perceived as "westernizing" Islamic discourse. The significance of the current period is that the discussion of critical or progressive Islam is taking place within Muslim communities and among Muslims. Social justice, gender justice, and pluralism are at the core of this discussion, Safi argues.

Is this the beginning of an Islamic Reformation? The question has been raised before by Muslim and non-Muslim alike. Safi's response is that it may be a hasty or too general attribution. "Reformation" signals a significant break with the past when what is advocated is a critical reengagement with the heritage of Islamic thought, rather than a casual bypassing of its accomplishments (16). This calls for a rigorous reengagement with classical Muslim liberal thinkers such as al-Ghazzali or Ibn Tamiya and concerted movement beyond apologetics and sloganeering. In a most pragmatic and urgent vein, Safi argues that contemporary discourse within the Muslim community must move beyond what he refers to as "pamphlet Islam," published by Da'wah groups promoting Islam, and such subjects as the status of women in Islam or Muslim relations to Christians and Jews. Moreover, advocating tolerance is meaningless without pluralism, and repeating the mantra that Islam is a religion of peace is hollow without equal rights and justice. Safi's quest amounts to a clarion call to Muslims to engage Islam with critical reflection combining this with activism for social justice. However, the message is one for non-Muslims as well. Liberal forces are reclaiming the faith and finding new meaning in its fundamentals.

Human Rights Movements

Human rights movements exist all over the Muslim and Arab world. These movements are built upon the same principles of the Universal Declaration of Human Rights and U.N. statements on the rights of women and the child, but they operate under regimes that are repressive and fear the truth they speak and where they are ignored by the world because of western support of the repressive regimes. Also, they may address international issues criticizing the Euro-American superpowers. Thus they are often caught between domestic oppression and foreign injustice. Active human rights organizations can be found in what the West often calls the "moderate countries": Egypt, Tunisia, Morocco, Palestine, Lebanon, Kuwait, Qatar, and Jordan. They are also struggling in Israel to equalize the rights of Arabs and Jews, and countries such as Syria, Iraq, Sudan, Algeria, Pakistan, and Afghanistan have human rights movements tied to their pro-democratic organizations, but many activists have been imprisoned or forced into exile. Feudal monarchies like Saudi Arabia and other kingdoms in the oil-rich Arab Gulf region shield their own repressive rule by saying that Islam is sufficient to protect all human rights. An outstanding organization is the Cairo Institute for Human Rights. It organizes international conferences and publishes position papers and conference volumes on Arab and Muslim human rights.

Arab Human Rights Organizations have called for a new democratic era in the region based upon the following:

- A call to armed Islamist groups to stop all forms of violence while supporting their right to advocate their principles in a peaceful manner.

- A call to all Arab governments to legalize the right of free assembly within a framework of democratic laws and constitution.
- A call to further the Arab Human Rights organizations and urge debate and intellectual engagement among peoples of Europe, the United States, and the Arab-Muslim world to defeat the erroneous idea of the inevitable clash of civilizations between the West and the Islamic societies, especially as this encourages extremism and bigotry in both regions.
- A call to recognize women's rights as an integral part of the universal human rights system of which the Muslim and Arab worlds form a part.

These movements and the people who support them are the true democrats of their respective countries. It is the United States and Western support of these movements that would win the hearts and minds of Muslims and Arabs. Unfortunately, human rights movements are often perceived as anti-state due to the human rights abuses of repressive states supported by the West.

The challenge to combine any reformulation of Arab society and Muslim culture with the powerful global principles of democracy and human rights is emerging as one of the most critical issues in the current debate. These competing traditions, Western and Eastern, secular and religious, with their economic and political ramifications, create the major tensions in Islamic communities today, from without and within. They are felt in very real ways, from stresses in the family, to debate over the proper role for women in society, to challenges for legitimacy in religious leadership and struggles for power in the state.

Modernism = Westernism: Colonial Legacies and Definitions of What Is Modern

The twentieth century was one of tumult for the whole world, as well as the Islamic nations within it. The special pressures and challenges that have been faced by a majority of the Muslim nations and their peoples include the basic historical fact that they began the century as colonial entities and ended it as independent nations, in most cases not yet economically secure or politically stable. The particular cultural challenge faced by Muslim peoples straddles the competing cultural traditions of the West—learned through colonialism and defined as modern, yet carrying with them that very legacy of colonialism—and the indigenous heritage, Arabic and Muslim, that was devalued in colonial times. The reclamation and restoration of that heritage and how it is to take on a modern form has been a major ideological question since independence. Further, the tensions between the secularism that was promoted by colonialism and the secular politics that grew into Arab nationalism, and the present challenge of religious alternatives under the banner of Islamic revival, fundamentalism, or political Islam are the current phase of this historical trend.

The most important part of the colonial legacy is the nation-state itself, which was created, in its modern form, by the European occupier, either British or French. In a number of cases, like Egypt and the Sudan, Syria and Lebanon, the state was created out of the remnants of the Ottoman Empire, while in others, for example, Kuwait, Saudi Arabia, and other Arabian Gulf nations, it was created *de nova*. The indigenous national movements were built upon the presumption that the nation-state, as defined, would continue, and there was little talk at the time of independence about the return to precolonial borders or territories. It may portend future developments to note that Saddam Hussein attempted to legitimize his claim to territory in Kuwait in Iraq's invasion in 1990 on the basis of colonial boundaries drawn by the British. Certainly both sides in the ongoing civil war in the Sudan would agree that the British policy of divide and rule between north and south Sudan exacerbated already hostile feelings left over from Turco-Egyptian rule and the slave trade. In this particular respect, the legacy of colonialism is usually brought up in a negative way.

Although the motives of colonialism were clearly economic and political, imperial control introduced to the colonies a number of basic institutions of government, law, education, and administration that have remained the mainstay of the postindependence nations. For the first several decades after independence, in many countries, these basic institutions remained intact, except for the fact that they came under local control. Even the transition to the use of Arabic as the official language of government was often delayed due to the dependence on the former colonial structures and procedures. Arabization was accomplished more slowly than the simpler personnel changes from European to indigenous control of offices and schools. And in some contexts, such as the Maghrib countries of Tunisia, Algeria, and Morocco, French has continued to be the language of education and cultivation, with its defenders arguing that literacy in French opens the student-intellectual to a wider world than does the Arabic language. The Sudan, despite many years of the call for the Arabization of the curriculum at the University of Khartoum, only accomplished this avowedly political goal under the Islamist regime in power since 1989.

Many would argue that the colonial legacy was carried on in more subtle cultural ways than language alone, in the cultural values conveyed by language and its heritage and context. The colonialist paradigm that political overseer translates into cultural superiority is a deeply entrenched belief in the minds of the colonizer and the colonized. Perhaps this is the most difficult part of the colonial legacy to excise. While for decades of colonialism the standard of the highest achievement, educational, political, or otherwise, was to emulate the British or French ways of speaking, thinking, and acting, the shift to an indigenous set of values created a tension in society, especially along class lines. Upper-class nationals continued to send their children, especially sons, out of the country for their education or to local institutions that continued to operate in the European fashion. Families that were not so well off sent their children to local schools where the language of instruction was Arabic and where they were socialized to think that their children were receiving an inferior education.

Outwardly, styles of dress and use of language became highly indicative markers of what Franz Fanon would have called the interior colonization of mind. It is not uncommon today to overhear two educated Tunisians, fashionably dressed in European suits, conversing in French. It is a sign of their education and breeding. French has so overtaken Tunisian literary culture that contemporary writers, dealing with themes of culture and the colonial legacy, write about the subject more passionately in French than in Arabic. Indeed, their formal education has abjured the use of Arabic, which was historically seen as limited to religious subjects.

In the Levantine countries of Syria and Lebanon, also colonized by France, the impact on local culture was, perhaps, not so profound as in the Maghrib, but the standard of education for elites was certainly training that included extensive involvement in the French language. Quite remarkably, in Egypt, only occupied by France for a brief period under Napoleon, the legacy of that encounter was the introduction of the Code Napoleon and the basics of French law, as well as an educational and cultural foundation in French that persisted through the two centuries of British cultural influence and colonialism. The cream of Egyptian elites, up to the present, are fluent in English and French.

The attitude of the colonial governments to the religion of Islam and its indigenous institutions was one of cautious respect but firm control. In some instances, where resistance was mounted against foreign control in the name of religion, like the Mahdi of Sudan, military suppression was coupled with a high degree of formal autonomy afforded to Muslim structures and leaders. Independent "Mohammedan" courts were established as a separate judicial entity, with its own Court of Appeals, but the final authority always rested with the English colonial government. The religious establishment may have done little to criticize or oppose colonialism, but religious opposition to foreign domination did develop in political organizations, like the Muslim Brotherhood, organized in Egypt during colonial times under the leadership of Hasan al-Banna. Their position on Islam was uncompromising and antireformist; Islam is a comprehensive system of religious thought and practice that is sufficient unto itself to solve every political and social problem. They opposed western imperialism on the ground that it circumscribed or denied Islam its full place; as such they represented a small but important voice in the struggle against colonialism.

The colonial governments were able to recognize and control the powerful yet competing legacy of the Islamic heritage by appointing their own guardians of that tradition. The state-appointed 'ulama during colonial times were called upon to confirm policies and legal changes that suited their political goals. The end of the practice of child betrothal, the so-called modernization and regulation of waqf and charitable trusts, and other changes regarded as reforms of an archaic system were accomplished by appropriate religious interpretations, fatwas, issued by these 'ulama. To be fair, there is evidence of both restraint on the part of the colonizers and resistance by Muslims and the 'ulama themselves on certain points of religious and social principles. The restraint is explainable in terms of the colonizer's desire not to alienate further a subjugated populace with unpopular reforms. Polygyny, for example, which was disdained by the Europeans on religious and cultural grounds, was not a target of reform. Female circumcision was outlawed in the Sudan in 1946 by the English on religious, medical, and social grounds; however, despite a fatwa that described infibulation as "mutilation" and therefore forbidden in Islam (Fluehr-Lobban 1987, 97), the practice has continued, although it has been modified by some contemporary midwives (Kenyon 1991). In virtually every colonial situation, both holy days for Muslims and Christians, Friday and Sunday, were observed, while the annual Muslim religious holidays were also respected.

The religious leaders who were appointed by the colonial state were, generally speaking, not controversial nor were they opposed during their time of government service. However, during the postcolonial secular rule by indigenous officials, their alleged role as apologists for state policy became more acute. A great deal of credibility was lost by the grand mufti and sheikh of Al-Azhar during the time of Nasser's secular, Arab socialist rule in Egypt when government policy was routinely sanctioned by the 'ulama on a range of subjects from legal reform to foreign affairs. At the same time, the Nasser regime was cracking down on the Muslim Brotherhood, so the impression was given that the highest religious authorities were, in fact, acting on behalf of the government's interests and against Islamic causes. The antagonistic relationship between the state and resurgent Islam is not new, and the beginning of the distrust of state-appointed 'ulama by Islamic activists is traceable to this early period of independence when colonialism could no longer be blamed for their subservience to government. This tension within various Islamic societies has sharpened over the decades since independence to the point where some contemporary Islamist activists openly condemn their official religious leadership and seek alternative guidance from more populist sheikhs and imams. From a perspective that is grounded in the twentieth-century development of Islamic society, this is an utterly modern phenomenon in that the relationship between the state and religion is being questioned in a fundamental way. Ideally, religion and the state would be merged in the perfect Islamic society, but not what has been described where religion is subordinated to the state's interests. Likewise, calls for the restoration of Arabic language education with Islamic and Arabic studies and for the restoration of Shari'a to a more central place in the rule of law in state government are viewed as modern demands.

The Proper Contemporary Role for Women: Being Both "Modern" and Muslim

The contradiction between modernity and Islam has been raised in the West and discussed in the East more as a response to questions raised in the West regarding the compatibility of Islam with modernism. Modernity is generally equated with Westernization, rather than simply meaning up-to-date. The developments taking place may not be viewed as modern by the West, but they are certainly current in the Islamic world. Muslim women are confronting conflicting definitions of what it is to be modern; the older secular models derived basically from European colonial contact have been challenged by alternative Islamic models in aspiration, behavior, and dress. This is a tension that is sharply felt in contemporary Islamic society and one that is increasingly falling to the side of Islamic interpretations of the proper modern role for women.

There are certain continuities and discontinuities between the end of colonialism, early independence, and the contemporary period. In the realm of education, this was established as a societal goal later for women than men in most formerly colonial situations. However, once established, education for women and girls became firmly embedded as a natural right and an expectation for the state to provide. Except for the poorest, most isolated locales, or those which are experiencing political disruption, education for girls is normal, at least through the middle school or secondary levels. Female literacy is promoted through development programs as well, at least so a young woman can read and understand her marriage contract, read the newspaper, or follow the instructions on a prepared food label.

This goal of supporting and promoting female education has not witnessed major setbacks in the current period of increased Islamism. If anything, it is a twentieth-century trend that has been reinforced through a reinvigorated Islam. Recalling that Islam encourages literacy in order to read and recite the Qur'an, it follows that a revived Islam will endeavor to

Fig. 26. Algerian women protest potential loss of rights in a possible Islamic state.

bring about a return to reading and studying the Qur'an. This is exactly what is happening, but what is remarkable is that it includes study groups led by women, especially in some of the clandestine Islamist movements in Egypt and Tunisia. Openly Islamic feminist groups, such as Sisters in Islam, challenge the absolute authority of the historical 'ulama in Malaysia and throughout the Muslim world. They have argued that Islam permits women to be judges, and indeed this is or has been the case in Malaysia, Indonesia, Tunisia, Turkey, Iraq, and Sudan and probably in other less well documented cases.

The study of the holy sources by women is a new phenomenon in the modern world. In the past, most *madrasas, khalwas,* or *kuttabs,* Islamic schools, were almost exclusively devoted to boys' education. However, education today, including religious education, is stressed for both sexes to the highest level attainable. Indeed, the highly motivated young men and women involved in contemporary Islamist movements are drawn from these highly educated segments of society. The goals of that education may have shifted away from the goals articulated by the generation of the newly independent states. Female education then stressed career training, while the Islamists argue that the education of women enhances their "natural" roles as mothers and educators. A seeming paradox, many of the women Islamist leaders are themselves professional women, as doctors, lawyers, and university professors. It is perhaps more telling that, during the recent period of the most intense Islamist political agitation and influence, the number of women formally entering the workforce has increased in Iran and Egypt.

This poses a unique problem for the Muslim woman of how to be both Muslim and modern. The problem has been successfully resolved by a large number of intellectual Muslim women. They have chosen to work outside the home for wages, primarily for the same reasons that women in the West have done so, that is, for a second income for a family (recall that women bear no financial responsibility for household maintenance, but they may wish to earn an independent income for "extras" for their children or for themselves) or for personal satisfaction. However, leaving the protection of the home for many hours a day, moving about in crowded streets or taking public transportation, and perhaps having male coworkers are all situations that place a woman in jeopardy, according to traditional values. Historically, male jurists have seen this as a kind of *fitnah,* the "chaos" caused by the association of unrelated males and females. Before colonialism and the introduction of Western styles of dress, women typically would don some type of outer covering, known in various cultural contexts as *milaya, chador,* or *tobe,* when they left the confines of the home and extended family to visit or shop. This was and continues to be means of providing modesty and offering protection from the unwanted gazes or physical jostling of strangers in public areas. In a few rare cases, particularly in the Arabian peninsula and parts of central Asia, such as Afghanistan, veiling of the face was also customary.

In the cultural reassessment and reawakening that has occurred since the end of colonialism, it is not surprising that women have revived and modernized forms of Islamic-inspired dress as a resolution to the conflict implicit in working or studying outside the home. These are no longer simple sheet-like pieces of material to cover the body; women now wear fashionable long skirts, long-sleeved blouses, and coverings for the head that both conceal the hair and flatter the contours of the face. Simple eye makeup, or no cosmetics at all, is the norm for the modern woman dressed in this "Shari'" way, inspired by Islamic teachings and referring to the type of dress as hijab, meaning covered or protected. Typically, these were homemade ensembles that were cost-efficient and involved collaborative sharing of patterns, sewing machines, and labor on the part of women, but with their increasing popularity, ready-made clothes are available in department stores. The hijab has become a symbol of revived Islam, and unobtrusive observers may attempt to gauge the depth or popularity of Islamist movements in a country by the number of women seen in public dressed in this way. In some countries where Islamist movements, like An-Nahda in Tunisia, represent a threat to the government, women dressed in the hijab may be harassed on the streets by public security agents. In other countries where the government has cracked down on radical Islamist movements but has adopted a laissez-faire attitude toward wearing the hijab, such as in Egypt, the growth of wearing some form of hijab has been dramatic and marked, by now an overwhelming majority of urban women. Studies of the adoption of Islamically inspired dress indicate that women have taken to this cultural-religious expression because of its authenticity and congruence with national heritage, because of its practicality and simplicity, and because of its religious meaning (El Guindi 1999). Also mentioned is the growing social pressure of so many women making the change. Wearing the hijab can also have its contextual usage. One woman with whom we were acquainted in Tunis wore the hijab when she was working at an open desk with direct contact with the public, but changed to a style of no head covering when she worked behind an enclosure.

The attitude of many modern Muslim women toward social and legal reform is similarly complex. Some of the legal reforms that offered women emancipation in the wake of the successful independence movements are viewed as Western-inspired changes that are more cosmetic and symbolic than real in terms of women's rights. Egypt is a case in point; a progressive body of laws inspired by Mrs. Sadat was abruptly overturned in the wake of her husband's assassination because of the undemocratic method in which the law was promulgated. Some years later, much of the substance of the law was reinstated through parliamentary means, leaving aside certain provisions thought to be offensive or contrary to Islam. The debate over this law revealed the tension between the secular feminists of Egypt's early post-independence period, who, perhaps, sought change in the status of women more along the lines of the Western woman, while the contemporary Islamic feminists are seeking greater restoration of the traditional Shari'a or change in the laws affecting the status of women that conforms to Islamic principles.

Restriction of, or the outright elimination of polygyny has probably been the most controversial change proposed by secularists and feminists who have sought to remove this allegedly archaic remnant of an older Islamic society. Since there is widespread consensus among the 'ulama internationally that polygyny is explicitly allowed in the Qur'an, its removal represents a denial of the truth and validity of the word of God. It is more this point which is defended by the Islamists than a steadfast adherence to the practice of polygyny. In fact, as was mentioned in the discussion of the contemporary Muslim family, a very small percentage of Muslim men practice polygyny today. So it is not so much the defense of the practice as the principle it represents. On the other hand, the right of the wife to receive adequate support, *nafaqa,* when her husband is away, during divorce proceedings while they are still legally married, and in certain cases for a period of time after a final divorce has been strongly defended as correct and appropriate in Islamic terms. And the right of the wife to seek judicial divorce has not been challenged by the Islamists, although the social conditions that drive a woman to seek divorce are often criticized.

A number of controversial points surrounding the degree of personal freedom that a woman or wife should be able to exercise represents another source of tension within contemporary Islamic society. Under traditional Muslim thought and practice, a woman lives under the protection and guardianship of her father, initially, and then her husband. This conforms to patriarchal ideas found in other Western and Eastern societies. However, twentieth-century life brought many changes that have physically and psychically freed women from traditional bonds. Women move about more openly to carry out errands and household tasks if they are housewives, and an increasing number of women are working outside the home. An Islamist view would argue for women working outside the home in "appropriate" jobs, such as physicians working at Mother-Child clinics or with pediatric or obstetrical-gynecological medicine. Likewise, an approved type of work for a female lawyer would be a practice that focuses on the personal status laws affecting women, such as divorce, child custody, or support cases, and primarily with female clients. Some of the stricter Islamists believe that a woman should remain at home after marriage and the birth of children, and that a woman seeking employment outside the home should obtain permission from her husband, father, or guardian. Likewise, these so-called fundamentalists would have women obtain permission from their male guardians to acquire a passport or to travel outside their countries. The Islamist regime in Sudan has invoked this idea to prevent academic women who are critical of the government from traveling abroad, while they have also removed some female government employees who are not aligned with the regime, using the Islamic rationale as a justification. Critics of the Islamist approach and human rights activists have opposed this strict and harsh interpretation that limits freedom and mobility for women.

Rather than signaling an end to women's participation in society and politics, the Islamist upsurge has provided a continuing outlet for women's involvement in the issues of the day. The current wave of Islamist activity can be seen as a continuation of their mobilization and participation in the nationalist movement a generation or more ago. The model and inspiration that the nationalist and feminist women provided has laid the foundation for the Islamist women, some of whom proactively describe themselves as "Islamic feminists." And why not, since much of the energy that has been generated by the movement has focused on the study and examination of the sources of the religion, the Qur'an and Sunna, from the perspective of the proper role of women in society, and this has its own liberating and emancipating dimension. Egyptian Muslim feminist Aisha Abdel Rahman argues that the "truly Islamic" and "truly feminist" option is neither immodest dress nor identical roles for men and women in the name of modernity; neither is it sexual segregation and the seclusion of women in the name of Islam. The right path is the one that combines modesty, responsibility, and the integration of women into public life, while honoring the Qur'anic and naturally enjoined distinctions between the sexes (Hoffman-Ladd 1987, 37).

Human Rights Organizations and Their Commitment to Women's Rights

Some Western observers and Arab and Muslim secularists are deeply concerned about the future status of women under Islamist regimes, insofar as the examples which have emerged in Iran, Saudi Arabia, Sudan, and Afghanistan are not encouraging on this question. On balance, it should be pointed out that dramatic progress in the area of women's rights was not achieved under secular regimes since independence and that the greatest advances have been made when women have agitated on their own behalf with their social and political agenda in hand (Hale 1996). There is not much reason to think that an enlightened Islamist government would be any worse than a secular regime, and it might do a better job if it incorporated activist women into the apparatus and policymaking realms of government. As yet, we have not seen this kind of consistent commitment to the inclusion of women by any secular or religious government in the Arab or Muslim world, but then we have not yet witnessed this in any Western government either. And it is important to recall that more Muslim women have become heads of state in the past several decades than women in the West.

Islamism and the Challenge to the State and Official Islam

So much has been written about the phenomenon of Islamic revival that it is difficult to say something new, except that it is important to point out that its potential or threat is very much in the mind and the eye of the beholder. Much of the popular discourse in the West on the subject has used the term *Islamic fundamentalism*, perhaps employing the term *fundamentalist* as it is commonly used in the West to describe Christian movements that seek to return to literal interpretations of the Bible and a basic Christian lifestyle that has been eroded by secularism. In some ways this is a fruitful comparison; however, few Arab or Muslim writers use the term, arguing that among Muslims there is no disagreement about the fundamentals (*'usul al-din*) of the religion, that it is based upon the holy sources of Qur'an and Sunna. Thus the Arabic translation of the word *fundamentalism, 'usuliyya,* conveys a different meaning and context than in contemporary English usage. Likewise, the tendency to lump all of the various Islamist movements under a single, simplifying term is misleading and, ultimately, confusing.

Islamist movements burst on the scene among Shiʻa and Sunni Muslims alike, and they have grown in response to decadent kings, such as the shah of Iran, as well as in reaction to military secular regimes, as in Egypt, and in single-party secular regimes, like Tunisia and Algeria, and in irredentist movements weary of the promises of Arab nationalism, such as the Palestinian movement. These historical contexts are too varied to be treated as a single phenomenon, and so scholars struggled to find more appropriate terms—*Islamic revival, resurgent Islam,* and *political Islam* before settling on *Islamist*. The terms that the Islamic activists are using themselves refer to "the call" (ad-Daʼwah), "Islamic renewal" and "renaissance" (an-Nahda), and "new dawn" (al-Fajr), and they are finding ways to live that conform to the teachings of Islam and the Shariʻa. The slogan "Islam, huwa al-hal" (Islam is the solution) summarizes and defines their approach.

To the Western politician, perhaps preoccupied with the uninterrupted flow of oil from the Middle East and Persian Gulf or the preservation of the status quo in Israel, the threat of Islamist movements and their mass appeal is very much a cause of concern to the stability of the region and the international order. Some conservative Western observers have voiced concern that, with the end of the cold war, the communist threat has been replaced by an Islamic threat in a now famous characterization as a "clash of civilizations" (Huntington 1996). This point of view has been underscored by the events of September 11, 2001, which seemed to pit the Islamic world against the Western world. This fear results more from an ignorance of Islamist movements that may not be more developed politically than the anger and impotence the United States felt at the time of the Iranian-American hostage crisis. We are still far too ignorant of the religion of Islam and Muslims, yet we seem to feel very comfortable in speaking about the "dangers" of Islamism and the inevitable backwardness that will ensue and the darkness that will descend upon nations and people who follow this path.

What Is the Islamic State?

The central goal of the contemporary Islamist movement is to establish an Islamic state. Of course, Islamic states are not new and were established in the early and medieval caliphates of Syria, Egypt, Moorish Spain, and Iraq as well as the Ottoman Empire. The Mahdist state that ruled in the Sudan from 1884 to 1898 was perhaps the first modern Islamist state in that it was created in armed resistance to the foreign colonial invasions and occupations of the Turks and the British during the nineteenth century. Contemporary Islamism is a combination of a response to European colonialism where

Muslim institutions were contained or abrogated, the failure of indigenous secular regimes in predominantly Islamic countries, and historic relations between the West and the Islamic world, especially the policies of the United States favoring Israel over Palestine and the support of undemocratic militarist and monarchist regimes in the Middle East and Islamic worlds.

Radical alternatives by a host of Muslim thinkers were developed as alternatives to Western models of state and governance. The Muslim Brotherhood called for the postindependence state to be governed by Islamic principles. Disciples in Egypt and elsewhere created a model of a contemporary Islamic state. Islamic states have been established in Iran, Pakistan, Saudi Arabia, Afghanistan under the Taliban, and de facto in Sudan. The essential features of an Islamic state include the following:

1. A Muslim head of the state, sultan, imam, khalifa, ayatollah, malik (king), or emir (prince) who rules in the name of the Islamic faith.
2. Shari'a is state law and the sole source of legislation.
3. State-enforced *zakat*, religious duty of almsgiving, becomes state law.
4. Islamic institutions are established, including banks, insurance, health care, and education.
5. The status of women may be compromised by mandatory veiling, seclusion, and lack of full rights as citizens, such as the right to vote, hold elective office, or become judges or heads of state.
6. Non-Muslims, especially Christians and Jews, are dhimmis, or "protected" people who pay a tax for their special status in Islamic states.

Mass Appeal of the Islamic State

To the disenfranchised and disempowered young Muslims in the Middle East or Islamic worlds, a resurgent Islam represents something quite different; it means the possibility of unified action of a more broadly based, mass character than the military or monarchical regimes that have ruled in the name of the people but are fundamentally undemocratic. The appeal of Islamism is that it draws from a rich and powerful religious heritage to challenge effectively the ideologies of Arab nationalism and socialism that have dominated the political arena since the advent of independence. Some regimes have used the promise of socialism with a distinctly Arab or Islamic character to offer their citizens the hope of economic development and prosperity at home while confronting the Zionist and imperialist ambitions of Israel and the West on the international front. The Arab Socialist Union of Nasser's Egypt, put into power and kept in power by the military, provided the inspiration and the model for a number of sincere imitators. In retrospect, it is clear that the 1967 war was the beginning of the end of the confidence of the masses of people in the idea of Arab nationalism, for it revealed that neither the Arab states invaded nor a wider Arab nationalist solidarity could salvage any measure of military or political victory out of this crippling defeat. On the domestic front the "socialist" regimes whose political rhetoric emphasized the central role of the masses were becoming elitist, personally corrupt, and more withdrawn from the needs of the rural peasantry and urban working classes. The word for "the masses" (al-Sha'ab) became a shopworn, hackneyed political term that lost its legitimacy for mobilizing anything but contempt among the masses.

Until the Bush administrations (presidents #41 and #43)—with their perceived hostility to Islam and the Arab world, particularly focused on Iraq—it was domestic politics that drove Islamist movements. Now it has become a combination of both, anti-Bush and American neo-imperial ambitions in the region and their regional allies, that are the targets of Islamist rhetoric. This continues a pattern of anti-Western sentiment traceable in the modern era to the Iranian Islamic revolution. The content of the many Islamist movements when examined closely reveals that their grievances are primarily with their own leaders' failures and secondarily their alliance with the West. The support of unpopular and undemocratic leaders by the West is often viewed as an extension of colonialism, evidencing the continued powerful influence of the West and the humiliating dependence of the East.

While it is the perceived failures of secular Arab nationalist regimes on both the international and domestic fronts that have fueled the Islamist movements, there is no denying the impact or the significance of the Iranian Islamic Revolution in 1979 that realized the dream of an Islamic solution to the problems of Muslims and Arabs. Whatever its weaknesses, and many are recognized by other Islamist leaders and followers, the Islamic revolution made possible the rebirth of the idea of Islamic government in the modern era. This presents another tension within Islamic and Arab societies, and that is the division in popular attitude toward the potential for Islamic governance. Obviously, the committed secularists and Islamists have divergent points of view, but for the majority of people who are politically neutral, there is a sincere division as to the correct path to follow toward economic development, peace, and the good society. Many people believe that the Arab nationalists and secularists have had their chance and have failed, so it is timely and appropriate to give the Islamic alternative an opportunity. Others are genuinely fearful when evaluating the current examples of Islamic Republics in the world: Saudi Arabia, Iran, Afghanistan, and Sudan. Serious questions about the rights of women and non-Muslim minorities have been raised without satisfactory answers in practice, although theoretical solutions by Muslim progressives now abound. Since the 2003 U.S. war in Iraq, the world may well witness both revival of Arab nationalism as well as an intensification of Islamist movements.

When the Iranian Islamic revolution occurred, there were demonstrations in support of it throughout the Shi'a and Sunni Muslim worlds, showing that its force was not felt along lines that might be characterized as sectarian. Some Western analysts attempted to comprehend this militancy in Iran in the context of the suffering and veneration of martyrdom that are a part of the observance of Shi'a Islam. However, when comparable sentiments were expressed by militant Islamic movements throughout the Sunni Muslim countries—and even in the Palestinian movement, historically dominated by Arab nationalist politics—alternative explanations had to be sought. The strength of Hamas, the Islamist Palestinian resistance movement, can be seen in the construction of the new Palestinian constitution in which Shari'a forms the basis of the legal system.

The dramatic growth and influence of the Islamic alternative quickly became a force with which secular nationalist governments had to contend. Hosni Mubarak, taking the lesson from the assassination of Sadat by a radical Islamic movement, moved to absorb some of this political heat by legalizing Islamist political parties and allowing them to run for office (they quickly earned 20 percent of the parliamentary seats). Bourgiba's successor in Tunisia, Zein Abdine Ben-Ali, moved to legalize the Islamic Tendency Movement (MTI) when it transformed itself to a political party, an-Nahda (Renaissance Party or Party of Renewal), and then delegitimized the party charging that they engaged in violence and proposed the overthrow of the government. Saddam Hussein, leader of the historically secular Ba'ath (also meaning renaissance) Party in Iraq under attack twice by the United States, employed the rhetoric of Islamic jihad against the Western allied attackers in the Gulf War, and changed the Iraqi flag to read "Allahu Akbar," God is almighty, as a co-optation of the strength of the Islamist sentiment. Remarkably, there was not a strong Islamist challenge to the regime of Saddam Hussein—probably due to his extremely repressive rule—while one directed against his fellow Ba'athist, President Hafez al-'Asad of Syria, was crushed.

Another source of tension within Muslim society exists between a populist Islam with its aid-related religious organizations, and official, state-supported Islam, with its government institutions established to speak for religion from a national standpoint. The state-appointed 'ulama have played a difficult and at times ambiguous role during the colonial and postindependence period. As officially anointed guardians of the religion, they were responsible for defending religious principles against the perceived encroachment of Western ideas and practice contrary to Islam, all the while beholden to the colonial government that employed them. Their work and position could not have been easy, and when they stood their ground on issues of fundamental interpretation, such as the protection of polygyny, defense of the inheritance laws, and protection of the Waqf system, their acts were courageous.

From my own work on Islamic law in Sudan, it is clear that there was an uneasy relationship between the colonial government's legal secretary, the final legal authority before the governor general, and the Shariʿa grand qadi, first among the government's appointed ʿulama. They differed on many points, and the colonial government's effort to impose certain "solutions" to social-religious problems was often met with resistance by these special government employees. Such a case involved the return by force of recalcitrant wives (bayt al-taʿa), which the English objected to on practical and moral grounds: First, wives repeatedly ran away and judges were enforcing decrees of "obedience" on the same wives many times, and second, the English thought, why force a woman to remain with a husband she obviously wants to escape. The ʿulama countered that, until the wife was legally divorced according to the rules of Shariʿa, she must continue to "obey" her husband by returning to his house and living with him, even if this must be accomplished by force. (This element of force has since been removed after independence in every country where it was practiced.) The ideological battle was waged for a number of years until a compromise was reached whereby the order of obedience would be imposed but no more than three times on the same woman. The ʿulama, whether in Sudan or Egypt, with its grand tradition of religious education and scholarship at al-Azhar Islamic University, or elsewhere, always publicly pledged their support of the colonial governments, but they surely waged many private struggles that, as yet, are not fully appreciated or documented. The public appearance was one of accommodation and acceptance of foreign, non-Muslim rule, while the struggles to end foreign rule were carried out by secular nationalists (who ultimately came to power) and anti-state religious organizations, like the Muslim Brotherhood. Once independence was won, this gave greater legitimacy to the popular nationalist movements, while the state ʿulama were seen to be peripheral to these events. While they did not lose their authoritative status, because they were and are still seen as religious men, they lost the glory of playing a pivotal role in the achievement of independence.

To a certain extent the sheikhs at the world's premier Islamic university, Al-Azhar University in Cairo, have seen themselves as conservators of a religious tradition of interpretation that has survived by resisting new ideas. I was invited to meet with some of the scholar-educators in the Law Faculty at Al-Azhar in 1983 while I was living in Cairo and conducting research on family law issues in Egypt. Before entering the university grounds, I was asked to cover my head and so obliged by purchasing a head scarf at a nearby store. As our meeting convened in the office of the chairman of the personal status law division, I was at once awed by being invited to this historic institution and acutely aware of being a non-Muslim, Western woman studying Islamic law. An oddity to them no doubt, I was nevertheless graciously and respectfully received as one with some background in Islamic legal studies, although my having studied with the Sudanese grand qadi did not seem to impress them much. We began discussing family law issues, especially my interest in the divorce law as interpreted and applied in Egypt. Our discussion in Arabic was progressing well, I thought, although they seemed amused by my Sudanese accent in Arabic. While discussing the gradual elimination of bayt al-taʿa, I was searching for a word in Arabic that conveyed development or change in the law, and mistakenly, and unfortunately, used the word *tatwir,* roughly translating as "evolution." I had just been reading some of the works of Islamic reformers in the Sudan, the Republican Brothers, who use the notion of evolution of Islamic institutions like the law liberally in their writings. I should have used the word for change, *ghayaar,* or some other more neutral term rather than the inflammatory tatwir, which denies or modifies the essential immutability of the Shariʿa upon which the conservative religious community relies. Having made my mistake, and having been "corrected" by the admonition that the Shariʿa "does not evolve," I felt my interview coming rapidly to a close, and indeed the chairman of the group was the first to excuse himself. Embarrassed by my own unthinking error, I nevertheless gained a valuable perspective on the religious sheikhs at Al-Azhar whose insularity has been a powerful defense.

As secular, Arab nationalist governments came to power, and Islamic institutions were seen as interfering with development and "progress," the ʿulama were further isolated and brought under more direct state control. After all, the state was no longer foreign, and it became more difficult to oppose it, formally and informally. As mentioned earlier, the Egyptian state-appointed mufti and sheikh of al-Azhar have been little more than rubber stamps for the government's policies and programs. It has only been the growing strength of the Islamist movement that has emboldened some ʿulama under Mubarak to speak out and oppose government ideas and acts. Some of the more heated battles have occurred in the attempted reform of the personal status laws regarding marriage and divorce, where the more conservative religious scholars have forestalled efforts to restrict polygyny and uphold the husband's right to divorce without a court order. As a result of these struggles with the government, the ʿulama have regained some of their credibility and thus their ability to influence the masses of Egyptians who have turned to Islamist alternatives.

In Tunisia, where secular politics still dominate but the Islamist an-

Nahda movement has challenged the existing order, the role that the ʿulama historically played under colonialism and the secular reformist Bourghiba has changed little. The state-supported ʿulama are viewed by the Islamists as a part of the same problem to be resolved in the struggle to restore freedom and democracy. Most telling is the fact that the leader of the an-Nahda Party, Rachid Ghannouchi, is not from the class of ʿulama, but was born into a rural farming family and was taught the Qurʾan by his father. Leaders of the Pan-Malaysian Islamic Party and its predecessor, the Islamic Party, came from outside the ranks of the politically cautious ʿulama.

Some religious sheikhs, whose influence has been curtailed by the state, meet privately with their followers to counsel them. I learned of several cases, while in Tunis, of Muslims disaffected by the government's alienation from Islam, who would choose to seek the clandestine advice of such sheikhs, preferring them to the use of the Tunisian official legal system.

In countries that have undergone a progressive political Islamization over the past two decades, like Sudan, the traditional ʿulama were bypassed in favor of former Muslim Brotherhood leader Hasan al-Turabi, who was made attorney general under President Jaʿafar Numeiri. During his time in office he oversaw the introduction of Shariʿa law as state law in 1983. The Muslim Brotherhood in Sudan, reborn as the National Islamic Front in 1985, came to power in 1989 and has steadfastly opposed any efforts to rescind the executive order making Islamic law state law, despite the fact

Fig. 27. Sudanese Islamist Dr. Hasan al-Turabi, founder of the Muslim Brotherhood/ National Islamic Front, in 1992.

that it is a central issue in the chronic civil war between north and south Sudan, where its one-third non-Muslim population has fought this decision since 1983.

The tension between the traditional 'ulama and the leadership of the various Islamist movements is palpable. Although the 'ulama can still command respect for their religious knowledge, if not their political alliances, the new Islamist leaders are largely self-taught and rely on the purity of the sources themselves and encourage collective study of the Qur'an, Sunna, and Hadith, independent of the interpretations of state 'ulama. This undermines the monopoly on knowledge and interpretation that the 'ulama once held and represents a dramatic democratization of access to and use of religious knowledge with wide-ranging implications.

The election of the Turkish Islamic or Islamist party in 2002, AKP (Justice and Development Party) under leadership of Tayyip Erdogan, proclaiming itself the face of moderate Islam in power, is another case in point. The AKP rejects the label "Islamist" and does not advocate applying Shari'a as state law, but it describes itself as a Muslim democratic party. It succeeded the Welfare Party, which was displaced because it allegedly attempted to overthrow Turkey's historical secular rule. It is viewed in the West and perhaps the East as more "moderate," but the fact is that the party picked up support from secular forces desiring a change. Jenny B. White, an anthropologist who has studied the Islamist trend in Turkey, sees something more fundamental than the usual exchange of elites at the top of political hierarchies. Her findings are typical of Islamist mobilization elsewhere, that is, that political mobilization has been from the bottom up with grassroots organizations working within communities providing health care, supplemental education, and even aid with home construction that the state has not provided for poor and impoverished communities. This is true in Egypt; it was true in Iran; and it is a fact that politicians in the region and in the West often ignore. However, AKP is not just a party of the working class. It is also a party of a new Muslim elite (Secor 2003b). Such figures have supported women's right to veil and attend universities and serve in Parliament donning the veil. Turkey's secularism made such "religious" displays illegal. When I visited Turkey in the mid-1980s and saw a small number of women veiling at that time, I asked a Turkish friend about this and was told these were Iranian girls, not Turks.

The AKP's platform speaks to universal human rights, civil society, and democracy that will be implemented with "God's help" (Secor 2003b). If the issue of the reintroduction of Shari'a emerges (that, of course, was in force until the end of the Ottoman Empire in 1918), another kind of debate will ensue, with questions of whether Shari'a can be applied in anything other than an Islamic state. The admission of Turkey to NATO and its seeing itself as the bridge between Europe and the Middle East will probably mollify any tendency toward conservative Islamism; however, regional instability from war could change this.

Islam, Democracy, and Human Rights

The greatest political challenge to the range of movements we in the West have called Islamic fundamentalism or Islamism is the accusation that Islamic movements, when they come to power, are undemocratic and weak in the application of basic human rights, especially as regards women and non-Muslims living in Islamic republics. This sentiment is so profound that, when a preemptive coup stopped the Islamists who had won the national election in Algeria early in 1992, hardly a complaint was heard from the Western editorial pages. What is to follow is not an apology for Islamist regimes currently in power but an exploration of the ideas and concepts that the West is using to judge the East, with the caution that we should not misrepresent ourselves or "the other" and that we must not operate by a double standard with respect to an evaluation of the Arab-Muslim world.

Notions of human rights and democracy are rooted in Western history, but only as recently as the French Revolution in the eighteenth century and its subsequent impact, primarily as a clarion call to those struggling for freedom from oppression in Western settings, such as the American colonies and the first "Black" Republic of Haiti in the eighteenth century. Islamic civilization has been apart and has been isolated or kept apart by language, government, and an historical antagonism with the West that can be traced at least as far back as the Crusades, if not the very introduction of the faith in the seventh century c.e. Since the creation of the United Nations, the upholding of basic human rights, outlined in its Universal Declaration of Human Rights, has been a part of the international agenda, and in the United States the administration of President Jimmy Carter placed human rights on the national agenda. Today it is a key concept by which nations and their actions are judged.

In the Islamic world two separate tendencies are present with respect to human rights, *al-huquq al-insan*. The first is a liberal view that argues that the essential ideas of Islamic thought and practice, properly interpreted, are fully compatible with democracy and international standards of human rights. The second is an Islamist view that places first priority on a religious foundation for the state that is essentially communitarian (based on the idea of Umma), where a just social order will necessarily emerge from the proper application of Islamic principles (Sisk 1992, viii). The struggle between these two points of view represents a tension within Muslim societies, while it also constitutes the most pressing tension between the Islamic world and the West.

The liberal tradition is one whose current ideas can be traced to the writings of the great Egyptian jurist, Muhammad Abduh, and the advocate of women's rights, Qasim Amin, both of whose writings had an impact in the region around the turn of the century.

The Islamist view of democracy rests with the principle of *shura*, or consultation, in which the ruler (the caliph or imam) may accept advice from counselors whom he has appointed, although he has no obligation to follow their advice, even if there is consensus among them. An allied concept is *ijma'*, meaning consensus of the legal scholars, used in Islamic jurisprudence to discuss changes in legal interpretation. Such consensus has been achieved regarding Islamic attitudes toward insurance and banking, but remains controversial on matters already discussed, such as polygyny and divorce. According to the former Islamist leader of Sudan, Dr. Hasan al-Turabi, shura and ijma' constitute the basis for legitimate Islamic government (1992). Democracy, he points out, is a Western concept developed in a secular context that has been applied to Islamic societies, whose premise is religious. This makes the comparison between them neither fair nor legitimate, and democracy need not necessarily mean political parties and ballot boxes. Consultation and consensus, in the Islamic model of government, are sufficient to satisfy the requirement of democracy in the Muslim state.

While Western notions of democracy need not be met to satisfy an Islamic concept of right government, in cases where Islamist political parties are achieving greater influence through democratic elections, such as in Algeria, Egypt, and Turkey, the clash between Western ideas of secular democracy and Islamist religious agendas is acute. Western and secular critics of Islamist politics cannot delegitimize the ballot box; democracy, as voiced through people voting directly in elections, is indivisible. In other words, democracy is democracy, even if the outcome is an Islamist regime. The popular election of Islamists in Algeria in 1991 was highly disturbing and controversial, for many critics of the Islamist approach contended that democracy, for women and for the secular parties, would ultimately be denied by an Islamic Republic using democratic means to come to power. Sa'id al-'Ashmawy (1998) agrees with this view, arguing that any religious state whose rule is based upon the exercise of the "Divine Will" will necessarily abuse power and justify it on religious grounds. Thus, democratically elected Islamists are likely to fail a basic test of democracy, that is, rely upon God's will above that of the people.

The difference between these two points of view represents the deepest and most serious fissure within contemporary Islamic societies. They are mutually exclusive ideologically and practically, and success of one of these viewpoints means the defeat of the other. In some countries it has become a matter of life and death, and Muslim liberals have been jailed and forced into exile where Islamic Republics have suppressed their point of view, such as in Iran and the Sudan, and Said Al-'Ashmawy has lived with a constant need of personal protection since 1986. Increasingly, the debate between them and with the West has sharpened to differences over human rights and the right to dissent within an Islamic context.

There exists a rather pessimistic view among some Arab intellectuals that democracy is a luxury of the "developed" countries, and that it is a stage of political maturity that will come only in the distant future for Arab and Muslim societies. The issue of human rights may be one that hastens that day. The experience of human rights activist Saad Eddin Ibrahim, who was tried twice in 2001 and 2003 for allegedly engaging in anti-state activities for the research carried out by his Ibn Khaldun Institute into the limits of democracy in Egypt, has already been mentioned. His scholarly activism found the limits of Egyptian democracy, ruled since independence by the military with "elections" that count 99 percent support for the ruler. A few years earlier, writer Muhammad Abu Zayd was forced to flee Egypt because of threats on his life and a specific threat of an imposed divorce on his wife for her marriage to one judged an "apostate."

Turkey's "Hunger Warriors" gained world attention for their protracted hunger strike to protest their government's repressive policies and violations of the human rights of political prisoners. When the story was reported (Anderson 2001), forty women had died of starvation. Taslima Nasreddin, author and advocate for women's rights from Bangladesh, has been in exile from her country for her years of intellectual and political resistance.

Over the past decade or more, the term used to refer to human rights, *al-huquq al-insan,* has gained a wide currency in the Arabic-speaking Middle East (Dwyer 1991, 8). In terms of formal organizations, there are many: the Cairo Human Rights Organization, the Tunisian Human Rights League, the Arab Organization for Human Rights, and others that have been formed in the midst of political struggle where basic human rights have been allegedly violated, such as the Sudan Human Rights Organization founded in the late 1980s. Since Islamists came to power in 1989, they have allied themselves with the secularist opposition, National Democratic Alliance (Mahmoud 1992). However, in Tunisia, where government repression of the Islamist An-Nahda has been criticized and cited by Amnesty International and the Tunisian Human Rights League, the call for democracy and human rights has been raised by an Islamic group against a secular government. Thus the human rights movement has joined forces with both secular and religious movements for democracy without any apparent contradiction raised between alleged violations by secular or religious regimes.

It has been alleged that Islamic rule is unable to deal equitably with women and with non-Muslim minorities as full citizens. This weakness has been raised when secular state constitutions weigh in against historical ideas about the status of women and the proper governance of non-Muslims in an Islamic state. Many secularly inspired constitutions provide equal rights for all citizens, irrespective of sex or religious affiliation. However, as the call for Islamic government has been heard, strict interpretation of Shari'a provisions regarding women and religious minorities has been enforced by Islamist regimes. This has meant that women and non-Muslims may be excluded from certain political and governmental positions, such as being appointed to or continuing in positions as judges. The Sudan, Tunisia, Iraq, and other states with strong secular feminist movements historically have admitted women to positions as judges in both civil and Islamic courts. Egypt did not share in this tradition, despite its influential feminist movement, and it has followed the more conservative Islamic interpretation that a woman cannot sit in a position of power and authority over a man. Egypt has many female lawyers, but no judges until 2003 when the first woman was appointed, while Tunisia has a high percentage of both female lawyers and judges. Other Shari'a restrictions on women that might violate secular constitutional guarantees of equality include the general rule of a half portion of inheritance to which women are entitled under Islamic law and their status as only half-witnesses in court, that is, two women witnesses are the equivalent of one man, who is considered a full witness. This latter rule is only applied where Islamic law is the sole law in force, or where it governs personal status affairs; otherwise, women are considered full witnesses with men in civil cases. The half portion in inheritance has not been challenged, since it is explicitly mentioned in the Qur'an and is justified by the injunction "Men are in charge of women because they spend of their property [for the support of women]" (sura 4:34). In fairness, men are obliged to support their wives, children, and other immediate family members, such as parents, while women have no such obligation, so the inequity alleged here may not be so great as it appears at first glance.

The position of non-Muslims is similar in that they may be relegated to second-class status in an Islamic government where they may also be denied the right to govern or hold positions of power over Muslims. The need for protection of dhimmis and the historical payment of a special tax for that purpose have been criticized as archaic and in need of reform by contemporary Islamic societies. The Sudanese Republican Brotherhood, an Islamic reformist movement, specifically rejects this inferior status of non-Muslims, saying that it is incompatible with the modern, multicultural, and multi-religious state. It is likewise critical of the incorrect interpretation that makes second-class citizens of women as well, basing its own more liberal interpretation upon the holy sources, especially the earlier, more universal texts of the Qur'an revealed at Mecca (Magnarella 1982).

Southern Sudanese, like other non-Muslim minorities, have justifiable fears for their protection as non-Muslims under Islamist regimes. In their case, past regimes have attempted to "solve" the problem of non-Muslim status through conversion, coerced Islamization, or political isolation, rather than integration. The spotlight on human rights abuses in Sudan and in Afghanistan under the Taliban has raised important practical questions about the treatment of women and non-Muslim minorities under Islamic rule. Critics charge that this is an abuse of Islam and that it is a misapplication of Shari'a to force women to cover themselves in certain "religiously correct" ways, or to limit their freedom of movement or free exercise of the right to work.

Some anthropologists have raised the question as to whether human rights is a universal doctrine or a Western idea that has gained currency in the world for political expediency; at least in these two cases the context appears to be less significant than the common call for democracy and political freedom. However, challenge to the Islamic law of inheritance was raised at the Beijing International Conference on Women in 1995 for the inequality in inheritance and lack of equal rights to divorce or as full citizens in Islamic nations. International standards of the exercise of full human rights as citizens of states, it is argued, should outweigh religious or cultural traditions. However, the free exercise of religion is also a basic human right, so the dilemma remains unresolved. The basic issue of any perceived or real Islamic limitation of human and civil rights is being addressed within Muslim communities by secularists who seek to keep religion separate from the state. However, in the model of Islamic governance, the state and religion are not separated.

Final Remarks

The tensions within Islamic communities and nations have sharpened as Islamist political movements have increasingly challenged Arab nationalist and secular regimes. The debates regarding proper government, the role of religion in government, the proper conduct and status of women, the definition of democracy, and the protection of human rights are both theoretical and practical. Differences of view engage Muslim and non-Muslim citizens from the Maghrib to northeast Africa and the Middle East. The outcome of this great internal dialogue and struggle is of utmost interest to the Western nations with long-standing economic and political interests in the region, as economic investors or former colonial powers with continuing interest in these nations. We in the West need to understand the nature of the debate and accept its outcome, even if it is not the most desirable one from the standpoint of our best interests. The Islamic religious and cultural system is too powerful in its ability to mobilize people, and it carries too much legitimacy for the West to confront and counter it successfully, apart from military confrontation. We must become better educated about the issues in the region so that we can become better communicators with its actors. Islamist or secular governments in the Muslim-Arab world will continue to want to foster dialogue and good relations with the West if we are prepared to come at least half of the distance and permit a forum where all sides engage in enlightened, mutually self-interested dialogue and relations between equals. In the current political environment, this is unrealistic, as the sole superpower dominates the region militarily, economically, and politically. However, in the long term, the lack of an engagement with Muslims as equals and Arab as full humans will have the predictable result of increased popular resistance directed against the United States and its allies and its own growing sense of insecurity.

This book is offered to those who seek a deeper understanding of Arab and Islamic cultures. The motivation can be self-serving, and if that is the case, then one purpose of the book will be achieved because information will replace ignorance. If greater mutual understanding is achieved, then a more valuable humanistic goal will have been reached.

As we in the West struggle to move beyond a bipolar world, driven for so many years by another East-West antagonism between the United States, Western Europe, and the Soviet Bloc, we can envision a multicentered world. This is one in which the West is one of several regional centers in an increasingly interdependent globe. The civilization of the Arab and Muslim peoples and the regions in which they predominate is surely one of the centers with which we must become better acquainted and with which we will surely contend time and again. If we accept that we have both influenced this cultural region and been influenced by it, then bilateral understanding can replace unilateral thinking. This means incorporating into our basic education and worldview the idea of a shared Judeo-Christian-Islamic heritage where both convergent and divergent forces have operated. Such an approach does not weaken the West, but it strengthens our world.

Glossary of Arabic Terms and Names

'**abd.** Slave or servant; used in Arabic names with one of the names of God, such as 'Abdallah or 'Abd al-Karim.

'**abid.** Enslaved persons, used as a derogatory reference, may mean "blacks" or Africans.

adat. Custom in Indonesia and Malaysia; recognized as a source of law in regional Shari'a so long as local custom does not conflict with Islamic precepts.

adhan. The call to prayer, heard five times a day in Muslim lands and just before Friday prayers at mosques all over the world.

Ahl al-Kitab/Kitabiyeen. "People of the Book," reference to Christians and Jews, protected in an Islamic state and eligible for marriage partners for Muslim men.

"**ahlan wa sahlan.**" Standard secular Arabic greeting meaning "hello" or "be at ease, you are safe here."

al-ajnabi. Any foreigner, or outsider; from Arabic root meaning "lateral" or "on the side."

'**Alawi sect.** Shi'a religious sect.

'**Ali.** Cousin and son-in-law of the Prophet Muhammad, and fourth caliph, whose rule precipitated a crisis over succession in the caliphate; those siding with 'Ali were known as the Shi'at 'Ali, or subsequently, Shi'a Muslims.

'**alim.** One who is educated, especially in religious subjects. See also 'ulama.

"**Allahu akbar.**" Religious expression meaning "God is great," used in prayers, expressions of personal piety, and mass political rallies.

'**aqd.** Muslim marriage contract signing.

'**Arab.** One who speaks Arabic as a first language; self-identifies as "Arab"; a collective term for people of Arab descent; also a pastoral nomad, Bedouin.

'asaba. Core group of patrilineally related males.

Ashura. Shi'a Muslim commemoration of the martyrdom of 'Ali and his son Husayn beginning on the tenth day of the first month (Muharram) of the Islamic calendar; men may flagellate or mutilate their bodies in memory of their suffering, much like the Christian passion plays.

"assalaamu alaykum." Universal greeting of Muslims, meaning "Peace be upon you all," to which the response is "wa alaykum assalaam," meaning "and upon you and yours peace."

'ayb. Shameful behavior.

Al-Azhar Mosque and al-Azhar University. The oldest and premier international university of Islamic studies, in Cairo (Jami'at al-Azhar).

baraka. Blessings from God, obtained by performing religious acts, or dhikr; remembrance of God.

Ba'th Party. "Renaissance" party of Arab nationalism in Syria and Iraq until the overthrow of Saddam Hussein by American military forces.

bayt al-ta'a. "House obedience"; the right of a husband to ask the court and police to bring back a wife who has fled the conjugal home; reformed in Sudan and Egypt.

bint 'amm. Father's brother's daughter, or patrilateral first cousin, the preferred marriage partner.

Coptic Christianity. Minority religious in Egypt following monophysite Eastern Christian rite.

Dar al-Islam. "The place of peace" where Islam prevails, as contrasted with *Dar al-Harb*, the "place of war" where non-Muslims predominate; used in the context of external jihad; enslavement of non-Muslims took place in historical jihads in Dar al-Harb.

Da'wa/Da'wah. The call to religion that is part of contemporary Islamic proselytizing associated with revival and Islamism.

Dawla. The state in the Arabic language, as distinguished from *jamhouriya* (republic) or individual states (*wilayaat*) or provinces that are part of a larger nation, as in al-Wilayaat al-Muttahidah (the United States).

dervish. Turkish; Persian referent to Sufi practitioners who may employ whirling on performance to produce a religiously ecstatic state; *darwish* in Arabic.

dhikr. "Remembrance"; Sufi rituals performed in veneration and remembrance of God.

dhimmi. Non-Muslim in an Islamic state.

Dhu al-Hijja. Literally, the "one of the pilgrimage," meaning the time of year for making the hajj or pilgrimage to Mecca.

'Eid. Religious holiday.

'Eid al-Adha. Feast of sacrifice commemorating the willingness of the prophet Abraham to sacrifice his son; also known as 'Eid al-Kabir, or Great Holiday.

'Eid al-Fitr. Holiday ending Ramadan, the month of fasting.

faqih (pl. foqaha). Person trained in the sources of Islam; interpreter of religious law (al-fiqh).

faranj. Foreigner, often used in historical reference to the "Franks" in the Crusades.

Farsi. Language of Persia (contemporary Iran).

fatwa (pl. fatawa). Religious interpretation made by an 'alim or a collective opinion issued by the 'ulama; fatawa only have the weight of legal opinion, not law.

fellahin/fellaheen. Arab peasantry at the core of Middle Eastern rural life.

al-fiqh. Islamic jurisprudence; interpretations by the foqaha.

al-gharib. "Foreign," "strange," refers to any stranger; derived from *gharb*, the direction of the west.

Hadith. The collected written traditions of the sayings and actions of the prophet Muhammad.

hadd (pl. hudud). Islamic punishments in criminal law "to the limits," including stoning for adultery, amputation of limbs for theft, or lashing for morality offenses; applied contemporarily in extremist Islamist nations.

hajj. Pilgrimage to the holy places of Mecca and Medina, one of the five pillars of Islam.

halal. Lawful or what is recommended in Islamic practice; *halal* meat is slaughtered properly by slitting the animal's throat; *halal* foods contain no pork or pork products; contrasts with that which is forbidden, or *haram*.

"al-Hamdulilah." "Praise be to God," a fundamental expression of faith and recognition of God's power used in everyday conversation.

Hanafi. One of the four schools of Islamic jurisprudence; spread with the Ottoman Turkish empire.

Hanbali. One of the four major schools of Islamic jurisprudence.

Haram. Forbidden practice in Islam, such as taking interest (*riba*) on loans, consuming alcohol or pork, or any other practice contrary to the precepts and teachings of Islam.

hareem. Female section of home where women are secluded from "stranger" (non-kin) males.

Hegira/Hijra. The flight of the Prophet and the early community of Muslims from Mecca to Medina in 622 C.E., thus marking the first year of the Muslim calendar, reckoning time after the Hegira (anno hegirae, A.H.).

Hezb Allah. "Party of God," Islamist political group active in Lebanon among Shi'a Muslims.

hijab. "Covering," most common reference for contemporary Islamic dress or veiling of Muslim women; hijab styles vary culturally, but usually include a head covering, long sleeves and dress, or loosely fitting blouse and pants.

Hijaz. Reference to the western shores of the Arabian peninsula where the Holy Lands of Mecca and Medina are located.

al-huquq al-insan. Human rights.

ibadat. Religious obligations.

ʿidda. Three-month period observed by a divorced wife or widow to ascertain that any pregnancy would result in a legitimate birth and assuring the paternity of the child.

ihram. Simple white garment worn by the pilgrim in performance of the hajj; also used as a burial shroud.

ijmaʿ. Consensus of the legal scholars on an issue of religious interpretation.

ijtihad. Legal interpretation or innovation of the holy sources, Qurʾan and Sunna.

ikhtalat. Open socializing between men and women that many Islamists criticize and abjure.

ʿilm. Knowledge or learning.

imam. A leader of prayer; used in reference to the leader of a mosque.

"insha Allah." "God willing," an expression of worldview and everyday conversation in Arabic.

intifada. "Uprising" or "rebellion," mostly associated with Palestinian resistance to Israeli occupation.

Islam. The peace that comes from submission to the one God, Allah; the last of the great prophetic traditions and revelations traceable to Abraham.

Islamism. Political Islam, where religion is used as a device for mobilization of the masses of Muslims; also referred to as militant Islam, or Islamic revival.

Islamist. Person advocating the political application of ideas generated from an Islamic framework using a variety of tactics from violent to nonviolent and electoral; examples include the Muslim Brothers, Hezb Allah, Jamiʿat al Islami, Hamas, or the National Islamic Front who advocate an Islamic state.

jahiliyya. The time of ignorance that preceded Islam in the Arabian peninsula.

jamhouriya. "Republic," used in postindependence Arab and Muslim states that are not monarchies.

jamiʿ. Mosque; see also **masjid**.

jamiʿa. University.

Al-Jazirah al-Arabiyya. "The Arab Island," refers to the Arabian peninsula.

jihad. "Struggle," or great effort by Muslims or Arabs, which can be either internal, as in the struggle within oneself to live an upright life, or external, as in the better-known "holy war" to defend the religion.

jinn. "Spirit" or supernatural force; in Arabic folktales refers to a mythical being endowed with supernatural powers; *genie* in English is derived from *jinn*.

jizya. Tax for protection of non-Muslims in an Islamic state.

Ka'ba. Sacred enclosure at the center of the Great Mosque in Mecca where sacred black stone is displayed; the focal point of Muslim prayer.

Al-kafa'a fi al-zawaj. "Equality of standard in marriage," ensured by a woman's marriage guardian (al-wali) that she marry a man whose family background is equivalent to her own in religion, education, and economic standing.

karama. Personal dignity, honor.

Karbala. Location of the martyrdom of 'Ali, whose mosque and tomb are venerated by Shi'a Muslims.

karim. Generosity, a basic value in Arab-Islamic society.

Khadijah. First wife of Prophet Muhammad and the first convert to Islam; fifteen years his senior whose income as an independent businesswoman enabled the Prophet to follow his religious calling.

khalifa. "Caliph"; rightful successor in an Islamic state.

khalwa. "Retreat" or "secluded place"; Islamic school for studying the Qur'an.

khawaja. Common term for a foreigner, usually European or of European extraction; colloquial for "mister" in the Levant.

khul'. Negotiated divorce by mutual consent; a type of traditional divorce before reforms permitted judicial divorce for women.

Kitabiyeen. "People of the Book," reference to Christians and Jews, protected in an Islamic state and eligible to marry Muslim men.

kuttab. Islamic school, from Arabic root *ktb,* to write.

loh/lawh. Writing board used in Qur'anic schools.

madhab (pl. madhahib). School of Islamic jurisprudence, as in Maliki, Hanafi, Shafi'i, or Hanbali.

madrasa. Muslim school for learning to read and write the Qur'an, and Islamic subjects.

Maghrib. "The West," or location of the setting sun; refers to the northwest African countries of Tunisia, Algeria, and Morocco.

Mahdi. An expected deliverer and religious purifier in the Messianic tradition of Judaism, Christianity, and Islam; one who is divinely guided and has come to save humanity; the Sudanese Mahdi is among the best known.

mahr. Islamic dower, without which a legal marriage cannot be contracted; this is a large amount of wealth subject to inflationary increases, which some reformers and Islamists have rejected by reducing the mahr to a modest or token amount of wealth.

maktub. "That which is written"; can refer to the completion of a marriage contract or a sense of one's fate having been "written."

Maliki. One of the four schools of Islamic jurisprudence.

mallam. Religious scholar in West African Islam.

makruh. "Reprehensible" practice, not forbidden (*haram*) but strongly discouraged.

marabout. A pious or holy one, a "saint," or one believed to have special abilities to communicate with God; subject to frequent veneration in North African traditions.

marhaba. Standard secular greeting in Arabic and Turkish meaning "welcome."

Mashriq. "The East"; refers to the eastern Arab countries, such as Egypt or Syria.

masjid. Mosque, place of worship, from Arabic root *sajada,* to prostrate oneself.

Mawlid al-Nabi. Holiday celebrating the birth of the Prophet Muhammad.

mihrab. Niche in a mosque indicating the qibla, or the direction toward Mecca for prayer.

millet. Political system of local autonomy for lands, religions, and cultures of the Middle East and North Africa occupied during Ottoman rule.

mudarabah. Limited or silent partnership in Islamic economics.

mufti. "One who opens the way"; one with legitimate authority of the state to issue an official religious opinion, or fatwa, also the official title of one of the highest Muslim authorities in a state, as the Mufti of Egypt.

mujahideen. "Struggler" or fighter for a cause, most often used in association with Islamist movements.

mulid. Festival commemorating a holy man or "saint," especially among Sufis.

mullah. Local religious teacher, or preacher among Shi'a Muslims in Iran and Iraq; comparable to a local sheikh in Sunni Islam.

mut'a. "Indemnity"; interpreted in Egypt as a divorce compensation or "gift" over and above the legal obligation of support (*nafaqa*).

mut'a marriage. Temporary marriage lawful only in Shi'a Islam; criticized by Sunni Muslims as legalizing temporary sexual liaisons or prostitution.

nafaqa. Alimony or child support legally owed by a man to his former wife and children.

nasab. Genealogy, determined by legitimate birth to a legally married couple; genealogy is reckoned patrilineally through the father's line.

Nation of Islam. "Black Muslims"; indigenous American Muslim movement begun by W. D. Fard in 1932 and continued by Elijah Muhammad, who was considered a prophet, contrary to Islamic teachings, along with its racial exclusivity; Malcolm X and Lewis Farrakhan are two of its most famous leaders; Malcolm X later joined mainstream Sunni Islam after his performance of the hajj.

niyah. Intention, one of the required steps in prayer.

Orientalism. The study of the East by the West, mostly associated with the period of colonization and colonialism of the "Orient" by European powers.

patrilineal. Descent and inheritance traced through males.

qadi. A judge in an Islamic or civil court in predominantly Muslim countries.

qaraba. "Nearness," or "closeness," both genealogical and physical within the extended family.

qasida. An ancient Arab ode, composed to be sung.

qiblah. The direction of prayer; toward the Ka'ba in Mecca.

Qur'an. The Holy Book of Islam; the word of God revealed to His last Messenger, the prophet Muhammad.

Quraysh. Descended from the extended family or lineage of the prophet Muhammad.

Ramadan. Lunar month of fasting (sawn, siyam); at the end of Ramadan is the great feast, 'Eid al-Fitr, when the fast is broken; during the month of Ramadan the revelation of the Qur'an to the prophet Muhammad is venerated by holding Qur'anic readings after the daily breaking of the fast.

raku. Bowing; bending forward in prayer.

riba. Usury, forbidden in Islam; charging interest on money loaned.

Salat. Prayer; five times a day at specified times; one of the five pillars of Islam.

sawm. Fasting from sunrise to sunset for the holy month of Ramadan, one lunar month.

Shafi'i. One of the four major schools of Islamic jurisprudence.

shahada. The testament of fundamental belief: "There is no God but God, and Muhammad is His Messenger."

sharaf. Honor conveyed to an individual or family by upright living within a community; sharif (m.), sharifa (f.).

shar'i. Proper, lawful behavior, often as interpreted by Islamists.

shar'i dress. Proper Muslim dress, implying wearing of the hijab.

Shari'a. "The correct path"; Islamic law as it has been interpreted by the 'ulama or foqaha of the four main schools of Islamic jurisprudence.

sheikh/shaykh. Religious and/or political leader of a group, from a local mosque or village, or a professor in an Islamic university.

Shi'a Islam. The branch of Islam traced to the historical dispute over the question of succession in the early decades of the faith; whether the rightful caliph should be from the family of 'Ali and thus the Prophet's line, or from among the pious Muslims.

shura. "Consultation"; a democratic method of discussion arriving at consensus by which Muslim rulers should govern.

Sufi/Sufism. The mystical path in Islam, possibly derived from the Arabic *suf* (wool), garments worn by some Sufis symbolizing a lack of regard for the material world; the Sufi way is characterized by performance of dhikr, rituals that emphasize music, dance, and a populist approach to religion.

sujud. Prostration in prayer; prayer rug is sajada.

Sunna. Practice of the Prophet during his lifetime; the ideal in Muslim behavior.

Sunni Islam. Islam's majority branch (over 90 percent of the world's Muslims), as contrasted with the minority branch of Shi'a Islam.

suq. Arab marketplace, bazaar.

sura. Verse from the Qur'an.

ta'a. "Obedience" required by a wife; interpreted as cohabitation.

tahara. Purification; used in purifying oneself for prayer.

tahuur. Circumcision, from tahara, to purify.

talaq. Divorce.

talaq thalatha/talaq talata (coll.). Divorce by triple pronouncement—"I divorce you three times"; restricted by legal reformers in the twentieth century.

tariqah (pl. turuq). Sufi religious brotherhood(s).

tawheed. The absolute oneness of God, constituting an uncompromising monotheism in Islam.

'ulama. Official interpreters of the Shari'a and holy sources of Islam; often associated with the power of the state.

Umma. The world community of believers; a powerful transcultural, international identity of 1.2 billion Muslims worldwide.

'umra. "Visitation"; the lesser pilgrimage lasting only four days.

Urdu. Language spoken in Pakistan, written in Arabic calligraphy.

usul. Foundation or fundamentals.

usul al-fiqh. Foundations of Islamic jurisprudence.

usuliyya. "Fundamentalism" in Arabic, referring to the "fundamentals" of the faith, Qur'an, Sunna, and the five pillars of practice.

al-wali. Guardian or protector, in personal or religious affairs, such as the marriage guardian.

waqf (pl. awqaf). Religious bequest for charitable purposes, such as the support of a mosque, hospital, or school; Ministries of Awqaf register and regulate such bequests.

wudu. Ablutions; washing before prayer.

zakat. Religiously inspired charity, one of the five pillars; often mandated as a religious tax in Islamic Republics.

zinji (pl. zunuj). Refers to non-Arab, generally non-Muslim Africans; may be used colloquially to refer to "blacks"; from Zanjabar or Zanzibar Island.

Bibliography

Abou El Fadl, Khaled. 2002. *The Place of Tolerance in Islam.* Oxford: One World.

Abu-Lughod, Janet. 1989. *Before European Hegemony: The World System, A.D. 1250–1350.* New York: Oxford University Press.

Abu Rabi', Ibrahim M. 1995. "Salat." In *The Encyclopedia of the Modern Islamic World,* ed. John L. Esposito, 469–73. New York: Oxford University Press.

Adams, William Y. 1984. *Nubia, Corridor to Africa.* Princeton: Princeton University Press.

Ahmed, Akbar S. 1986/1406 A.H. *Toward an Islamic Anthropology.* Herndon, Va.: International Institute of Islamic Thought.

Ahmed, Leila. 1992. *Women and Gender in Islam.* New Haven: Yale University Press.

An-Na'im, Abdullahi Ahmed. 1990. *Toward an Islamic Reformation: Civil Liberties, Human Rights, and International Law.* Syracuse: Syracuse University Press.

Anderson, Scott. 2001. "The Hunger Warriors." *New York Times Magazine,* October 21, pp. 43–47, 74–127.

Aramco World. 1991. *Islam's Path East.* Special Issue, vol. 42, no. 6.

al-'Ashmawy, Muhammad Sa'id. 1998. *Against Islamic Extremism: The Writings of Muhammad Sa'id al-'Ashmawy.* Introduction by Carolyn Fluehr-Lobban. Gainesville: University Press of Florida.

Atterbury, Anson P. 1899. *Islam in Africa.* New York: Putnam.

Austin, Allen D. 1984. *African Muslims in Antebellum America.* New York: Garland.

Azoy, G. Whitney. 2003. *Buzkashi, Game, and Power in Afghanistan.* 2d ed. Prospect Heights, Ill.: Waveland Press.

Callaway, Barbara, and Lucy Creevy. 1994. *Women, Religion, and Politics in West Africa.* Boulder: Lynne Rienner.

Canedy, Dana. 2002. "Lifting Veil for Photo ID Goes Too Far, Driver Says." *New York Times,* June 27.

Chelkowski, Peter. 1995. "Ashura." In *The Oxford Encyclopedia of the Modern Islamic World,* 1:141–43. New York: Oxford University Press.

Coulson, N. J. 1971. *Succession in the Muslim Family.* Cambridge: Cambridge University Press.

Demick, Barbara. 2000. "Arabs Pay Painful Price for a Powerful Tradition." *Philadelphia Inquirer,* May 8.

Deng, Francis. 1978. *Africans of Two Worlds: The Dinak of the Afro-Arab Sudan.* New Haven: Yale University Press.

Dwyer, Kevin. 1991. *Arab Voices: The Human Rights Debate in the Middle East.* Berkeley: University of California Press.

Eickelman, Dale F. 1976. *Moroccan Islam.* Austin: University of Texas Press.

———. 1989. *The Middle East: An Anthropological Approach.* 2d ed. Englewood Cliffs, N.J.: Prentice Hall.

———. 1993. *Russia's Muslim Frontiers.* Bloomington: Indiana University Press.

———. 1998. *The Middle East and Central Asia: An Anthropological Approach.* 3d ed. Upper Saddle River, N.J.: Prentice Hall.

———. 2001. *The Middle East and Central Asia: An Anthropological Approach.* 4th ed. Upper Saddle River, N.J.: Prentice Hall.

———. 2002. *The Middle East and Central Asia: An Anthropological Approach.* 4th ed. Upper Saddle River, N.J.: Prentice Hall.

Eickelman, Dale F., and James Piscatori, eds. 1990. *Muslim Travelers: Pilgrimage, Migration, and the Religious Imagination.* Berkeley: University of California Press.

El Guindi, Fadwa. 1999. *Veil: Modesty, Privacy, and Resistance.* New York: Berg.

Esposito John L. 1982. *Women in Muslim Family Law.* Syracuse: Syracuse University Press.

———. 1988. *Islam, the Straight Path.* New York: Oxford University Press.

———. 1999. *The Islamic Threat: Myth or Reality?* 3d ed. New York: Oxford University Press.

———, ed. 1983. *Voices of Resurgent Islam.* New York: Oxford University Press.

Fernea, Elizabeth W., and Robert A. Fernea, with Aleya Rouchdy. 1991. *Nubian Ethnographies.* Prospect Heights, Ill.: Waveland Press.

Fluehr-Lobban, Carolyn. 1976. "An Analysis of Homicide in the Afro-Arab Sudan." *Journal of African Law* 20(1): 20–38.

———. 1980. "The Political Mobilization of Women in the Arab World." In *Women in Contemporary Muslim Societies,* ed. Jane Smith, 235–52. Lewisburg: Bucknell University Press.

———. 1982. "Issues in the Shariʿa Custody Law in the Sudan." *Northeast African Studies* 4(1): 1–9.

———. 1983. "Challenging Some Myths: Women and Islamic Law in Sudan." *Expedition* 25: 32–39.

———. 1987. *Islamic Law and Society in the Sudan.* London: Frank Cass.

———. 1990. "Islamization in Sudan: A Critical Assessment." *Middle East Journal* 44(4): 610–23.

————. 1995; 1998. "Cultural Relativism and Universal Rights." *Chronicle of Higher Education,* June 9; *AnthroNotes* 20(1).

————. 2001. "Against Islamic Extremism." Lecture delivered to Providence Public Library and URI/CCE, November 18 and 26, 2001.

————, ed. 1998. *Against Islamic Extremism: The Writings of Muhammad Saʿid al-ʿAshmawy.* Gainesville: University Press of Florida.

Fluehr-Lobban, Carolyn, and Lois Bardsley-Sirois. 1990. "Obedience (Taʿa) in Muslim Marriage: Religious Interpretation and Applied Law in Egypt." *Journal of Comparative Family Law* 21(1):39–53.

Fluehr-Lobban, Carolyn, and Patricia Moore. 2000. "Changing Family Law in Egypt." *Providence Journal,* December 17.

Fluehr-Lobban, Carolyn, and Kharyssa Rhodes, eds. 2003. *Race and Identity in the Nile Valley: Ancient and Contemporary Perspectives.* Metuchen, N.J.: Africa World Press.

Gerges, Fawaz. 1999. *America and Political Islam: Clash of Cultures or Clash of Interests?* Cambridge: Cambridge University Press.

Ghattas, Kim. 2000. "Tradition Endures, Episode at a Time." *Philadelphia Inquirer,* September 29.

Gilmore, David. 1987. *Honor and Shame and the Unity of the Mediterranean.* Special Publication no. 22. Washington, D.C.: American Anthropological Association.

Grady, Denise. 2002. "Few Risks Seen to the Children of First Cousins." *New York Times,* April 4.

Grotberg, Edith, and S. Washi. 1991. "Critical Factors in Women's Status Predictive of Fertility Rates in the Sudan." Paper presented at the eleventh annual conference of the Sudan Studies Association, Vassar College.

Gruenbaum, Ellen. 2001. *The Female Circumcision Controversy.* Philadelphia: University of Pennsylvania Press.

Haeri, Shahla. 1989. *Law of Desire: Temporary Marriage in Shiʿi Iran.* Syracuse: Syracuse University Press.

Hale, Sondra. 1996. *Gender Politics in Sudan: Islamism, Socialism, and the State.* Boulder: Westview Press.

Handal, Najoua Kefi. 1989. "Islam and Political Development: The Tunisian Experience." Ph.D. diss., Louisiana State University.

Hicks, Esther K. 1993. *Infibulation: Female Mutilation in Islamic Northeastern Africa.* New Brunswick, N.J.: Transaction.

Hoffman-Ladd, Valerie. 1987. "Polemics on the Modesty and Segregation of Women in Contemporary Egypt." *International Journal of Middle Eastern Studies* 19: 23–50.

Hourani, Albert. 1991. *The History of the Arabs.* Cambridge: Harvard University Press.

Huntington, Samuel P. 1996. *The Clash of Civilizations and the Remaking of World Order.* New York: Simon and Schuster.

Hussain, Afaf, Robert Olson, and Jamil Qureshi, eds. 1984. *Orientalism, Islam, and Islamists.* Brattleboro, Vt.: Amana Books.

Jehl, Douglas. 1999. "Arab Honor's Price: A Woman's Blood." *New York Times*, June 20.

Jennings, Anne M. 1995. *The Nubians of West Aswan*. Boulder: Lynne Rienner.

Jok, Jok Madut. 2001. *War and Slavery in Sudan*. Philadelphia: University of Pennsylvania Press.

Kenyon, Susan. 1991. *Five Women of Sennar*. Oxford: Clarendon Press.

Kurzman, Charles, ed. 1998. *Liberal Islam, a Sourcebook*. New York: Oxford University Press.

Labid Ibn Rabiah. 1977. *The Golden Ode*. Translated with an introduction by William Polk. Cairo: American University in Cairo Press.

Lerner, Gerda. 1986. *The Creation of Patriarchy*. New York: Oxford University Press.

Lewis, Bernard. 2002. *What Went Wrong? The Clash between Islam and Modernity in the Middle East*. New York: Oxford University Press.

Libidi, Lilia. 1987. *Al-Harakah al-Nisa' fi Tunis* (The women's movement in Tunisia). Tunis.

Lobban, Richard. 1982. "Class and Kinship in Sudanese Urban Communities." *Africa* 52(2): 51–76.

———. 1998. *Women in the Informal Economy in the Middle East*. Gainesville: University Press of Florida.

———. 2003. *Historical Dictionary of Nubia*. Lanham Park, Md.: Scarecrow Press.

Maalouf, Amin. 1984. *The Crusades through Arab Eyes*. Trans. Jon Rothschild. London: Al Saqi Books, distributed by Zed Press.

Magnarella, Paul J. 1982. "The Republican Brothers: A Reformist Movement in the Sudan." *Muslim World* 72(1): 14–21.

Mahmoud, Ushari, and Suleyman Ali Baldo. 1987. *Ed Diein Massacre: Slavery in the Sudan*. Khartoum.

Marmon, Shaun, ed. 1999. *Slavery in the Islamic Middle East*. Princeton: Marcus Wiener.

Mernissi, Fatima. 1975. *Beyond the Veil*. Cambridge: Cambridge University Press.

Mukhtar, al-Baqie al-Afif. 2003. "The Crisis of Identity in Northern Sudan, the Dilemma of a Black People with a White Culture." In *Race and Identity in the Nile Valley: Ancient and Contemporary Perspectives*, ed. Carolyn Fluehr-Lobban and Kharyssa Rhodes. Metuchen, N.J.: Africa World Press.

Musallam, Basim F. 1986. *Sex and Society in Islam*. Cambridge: Cambridge University Press.

Nawwab, Ni'mah Isma'il. 1992. "The Journey of a Lifetime." *Aramco World* 43(4): 27–35.

Passmore Sanderson, Lilian. 1981. *Against the Mutilation of Women: The Struggle to End Unnecessary Suffering*. London: Ithaca Press.

Peletz, Michael. 1995. "Neither Reasonable nor Responsible: Contrasting Representations of Masculinity in a Malay Society." In *Bewitching Women, Pious Men: Gender and Body Politics in Southeast Asia*, ed. Aihwa Ong and Michael Peletz. Berkeley: University of California Press.

———. 2002. *Islamic Modern Religious Courts and Cultural Politics in Malaysia.* Princeton: Princeton University Press.

———. 2004. "Islam and the Cultural Politics of Legitimacy: Malaysia in the Aftermath of September 11th." In *Civil Democratic Islam: Prospects and Policies for a Changing Muslim World,* ed. Robert H. Hefner. Santa Monica, Calif.: Rand.

Peristiany, J. G. 1966. *Honor and Shame: The Values of Mediterranean Society.* Chicago: University of Chicago Press.

Peters, F. E. 1982. *Children of Abraham: Judaism/Christianity/Islam.* Princeton: Princeton University Press.

Pickthall, Muhammad M. 1977. *The Meaning of the Glorious Qur'an.* New York: Muslim World League.

Powell, Eve Troutt. 2001. "Burnt Cork Nationalism." In *Colors of Enchantment,* ed. Sherifa Zuhur, 27–38. Cairo: American University in Cairo Press.

El-Rasoul, Rawsla Hasib. 1991. "Unifying the Application of Shariʿa." *Sudanow* 29 (September).

Rugh, Andrea. 1984. *Family Life in Contemporary Egypt.* Syracuse: Syracuse University Press.

Rúmi, Maulana Jalálu-ʿd-Din Muhammad i. 1979. *Masnavi i Maʾnavi: The Spiritual Couplets.* Trans. E. H. Whinfield. With an introduction by Idries Shah. London: Octagon Press for the Sufi Trust.

Safi, Omid, ed. 2003. *Progressive Muslims: On Justice, Gender, and Pluralism.* Oxford: One World Press.

Said, Edward W. 1981. *Covering Islam.* New York: Pantheon Books, 1981.

Secor, Laura. 2003a. "Covering Law: The Headscarf That Infuriated Turkey's Rulers." *Boston Sunday Globe,* February 9.

———. 2003b. "What Went Right: Turkey's Promising Experiment with Muslim Democracy." *Boston Sunday Globe,* February 9.

Shaheen, Jack G. 2001. *Reel Bad Arabs: How Hollywood Vilifies a People.* New York: Olive Branch Press.

Shahin, Emad Eldin Ali. 1990. "The Restitution of Islam: A Comparative Study of the Islamic Movements in Tunisia and Morocco." Ph.D. diss., Johns Hopkins University.

Sherif-Stanford, Nahla. 1984. "Modernization by Decree: The Role of the Tunisian Woman in Development." Ph.D. diss., University of Missouri, Columbia.

Singerman, Diane. 2003. "Rewriting Divorce in Egypt: Reclaiming Islam, Legal Activism, and Coalition Politics." Paper prepared for "Civil Islam" project, Boston University, January.

Sipress, Alan. 1995. "Egyptian Rights Group Sues Sheikh on Support of Female Circumcision." *Philadelphia Inquirer,* April 13.

Sisk, Timothy. 1992. *Islam and Democracy: Religion, Politics, and Power in the Middle East.* Washington, D.C.: United States Institute for Peace.

Smith, Elizabeth. 2004. "Tributaries in the Stream of Belonging: Crafting National Belonging in the Nubian Museum." In *TransActions: Tourism in the Southern*

Mediterranean, ed. Kamran Ali and Martina Rieker. Bloomington: Indiana University Press.

Sonbol, Sherif, and Tarek Atia. 1999. *Mulid! Carnivals of Faith.* Cairo: American University in Cairo Press.

Sudan Archives, University of Durham, Durham, U.K.

Taha, Mahmoud Mohamed. 1987. *The Second Message of Islam.* Translation and introduction by Abdullahi Ahmed An-Na'im. Syracuse: Syracuse University Press.

El-Tigani Mahmoud, Mahgoub. 2002. "Sudan Law and Human Rights: Comparative Research on Sudan Law and International Human Rights." Unpublished ms.

Toubia, Nahid. 1995. *Female Genital Mutilation: A Call for Global Action.* New York: Woman Ink.

Tucker, Judith. 1984. *Women in Nineteenth-Century Egypt.* Cairo: American University in Cairo Press.

Vitray-Meyerovitch, Eva de. 1987. *Rumi and Sufism.* Translated by Simone Fattal. Sausalito, Calif.: The Post-Apollo Press.

Voll, John O. 1995. "Sufism: Sufi Orders." In *The Oxford Encyclopedia of the Modern Islamic World,* vol. 4, ed. J. L. Esposito, 109–17. New York: Oxford University Press.

White, Jenny B. 2002. *Islamist Mobilization in Turkey: A Study in Vernacular Politics.* Seattle: University of Washington Press.

"Women whirling in face of religious traditions." *Providence Sunday Journal,* December 12, 2000.

Suggestions for Further Reading and Reference

Abou El Fadl, Khaled. 2001. *Speaking in God's Name: Islamic Law, Authority, and Women*. Oxford: One World.

Abu-Lughod, Lila. 1986. *Veiled Sentiments: Honor and Poetry in a Bedouin Society*. Berkeley: University of California Press.

Ahmed, Leila. 1992. *Women and Gender in Islam*. New Haven: Yale University Press.

Altorki, Soraya, and Camillia Fawzi El-Solh, eds. 1988. *Arab Women in the Field: Studying Your Own Society*. Syracuse: Syracuse University Press.

Antoun, Richard T. 2001. *Understanding Fundamentalism: Christian, Islamic, and Jewish Movements*. Walnut Creek, Calif.: AltaMira Press.

Eickelman, Dale F., and James Piscatori. 1996. *Muslim Politics*. Princeton: Princeton University Press.

El-Guindi, Fadwa. 1999. *Veil: Modesty, Privacy, and Resistance*. New York: Berg.

Haddad, Yvonne Yazbeck, and Adair T. Lummis. 1987. *Islamic Values in the United States*. New York: Oxford University Press.

Haddad, Yvonne Yazbeck, and Jane I. Smith, eds. 2002. *Muslim Minorities in the West, Visible and Invisible*. Walnut Creek, Calif.: AltaMira Press.

Ibrahim, Saad Eddin. 2002. *Egypt, Islam, and Democracy: Critical Essays*. Cairo: American University in Cairo Press.

Jok, Jok Madut. 2001. *War and Slavery in Sudan*. Philadelphia: University of Pennsylvania Press.

Lewis, Bernard. 1971. *Race and Color in Islam*. New York: Harper and Row.

Murray, Stephen O., and Will Roscoe. 1997. *Islamic Homosexualities, Culture, History, and Literature*. New York: New York University Press.

Musallam, Basim. 1983. *The Arabs: A Living History*. London: Collins/Harvill. Also produced as a series of videos, *The Arabs: A Living History*.

———. 1983. *Sex and Society in Islam*. Cambridge: Cambridge University Press.

Pickthall, Muhammad M. 1977. *The Meaning of the Glorious Qur'an*. New York: Muslim World League.

Rahman, Fazlur. 1966. *Islam.* New York: Holt, Rinehart and Winston.

Rodinson, Maxime. 2002. *Europe and the Mystique of Islam.* London: I. B. Tauris.

Said, Edward. 1979. *Orientalism.* New York: Random House.

Al-Sayyad, Nezar, and Manuel Castells, eds. 2002. *Muslim Europe or Euro-Islam: Politics, Culture, and Citizenship in the Age of Globalization.* New York: Lexington Books.

Young, William C. 1996. *The Rashaayda Bedouin, Arab Pastoralists of Eastern Sudan.* New York: Harcourt Brace.

Recommended Journals and Periodicals

Arab Studies Quarterly. Published by the Association of Arab-American University Graduates.

Aramco World. Published bimonthly, features on Arab and Islamic worlds. Escondido, Calif.

International Journal of Middle East Studies. Published by Cambridge University in association with the Middle East Studies Association.

Middle East Journal. Published by the Middle East Institute, Washington, D.C.

Muslim World. Published by the Duncan Black Macdonald Center, Hartford Seminary.

American Muslim magazines: *Minaret* and *Islamic Horizons*

Recommended References

Encyclopedia of the Middle East and North Africa. 2003. 2d ed. Ed. Philip Mattar. New York: Macmillan Reference.

Encyclopedia of the Modern Islamic World. 1995. Ed. John L. Esposito. 4 vols. New York: Oxford University Press.

Index

Carolyn Fluehr-Lobban is professor of anthropology at Rhode Island College, where she teaches courses in anthropology and Islamic, African, and Afro-American studies. She received the college's Award for Distinguished Teaching in 1990 and the Award for Distinguished Scholar in 1998. She is the author of *Islamic Law and Society in the Sudan* (1987) and the editor of *Ethics and the Profession of Anthropology: Dialogue for a New Era.*